Labor, Church, and the Sugar Establishment

Labor, Church, and
___the Sugar Establishment___

Louisiana, 1887–1976

THOMAS BECNEL

Louisiana State University Press
BATON ROUGE AND LONDON

Designer: Joanna Hill
Typeface: Linotype Garamond
Typesetter: Service Typesetters
Printer: Thomson-Shore
Binder: John H. Dekker & Sons

LIBRARY OF CONGRESS CATALOGING IN PUBLICATION DATA
Becnel, Thomas, 1934–
    Labor, church, and the sugar establishment.
    Bibliography: p.
    Includes index.
      1.   Trade-unions—Sugar workers—Louisiana—History.
    2.   National Agricultural Workers Union—History.
    3.   Church and labor—Louisiana—History.   I.   Title.
HD6515.S852L82   331.88'13361'09763   80-10572
ISBN   0-8071-0660-7

Contents

Preface

Early labor historians usually neglected industrial strife in the agricultural South. Until William Hair wrote about the sugarcane strike of 1887 that ended in the Thibodaux Massacre, few persons knew of the efforts by the Knights of Labor to organize in Louisiana. Roger Shugg revealed the New Orleans general strike of 1892 to modern readers. Recent studies show that before World War I the Industrial Workers of the World organized timber workers in Louisiana and conducted strikes, and under the New Deal several agricultural unions sprang up to stop the eviction of tenants by landlords who refused to share Agricultural Adjustment Act benefit payments with them.

For forty years H. L. Mitchell led the most famous of these unions, the Southern Tenant Farmers Union. After World War II the remnants of Mitchell's union, actively supported by New Orleans Archbishop Joseph Francis Rummel, ventured into Louisiana to organize the sugar industry. I have attempted to trace that union's activity in the cane fields of Louisiana and to assess the roles of the Catholic church and the agricultural establishment. I have sought to explain how union leaders reacted when sugar industry spokesmen refused to grant even token concessions to plantation workers whose cause both union and church supported and how the cane country of Louisiana thus became the setting for a three-sided confrontation. Even though many sugar planters were Catholic and many plantation workers were black, race and religion had less impact on the outcome than economics.

The Louisiana experience reflected a national pattern of defeat for agricultural unions, and therefore, the work occasionally extends beyond Louisiana. Mitchell's union, for instance, attempted to win support from both the AFL and the CIO when the two national unions worked out preliminary merger arrangements. The American Sugar Cane League, principal lobbyist for the domestic sugar industry, maintained a full-time office in Washington and worked effectively with the national bureaucracy. Senator Allen J. Ellender, the "first friend of the domestic sugar industry," sat on the Senate Committee on Agriculture and

watched over several farm programs. The right-to-work controversy in
Louisiana, too, should be viewed as part of a national phenomenon.
Ironically, however, the organization often thought of as monolithic,
the Catholic church, became involved through the efforts of clergymen
in the Archdiocese of New Orleans, not through national Catholic programs.

Strong-willed personalities are prominent in this study. H. L. Mitchell
proved his toughness and willingness to battle unfavorable economic
and political odds in many sections of the country. Archbishop Rummel
advocated a vigorous social action program despite spirited opposition
from influential Catholics. Articulate spokesmen for the sugar industry
consistently refused to deal with or recognize agricultural unions.

Many people aided and advised me in this study; naturally, they are
absolved of any responsibility for my errors of fact or judgment. Pro-
fessors Burl Noggle and M. T. Carleton of Louisiana State University
helped shape preliminary drafts and plans. The Reverend Charles
O'Neill, S.J., and Monsignor Charles Plauché, who read the chapter on
the church, prevented several embarrassing blunders and broadened my
understanding of Catholicism. Monsignor Plauché also facilitated my
entry into private church archives. Professor Ben Wall reviewed the
chapter on the agricultural establishment and, in typical good humor,
shared his knowledge of southern life and politics. My colleague at
Nicholls State, Philip Uzee, gave sound advice and, ably assisted by
Florence LeCompte, his secretary in the archives, introduced me to the
voluminous Allen J. Ellender Papers. Alfred Delahaye, a dedicated
journalist and a keen student of human nature, was my most patient
proofreader and advisor. However, no reader knew *Labor, Church, and
the Sugar Establishment* better than Judy Bailey, a talented copy editor
at Louisiana State University Press, who skillfully directed the work
through production.

A grant from the Nicholls College Foundation assisted me in the
final stages of manuscript preparation. Veldene Delatte, who sometimes
took on the duties of proofreader, typed the manuscript with help occasionally from Jan Leger. My talented friends, Dale Rogers and Dwight
Schakelford, prepared the map of the cane country with the help of
Pamela Vesterby.

Beverly Jane Walker's assistance was inestimable: she typed and
proofread copy, helped with the index, and took more than ordinary
interest in the study. Above all, when I had despaired of ever seeing
this work in print, she gave me hope.

Chronology

1886   Knights of Labor organized workers in the South
American Federation of Labor organized
1887   Thibodaux Massacre—outgrowth of cane-field strike
1891   *Rerum Novarum*, Papal Encyclical on Labor
1892   New Orleans General Strike
1905   Industrial Workers of the World organized
1913   United States Department of Labor organized
1916   First federal child-labor law was passed
1920   Women's Bureau established in the Department of Labor
1922   American Sugar Cane League organized
1926   Railway Labor Act required employers to bargain collectively with railroad employees
1932   Norris-LaGuardia Act restricted use of federal injunctions and outlawed yellow-dog contracts
1933   Congress passed the Agricultural Adjustment Act to aid distressed farmers
Section 7(a) of the National Industrial Recovery Act guaranteed right of workers to organize and bargain collectively with employers
1934   H. L. Mitchell and others formed the Southern Tenant Farmers Union (STFU) to halt eviction of tenants from cotton lands in Arkansas
1935   *Schechter* case nullified Title I of the NIRA
Congress passed the Wagner Act which created the National Labor Relations Board and guaranteed workers the right to join organizations of their own choosing and to bargain collectively with employers
John L. Lewis and others formed the Congress of Industrial Organizations (CIO) and attempted to organize the steel, rubber, and auto industries
1936   Sit-down strike became the new weapon of organized labor
1937   Congress passed the Sugar Act which restricted domestic produc-

tion, limited imports, and boosted prices paid for domestic sugar

1938   Fair Labor Standards Act established a twenty-five–cent minimum wage

1939   Archbishop Rummel appointed Father O'Connell to head his Archdiocesan Social Action Committee

Gordon McIntire of the Louisiana Farmers Union spoke in behalf of sugarcane workers at wage hearings conducted by the U.S. Department of Agriculture

Sugarcane farmers resisted acreage reduction rulings from the USDA

1940   Monsignor John Ryan addressed a conference on industrial problems hosted by Archdiocese of New Orleans

1941   United States became an active participant in World War II and soon faced a serious manpower shortage

AFL and CIO pledged a no-strike policy for duration of the war

1943   POW labor (mostly German) sent to the sugarcane fields of Louisiana

1946   Displaced Persons (DPs) sent to work in sugarcane fields complained to priests about poor housing and working conditions; many left

H. L. Mitchell's farm union joined the AFL and worked among Mexican-Americans in California

National labor unions organized "Operation Dixie," a drive to unionize the South

Louisiana Governor Jimmie Davis vetoed a right-to-work law passed by the legislature at the urging of labor leaders and priests involved in social action

1947   Congress passed the Taft-Hartley Act

Lou Twomey organized Institute of Industrial Relations at Loyola University

1948   H. L. Mitchell sent Hank Hasiwar and I. Lee Parker to Louisiana to organize strawberry, dairy, and truck farmers

1951   Allen Ellender became Chairman of the Senate Committee on Agriculture and Forestry

1952   Hasiwar conducted drive to organize sugarcane workers with assistance of Archbishop Rummel

Rummel met with sugar growers and asked them to discuss working conditions and pay with representatives of Mitchell's National Agricultural Workers Union

Sugar growers refused to negotiate with NAWU representatives

William Green (AFL) and Phillip Murray (CIO) died and were replaced by George Meany and Walter Reuther, respectively

1953 Sugarcane strike by Mitchell's NAWU

1954 Mathews sugar refinery strike
      Louisiana legislature passed a right-to-work law

1955 AFL-CIO merger convention; merger completed in January, 1956

1956 Louisiana legislature repealed the general right-to-work law, but retained an agricultural right-to-work statute
      Agricultural union activity declined in Louisiana

1964 Archbishop Joseph Francis Rummel died

1972 Senator Allen Ellender died

1974 Sugar Act expired

1975 Sugar prices in the U.S. soared

1976 Louisiana legislature passed a general right-to-work law

Abbreviations

ACTU	Association of Catholic Trade Unionists
AEP	Allen Ellender Papers, Division of Archives, Nicholls State University, Thibodaux, Louisiana
CCS	Catholic Committee of the South Papers, Amistad Research Center, Dillard University, New Orleans, Louisiana
JFR	Joseph Francis Rummel Papers, Archives, Archdiocese of New Orleans
K of L	Knights of Labor
LTC	Louis Twomey Collection, Documents Center, Loyola University, New Orleans, Louisiana
NAWU	National Agricultural Workers Union
NCWC	National Catholic Welfare Conference
NFLU	National Farm Labor Union
NLRB	National Labor Relations Board
NSF	National Sharecroppers' Fund
PAC	Political Action Committee
SCU	Sharecroppers' Union
STFU	Southern Tenant Farmers Union Papers, Southern Collection, University of North Carolina, Chapel Hill
USDA	United States Department of Agriculture
UCAPAWA	United Cannery, Agricultural, Packing and Allied Workers of America
UPWA	United Packinghouse Workers of America

Labor, Church, and the Sugar Establishment

Prologue

Agricultural Labor in Nineteenth-Century Louisiana

When Louisiana sugarcane field workers struck in October 1953, many observers in the cane country predicted a rash of strike activity against agricultural operations in the South. Cane growers thought the strike an ominous indication of future complex farm problems. Agricultural union leaders optimistically expected trade union tactics to bring real change in working conditions in the sugar industry. Both sides in the dispute called the strike unprecedented.

Actually, however, the agricultural labor movement in the United States has a long history of strikes and other activities that contradicts the popular view of the idyllic, small farmstead. Agricultural unions were less visible and less successful than other unions because they faced special problems in organizing farm workers: the temporary nature of farm employment, farmers' anti-union sentiment, the ease of replacing unskilled workers, the smallness of many farms, the heterogeneity of farm labor, the instability of farm employment, the difficulty of collecting dues, and the seasonal lack of demand for farm labor.[1] Nevertheless, the unions have continued to battle for the rights of farm laborers since Reconstruction.

During the Civil War, when military activities disrupted slave labor operations, black plantation workers came under several working arrangements. General Benjamin Butler, who arrived with conquering United States Army forces in 1862, confiscated slaves only on those plantations whose owners had supported the Confederate States of America and who, technically, had committed treason. When news of Butler's action spread to the countryside, hordes of liberated slaves

1 Stuart Jamieson, *Labor Unionism in American Agriculture* (Washington: U.S. Government Printing Office, 1945), 3–4.

flocked to the camps of invading United States armies, taxing the logistical capability of the military. Butler assigned them to jobs cleaning up New Orleans or sent them back to their former plantations. Often he used New Orleans city police for this task because War Department orders prohibited soldiers from returning slaves to their owners.[2]

Butler's successor, General Nathaniel Banks, helped planters in the sugarcane areas of Louisiana cope with plantation labor problems in federally occupied sections of the state. A delegation of planters from Terrebonne Parish visited Banks in New Orleans in January, 1863, hoping to establish work regulations for blacks who, according to grower complaints, came and went as they pleased and worked only sporadically. Planters considered the meeting a failure since Banks did not agree to their demands, but on February 3, 1864, they received nearly everything they had requested when he issued General Order No. 23. The order set the monthly rate of pay for blacks (three to eight dollars), established the ten-hour workday, prohibited floggings and the separation of families, and stipulated that each worker sign a one-year contract that withheld one-half of his pay until the end of the year. In addition, the contract allowed the provost marshal of the parish to assign blacks who refused employment to public works projects without compensation. These provisions effectively prevented black workers from joining unions and from moving about freely since the worker forfeited his wages if he reneged on his contract. In 1865 the Louisiana legislature added stipulations designed to prevent planters from enticing away workers already under contract or from harboring fugitives and contract jumpers.[3]

Whites, afraid of potential violence, established a system that maintained the subordination of black laborers to white employers. General Butler promised planters that the military would keep order, and unfortunately for the many freedmen who eventually returned to the plantations where they had lived and worked as slaves, some military guards acted as overseers and even helped growers cheat workers of their pay.

2 William F. Messner, "Black Violence and White Response: Louisiana, 1862," Journal of Southern History, XLI (1975), 24–25; Joe Gray Taylor, Louisiana Reconstructed, 1863–1877 (Baton Rouge: Louisiana State University Press, 1974), 4–11.

3 J. Carlyle Sitterson, Sugar Country: The Cane Sugar Industry in the South, 1753–1950 (Lexington: University of Kentucky Press, 1953), 220, 223; Roger Shugg, Origins of the Class Struggle in Louisiana (Baton Rouge: Louisiana State University Press, 1939), 213.

Yet whites evidenced confusion about the status of blacks. Some favored writing a new constitution to relegate freedmen to peasant standing, but General Butler felt that those freedmen who did not go into military service should work in a free labor market under a wage system. Between 1863 and 1865 authorities in Louisiana developed a wage system that whites, at least, considered successful.[4]

A year after Butler effected his labor policies, white attitudes toward blacks had changed dramatically. As fear of black violence gave way instead to a realization of widespread black docility, growers assumed administrative control of the wage-labor system and managed it to their own advantage. Freedmen suffered further when military commanders, impatient at having to feed nonmilitary personnel, delivered their black charges to planters without securing adequate guarantees for their protection. Some freedmen themselves considered returning to plantation work preferable to languishing in the contraband camps established by military commanders. Nevertheless, freedmen, apparently unhappy about plantation conditions, once again flocked to military camps early in 1863.[5]

The Freedmen's Bureau, created by Congress in 1865 to help former slaves adjust to freedom, became intimately involved in problems related to plantation labor. It returned blacks to the plantation, for many whites assumed freedmen would not return to plantation work voluntarily. Some bureau agents accepted bribes from planters and stole funds from the bureau, but in clashes between planters and freedmen, the bureau sided with growers in only about half the cases. In Louisiana the bureau never exceeded one hundred employees, some of whom distrusted the planters, while others tried to help them, sometimes even acting as unofficial agents in obtaining black laborers. By 1866, when the blacks' unwillingness to work no longer posed serious problems, the bureau had established a labor system.[6]

General Absalom Baird became head of the Louisiana Freedmen's Bureau in November, 1866, and established rules governing working conditions on plantations, which became standard bureau procedure in

---

4 Messner, "Black Violence," 25–26, 33–34, 35; Taylor, *Louisiana Reconstructed*, 84; C. Peter Ripley, "The Black Family in Transition: Louisiana, 1860–1865," *Journal of Southern History*, XLI (1975), 377.

5 Messner, "Black Violence," 33, 21, 37–38.

6 Howard A. White, *The Freedmen's Bureau in Louisiana* (Baton Rouge: Louisiana State University Press, 1970), 37, 102; Taylor, *Louisiana Reconstructed*, 93, 325, 330–31.

the state. A major regulation set wages due to freedmen as equivalent to a first mortgage on the property of the planter. In keeping with other Baird directives, planters kept families together whenever possible. Workers labored twenty-six days a month with Sundays off, and the workday was ten hours in summer and nine hours in winter. Rules required the planter to provide extra pay for extra work and a garden plot for each family. If a planter and his tenant worked the land on shares, one-twentieth of the proceeds went into a bureau fund for the support of education. Fines also went into the education fund. In addition, each planter was required to contribute one dollar per month to help support the bureau.[7]

Radical Reconstruction leaders referred to various state labor and vagrancy laws for policing freedmen as Black Codes. Each state had its own vagrancy law or a similar device for forcing freedmen to return to work, and in Louisiana the labor regulations in Nathaniel Banks's General Order No. 23 set a precedent for a law that northerners considered to be an attempt to restore blacks to peonage. General Butler had forced freedmen to work for wages, but Banks developed a "work or fight" policy and declared "labor is a public duty and idleness and vagrancy a crime." The law that was developed from this policy had vagrancy provisions meant to be enforced against blacks only. It also prohibited blacks from carrying firearms, trespassing on plantations, and tampering with employees under labor contract. Joe Gray Taylor described the conditions it created as "not far removed from slavery." But the Louisiana constitution of 1868, written after Radical Republicans had regained supervision of Reconstruction, outlawed many objectionable features of the code.[8]

Clearly, farm workers could not depend on the emerging agricultural system to take care of their needs. Given the economic, political, and racial attitudes of most white planters toward agricultural workers, the predominantly black laborers needed outside help. They required—and demanded—more protection than was provided by the whimsical and flimsy rules and policies instituted during Reconstruction and afterward.

A labor shortage in the late 1860s improved conditions somewhat for black agricultural workers. The law of supply and demand raised wages but created tension in the Louisiana sugarcane fields. In 1869 first-class

7 White, *Freedmen's Bureau*, 122–23; Taylor, *Louisiana Reconstructed*, 332–33.

8 Taylor, *Louisiana Reconstructed*, 324, 96, 38, 100–101, 152, 121.

sugarcane field hands earned from $15.00 to $20.00 per month, and by 1871 growers, fearing a further labor shortage, offered as much as $1.25 per day without rations. This upward wage spiral ended, however, when the Panic of 1873 drastically lowered sugar prices and a movement of blacks into the cane country produced a temporary labor surplus. Growers fixed wages in January, 1874, at $14.00 to $15.00 per month, but when they tried to effect this wage cut, freedmen in Terrebonne Parish, who had sought greater autonomy in managing sugarcane operations, called a strike on the Henry W. Minor plantation near Houma. A posse headed by the black sheriff of Terrebonne prevented the strikers from recruiting their fellow workers. The sheriff arrested twelve of the strikers, whom Minor charged with violating his civil rights, and sent them to New Orleans, but authorities there soon released them.[9]

J. Carlyle Sitterson, historian of the South's cane sugar industry, ranked labor problems above the scarcity of capital as a deterrent to the industry's recovery during Reconstruction. He cited grower complaints of rising labor costs and decreasing efficiency. Viewing the labor problem from the perspective of the grower, he considered stratagems to counteract union activity to have been in the interest of the entire sugar industry. One such stratagem was the formation of permanent grower organizations such as the Louisiana Immigration and Homestead Company, which sugarcane farmers helped to found in 1871 to encourage workers to settle in the sugar country. Some farmers wanted to use convict labor in the cane fields. Donelson Caffery, Sr., a St. Mary parish planter, formed an organization in 1877 to end cutthroat competition for labor. Following Caffery's lead, Duncan Kenner, a wealthy planter, established the Louisiana Sugar Planters' Association that same year.[10]

Blacks, feeling oppressed by the wage-setting policies of such agricultural associations, found ways to deprive planters of their agricultural labor supply without resorting to strikes. A threatened exodus of plantation workers from the South in the late 1870s, for example, alarmed growers more than did isolated small-scale strikes. Although the phenomenon, known as Kansas Fever, did not affect the sugar as much as the cotton regions of Louisiana, sugar planters disliked the prospect of blacks leaving *en masse* to homestead in Kansas. T. T. Allain of Iber-

9 Sitterson, *Sugar Country*, 244–45; Taylor, *Louisiana Reconstructed*, 386.
10 William Ivy Hair, *Bourbonism and Agrarian Protest: Louisiana Politics, 1877–1900* (Baton Rouge: Louisiana State University Press, 1969), 55–56; Sitterson, *Sugar Country*, 291, 323, 239, 316–18.

ville Parish, a black Louisiana legislator, speaking of the exodus, said "I have urgently invited people who are leaving North Louisiana to come to our sugar region, where they will obtain excellent wages, [and] good opportunities for their children." Even though planters armed with shotguns attempted to prevent their boarding steamboats along the Mississippi River, Henry Adams, a black leader from Caddo Parish, led many blacks to Kansas. When black settlers experienced hard times there in 1879, Louisiana planters, eager to regain their labor force, paid passage for their return trip to Louisiana.[11]

The agricultural labor situation changed dramatically during the 1880s when the Knights of Labor came to Louisiana determined to organize all workers regardless of skill, color, or sex. The union promised sugar workers higher wages and payment in legal tender instead of scrip. After 1885 many Negroes flocked to the K of L which did more to combat racial prejudice among workingmen than any of its predecessors—and more than its successor, the American Federation of Labor. The Knights successfully organized many sugar plantation workers, both black and white, into labor unions, but the presence of large numbers of Acadians and other poor whites in the sugar country, all potential strikebreakers during the cane-grinding season, weakened the efforts of the predominantly black union.[12]

In March, 1880, Richard Gooseberry a black leader from the cane fields of St. Charles Parish, led his followers in a strike—one of several that year—because planters refused demands for a pay increase from seventy-five cents to one dollar per day. Strikers printed posters proclaiming their slogan "Dollar or Fight." At the request of growers, Governor Louis Wiltz sent in the militia to put down the strike. Then, local judge James d'Augustin charged strikers with trespassing, inciting work stoppage, and intimidating workers who refused to join the movement. The strike leaders were arrested, tried, and sentenced to jail. Workers in St. John the Baptist Parish struck later in March as former President U. S. Grant visited New Orleans. Carrying banners proclaiming A DOLLAR A DAY OR KANSAS, the strikers expected support from the

---

11 Hair, *Bourbonism and Agrarian Protest*, 87–88; Morgan Peoples, "Kansas Fever in North Louisiana," *Louisiana History*, XI (*Spring*, 1970), 131, 135.

12 F. Ray Marshall, *Labor in the South* (Cambridge: Harvard University Press, 1967), 21–22; Hair, *Bourbonism and Agrarian Protest*, 176, 171–72; Sterling Spero and Abraham Harris, *The Black Worker: The Negro and the Labor Movement* (New York: Antheneum, 1968), 43; Shugg, *Origins of the Class Struggle*, 264–65.

former president but dispersed when Governor Wiltz once again sent in the militia. State Senator Henri Demas, a black who intervened on behalf of the strikers, submitted a petition to Governor Wiltz admitting his clients trespassed on private property in order to organize workers. The petition sought a remission of their sentences and Wiltz granted clemency. Other strikes of the brush-fire variety occurred in April, 1880, in Ascension, St. James, St. Bernard, Jefferson, and Plaquemines parishes. Authorities summarily arrested and jailed leaders without needing to resort to the militia.[13]

A poor sugar crop in 1886 prompted the Louisiana Sugar Planters' Association to propose cutting wages during the next year to sixty-five cents a day. District Assembly 194 of the Knights of Labor, expecting higher wages, hoped to negotiate new rates with the Planters' Association. After planters refused to even reply to communications from the K of L, members of District Assembly 194 distributed a circular letter on October 24, 1887, to growers in Iberia, Lafourche, St. Martin, St. Mary, and Terrebonne parishes requesting biweekly payment of wages of $1.25 per day without rations or $1.00 per day with rations. When growers refused these terms, the union's six to ten thousand members decided to strike, and the result of the strike was the Thibodaux Massacre of 1887.[14]

Planters claimed that the market price of sugar precluded wage increases and labeled the strikers Communists, but union leaders held fast. Three whites in Thibodaux, J. R. H. Foote, D. Monnier, and P. O. Rousseau, a former planter, helped black leaders Henry Cox and his brother George direct strike activity along Bayou Lafourche; Jim Brown, a black, led the strike in Terrebonne. Fearing trouble when they evicted strikers who refused to return to work, growers, through the Sugar Planters' Association, asked Governor McEnery to send the militia. He dispatched two batteries and ten companies, a Gatling gun among their weapons, but they left once workers had peacefully vacated their plantation cabins.

In Thibodaux a group of "organized citizens," reinforced by "Shreveport guerrillas," kept watch. Blacks from nearby plantations trudged into town, and soon it resembled a refugee center. They occupied houses rented for them by the Knights of Labor. On November 21, when the

---

13 Hair, *Bourbonism and Agrarian Protest*, 172–73, 175; Sitterson, *Sugar Country*, 248–49.
14 Hair, *Bourbonism and Agrarian Protest*, 164, 177–78.

first freeze of the year damaged the uncut sugarcane, the local judge, Taylor Beattie, realizing there would be a pressing need of labor, declared martial law. Shooting broke out the following night. Gunmen killed at least thirty blacks and two whites and wounded scores of others. The Cox brothers, who had been jailed, disappeared during the confusion, never to be traced. Perhaps they were among the unidentifiable dead later found in remote swamps. The Thibodaux Massacre broke the strike; workers returned to the fields and labored thenceforth under conditions set by growers.[15]

The 1887 disaster left cane-field workers unrepresented and without a unified voice. For the next sixty-five years no unions operated in the cane fields. Other organizations, such as the Colored Farmers' Alliance and the Grange, made no significant inroads in the sugar-producing areas of Louisiana. The Knights of Labor conducted scattered strikes in Ascension, Lafourche, and Terrebonne parishes in 1888, but the blacklisting of union activists made it impossible for the union to continue. One Bayou Lafourche planter expressed a hope in 1888 that "the reign of terror" against Negroes would not be repeated by reckless whites who seemed to enjoy shooting blacks.[16] By 1891 the K of L mattered only in the City of New Orleans.

Meanwhile, an extensive system of sharecropping and tenant farming was gradually becoming the dominant mode of operation in the South, especially in cotton production. Planters eventually obtained legislation emasculating the laws that protected workers' wages. In 1867 the Louisiana legislature passed an amendment to the state Civil Code giving indebtedness to growers precedence over tenants' rights to wages. This became the basis for the crop lien system in Louisiana. The historian Joe Gray Taylor termed it harsh, but concluded that planters and merchants did not regularly cheat tenants, although they charged the tenants higher rates of interest than they themselves paid when cotton prices fell below a profit level. If, as Taylor contends, tenants did not feel cheated by growers in the second half of the nineteenth century, their

15 Richard Hofstadter and Michael Wallace, *American Violence: A Documentary History* (New York: Vintage Books, 1971), 140; Hair, *Bourbonism and Agrarian Protest*, 179–84.

16 Marshall, *Labor in the South*, 287; Sitterson, *Sugar Country*, 320–21; Hair, *Bourbonism and Agrarian Protest*, 184–85, 195, 67; Theodore Saloutos, *Farmer Movements in the South, 1865–1933* (Lincoln: University of Nebraska Press, 1960), 35.

twentieth century counterparts certainly considered the planter to be one of the major reasons for their economic distress.[17]

In time, rambunctious farm leaders joined together and sought ways to fight against economic distress and political oppression. Keenly aware that America was experiencing an industrial revolution which made the country the leading manufacturing nation in the world, they reacted to agricultural depression in numerous ways. First they turned to political solutions, and when these failed, they looked to unions and to more drastic measures.

In the 1890s they helped America's rural poor wage a valiant political struggle to ameliorate economic distress. Calling for programs to aid farmers and to regulate big business, they established the Populist party, which appealed to urban workingmen as well as impoverished farmers. The Populists failed because of serious internal problems and, in Louisiana, vote-stealing on an unprecedented scale in the 1896 gubernatorial election. In order to add their support to the Democratic candidate William Jennings Bryan, a Nebraskan with distinct Populist proclivities, the Populists decided not to nominate a candidate of their own for president. Meanwhile, Louisiana Populists confused matters by fusing with Republicans against an entrenched Bourbon Democratic regime. Forced to steal votes at a surprising rate, even for Louisianians, in order to win in 1896, the Bourbons, in 1898, rewrote the Louisiana constitution to prevent this problem from reoccurring. They disfranchised blacks and thereby emasculated the Republican party. Similar tactics, carried out in every other southern state, created a solid, one-party South, safely in the hands of Democrats, who made few serious efforts to alter the pattern of poverty, ignorance, and poor health which usually accompanied sharecropping and tenant farming. Not until the 1930s and the New Deal was there a significant effort to break the system that held over seven million black and white Americans in the doldrums of tenancy.[18]

17 Taylor, *Louisiana Reconstructed*, 88, 402, 405.

18 Hair, *Bourbonism and Agrarian Protest* is the best published account of the Louisiana Populists.

Part I
The Setting, 1900—1949

Chapter 1

Louisiana Labor in the First Half of the Twentieth Century

Labor relations in Louisiana in the early twentieth century differed little from those in the rest of the South, where few significant innovations occurred. In industrial sectors of the United States organized labor experienced lean years prior to 1933 and enjoyed only limited successes during the New Deal period. The rural South, with strong provincial ties to its agricultural tradition and few contacts with industrial unions, presented formidable obstacles to the labor movement. Wilbur Cash concluded that intense individualism, unfortunate labor experiences, fear of communism, and a strong conviction that prosperity was imminent were factors in "a curious, widespread, and active antagonism" by southerners toward unionism. Unions tended to be even weaker in rural and agricultural states that restricted suffrage.[1]

During the first four decades of the twentieth century, agricultural unions failed to achieve the organizational levels of the cane-field unions affiliated with the Knights of Labor in the 1880s. Increasingly, tenant farming and sharecropping became the *modus operandi* for southern agriculture while industrial growth swept the rest of the United States. In Louisiana the Populists briefly posed a political threat to Bourbon Democrats, many of whom were cotton or sugar planters. However, when southern Populists attempted to unify a biracial agrarian proletariat in the 1890s, Democrats took steps that had disfranchised black voters throughout the South by about 1911. Sugar growers complained of railroads "unfairly" hiring away their natural labor supply in 1907 and 1908. Planters also called for stringent enforcement of New Orleans vagrancy laws, hoping to make idle men available for farm labor.

---

1 Wilbur Cash, *The Mind of the South* (New York: Vintage Books, 1941), 304.

In the 1920s, when even industrial unions were weakened, many agricultural unions disappeared completely, victims of economic setbacks and political policies.[2]

For many reasons, when organized labor set agricultural rather than general goals, its chances for success declined considerably. With the exception of the Bankhead-Jones Farm Tenancy Act of 1937, every major farm and labor bill excluded agricultural workers from its definition of labor. The Agricultural Adjustment Act did not specifically grant them benefit payments; Section 7(a) of the National Recovery Administration did not guarantee them collective bargaining rights; Social Security did not cover them at first; the Wagner Act's National Labor Relations Board did not assure them arbitration; the Fair Labor Standards Act of 1938 specifically exempted them from its minimum wage provisions; and Section 14(b) of the Taft-Hartley Act allowed states to pass right-to-work laws that operated to the detriment of farm workers.[3]

Unions representing timber workers, who are usually more radical and vociferous than craftsmen, failed to improve the legal standing or the economic lot of their constituents in Louisiana before World War I, but noisy campaigns alarmed antiunion forces and often encouraged retaliatory countermeasures. In 1906 John H. Kirby, a wealthy Texan, rallied lumbermen to form the Southern Lumber Operators' Association (SLOA) to counter union threats in the pine forests of Louisiana. Nevertheless, in 1910 unionized timber workers organized the Brotherhood of Timber Workers in Louisiana, and two years later it merged with the Industrial Workers of the World at a meeting in Alexandria. In southwest Louisiana, at Graybow and Merryville, timber workers walked off their jobs in 1911 and 1912 over wages and working conditions. Authorities arrested union leaders in Graybow, charging them with conspiracy, but most workers were acquitted or never brought to trial. After this incident, harassment inspired by the SLOA diminished union activity in Louisiana lumber camps.[4]

2 U.S. Department of Agriculture, *The Yearbook of Agriculture, 1940: Farmers in a Changing World* (Washington: U.S. Government Printing Office, 1949), 888–93; Stuart Jamieson, *Labor Unionism in American Agriculture* (Washington: U.S. Government Printing Office, 1945), 12–13.

3 H. L. Mitchell, interview, June 23, 1970.

4 James Fickle, "The Louisiana-Texas Lumber War of 1911–1912," *Louisiana History*, XVI (Winter, 1975), 59–85; F. Ray Marshall, *Labor in the South* (Cambridge: Harvard University Press, 1967), 94–98; Merl Reed, "The IWW

Public policy in the South favored the most prosperous rural land-owners, but few politicians could ignore southern labor. Vocal labor minorities asserted their demands while the southern business community helped to perpetuate the myth that labor unions were large, wealthy, and influential. This misconception of union strength was applied especially to the Congress of Industrial Organizations, whose Political Action Committee encouraged voter registration by paying poll taxes for prospective voters. In some cases, endorsement of a candidate for public office by the PAC meant sure defeat.[5]

Southern politicians, generally inexperienced in dealing with organized labor, reacted in a variety of ways to labor demands. Governor Cole Blease of South Carolina, although he was one of the first demagogues to appeal to cotton mill workers, developed no program for them. In a successful reelection campaign in 1946, Senator Harry Byrd of Virginia accused his rival of receiving support from the powerful CIO, but Senator Claude Pepper used union support to win in Florida, where union members were numerous. Florida Attorney General J. Tom Watson worked to undermine the influence of organized labor, and Georgia's Governor Eugene Talmadge generally opposed the labor movement. Talmadge's campaigns dramatized the support he received from small farmers, but he pleased business leaders, who financed the campaigns, with his low tax policy and his assault on textile unions in 1934. Textile union leaders were employing caravans of strikers in "flying squadrons" who traveled about persuading or forcing workers to shut down mills. Talmadge declared martial law and placed the leaders behind barbed wire enclosures at Fort McPherson in Atlanta. But because the Talmadges—Eugene and later his son, Herman—enjoyed long tenure in office, organized labor did not antagonize them unduly. E. H. "Boss" Crump of Tennessee, who chased off CIO poll watchers in 1946, blamed organized labor for his defeat in the 1948 gubernatorial campaign, and Estes Kefauver, a liberal on civil rights and labor matters, moderated his views to appease conservative constituents and win his 1948 race for a U.S. Senate seat. He denied receiving campaign funds from the CIO Political Action Committee in Tennessee. In Virginia the

---

and Individual Freedom in Western Louisiana, 1913," *Louisiana History*, X (Winter, 1969), 61–69.

5 V. O. Key, Jr., *Southern Politics in State and Nation* (New York: Alfred A. Knopf, 1949), 528, 57, 673–74, 480, 32.

CIO intervened in 1946 to secure the Democratic nomination of Willis Robertson who defeated Howard Smith, an ultraconservative, in the gubernatorial election. In Texas, Governor W. Lee O'Daniel supported legislation requiring union members to carry identification cards and submit detailed reports regarding their activities, and the legislation passed, although it was later struck down in the courts.[6]

Obviously, the strength of organized labor in the South varied from state to state. In the years after World War II, Tennessee had the highest percentage of unionized workers in the South (20.6 percent) and North Carolina the lowest (7.8 percent). Few southern steel and textile workers joined unions. Florida had a regressive tax system and right-to-work policy that William Havard associated with the conservatism supported by the Farm Bureau, chain stores, and the liquor industry. Labor in Mississippi had little influence partly because potential white supporters were alienated by the civil rights activities of blacks. Only 12.5 percent of Louisiana's labor force joined unions in the years after World War II, compared to 28 percent nationwide.[7]

Louisiana experienced the same labor disabilities that stymied other southern states during the 1930s, and, in addition, the state had unique problems brought on by local politicians and labor leaders. Allan Sindler blamed self-serving labor leaders for Louisiana's failure to enact child-labor, minimum wage, or workmen's compensation legislation. All too often the AFL leaders in the state resorted to personal bargaining that won them high posts in government but gained workingmen nothing. A Huey Long associate remembered that Long often said organized labor in Louisiana never defeated or elected a candidate in a statewide race.[8]

6 Cash, *Mind of the South*, 250; Marshall, *Labor in the South*, 241–45; William Anderson, *The Wild Man from Sugar Creek: The Political Career of Eugene Talmadge* (Baton Rouge: Louisiana State University Press, 1975), 110–11, 237; George Tindall, *The Emergence of the New South, 1913–1945* (Baton Rouge: Louisiana State University Press, 1967), 511; Key, *Southern Politics*, 413, 125–26, 64, 73, 24–25; Joseph B. Gorman, *Kefauver: A Political Biography* (New York: Oxford University Press, 1971), 56.

7 Charles Roland, *The Improbable Era: The South Since World War II* (Lexington: University of Kentucky Press, 1975), 17; William Havard (ed.), *The Changing Politics of the South* (Baton Rouge: Louisiana State University Press, 1972), 152, 161, 505, 517, 537–38, 587.

8 Allan P. Sindler, *Huey Long's Louisiana: State Politics, 1920–1952* (Baltimore: The Johns Hopkins University Press, 1956), 254; Fred Benton to Allen

Huey Long failed to alter labor's plight directly, but labor consistently supported him. "Huey's sorry labor record," Allan Sindler wrote, "typed him, at best, a rural liberal." Long put in no strong labor legislation, Sindler noted, not even a workmen's compensation bill. Yet even though Long produced no important labor legislation—despite his nearly complete control over the legislature—his biographer, T. Harry Williams, thinks he helped workingmen in other ways. Williams attributes Long's failure to help labor to the agricultural power structure of Louisiana, where the organized labor movement was too small to realize legislative success. Yet Long's road and bridge construction, free hospital service, free textbooks, and homestead exemption law benefited the masses directly and seemed a logical outgrowth of his early struggles to increase workmen's compensation benefits. Furthermore, his vocal opposition to big business won him labor support while alienating mercantile, banking, shipping, timbering, and cane- and cotton-growing interests.[9]

The Long faction continued to receive labor's endorsement after Huey's death. Governor Richard Leche made overtures to the State Federation of Labor and sounded like a labor supporter at Labor Day rallies. But one observer considered Leche "favorable to business" with his tax exemptions for business and his termination of the Huey Long-Standard Oil feud. Although he did not attempt to suppress labor organizations, Leche encouraged an anti–sit-down strike bill, vetoed a bill limiting the work week for women in 1936, and usually allowed the business-oriented state Board of Commerce and Industry a free hand.[10]

New Deal legislation changed the economic life of Louisiana and the South. For example, the National Labor Relations Board, created by the Wagner Act in 1935, helped to settle countless labor disputes. In the 1930s Charles Logan, who was hired and trained by William Leiserson, the NLRB director, became director of NLRB Region 15, which included Louisiana. He followed Leiserson's precedent of refusing to recognize company unions as bargaining agents. In 1940 he recognized the Oil Workers' International Union (CIO) as bargaining agent rather than the Solvay Employers' Council, a company union that Solvay had helped

Ellender, October 2, 1943, in "Gubernatorial Campaign—1944" folder, Box 408, Allen J. Ellender Papers, Division of Archives, Nicholls State University, Thibodaux, La., hereinafter cited as AEP.

9 Sindler, *Huey Long's Louisiana*, 105, 254; T. Harry Williams, *Huey Long, A Biography* (New York: Alfred A. Knopf, 1969), 857–58, 109–11.

10 Sindler, *Huey Long's Louisiana*, 131.

to set up in Baton Rouge. Short and red-faced, he had worked for eight years with Monsignor Peter Wynhoven at Hope Haven, a home for wayward boys in the Archdiocese of New Orleans.[11]

Organized labor especially concerned itself with two aspects of the Louisiana seafood industry. One dealt with child labor in seafood processing plants and, therefore, fell under the jurisdiction of the Children's Bureau of the Department of Labor. The other involved strikes in processing plants, which, ironically, did not always concern the Department of Labor since seasonal workers were not covered by the Wagner Act and therefore did not qualify for the protection provided by the National Labor Relations Board. Although denied basic New Deal labor law benefits, seafood industry workers were, at times, amazingly militant, considering their isolation from urban life, their high illiteracy rate, and, for many, their inability to communicate except in French.

Managers of seafood-processing plants employed child labor, in defiance of compulsory school attendance and child-labor laws, until the 1940s. In 1919 the findings of a Children's Bureau study of shrimp and oyster plants were bleak: many child workers in seafood plants endured sore hands and infections from shrimp spines embedded beneath the skin. Work also curtailed school attendance. The illiteracy rate in shrimp and oyster areas for working children ten to fifteen years of age was 25 percent compared to about 4 percent elsewhere in the nation. The rate of pay at Louisiana's twenty-eight large shrimp canneries in 1930 for young boys and girls was $.01 per pound of peeled, or about $2.50 per day. Federal authorities indicted shrimp-processing firms in Arabi, Houma, and Lafitte for child-labor violations of the Fair Labor Standards Act in 1940, and dealers who sold shrimp in interstate commerce within thirty days of using child labor in their plants became subject to Interstate Commerce Commission regulations which forbade child labor.[12] But even in the late 1940s, children regularly left school to catch or process shrimp when the May season opened in south Louisiana.

In 1938 shrimpers' unions in several gulf coast ports decided to withhold shrimp from canneries unless fishermen received more than the $7.00 per barrel the canneries offered. Some unions held out for the

11 Charles Logan, interview, September 26, 1974; Logan to Ellender, May 11, 1949, in "Federal Trade Commission, 1949," folder, Box 9, AEP.

12 Viola I. Paradise, *Child Labor and the Work of Mothers in Oyster and Shrimp Canning Communities on the Gulf Coast* (Washington: U.S. Government Printing Office, 1922), 5–6.

$8.50 price set by members representing the Gulf Coast Fishermen's and Oystermen's Association of Biloxi and the Fishermen's, Oystermen's, and Fur Trappers' Producers' Cooperative Association of Louisiana both of which had applied to the American Federation of Labor for charters. When the shrimp season opened on August 10, plants in Houma, Morgan City, Golden Meadow, Buras, Westwego, Harvey, Grand Isle, and New Orleans remained closed. Violence broke out when nonunion fishermen attempted to sell shrimp to factories at the cannery-set price of $7.00 per barrel. Union men, armed with shotguns, roamed the shrimping area. They poured kerosene on shrimp en route to market and dumped two hundred barrels of shrimp into Bayou Lafourche at the Lafourche Ice and Shrimp Company dock in Golden Meadow. Authorities arrested twelve fishermen for destroying several truckloads of shrimp in the Barataria-Lafitte area. Nonunion shrimpers finally rallied behind several rebel unions and worked for a compromise settlement. Jesty Collins of Golden Meadow revived the Louisiana Shrimp Fishermen's Cooperative Association with a fiery speech—in French—in Golden Meadow. He charged large canneries with intentionally causing the strike so they could unload surplus holdings from the 1937 season while prices remained high. His efforts increased support for the rebel unions and hastened the settlement that came on August 27 when a large cannery agreed to a compromise of $8.00 per barrel and the strike ended.[13]

A year later, a picketer was killed when the Violet Seafood Workers' Association struck the Dunbar-Dukate Company in Violet. The union was seeking wages of twenty-five cents per hour for its members. Mrs. Angelina Treadaway was standing in the picket line when she was struck by shots fired from a speeding car. She died three days later, and although the case was brought before the St. Bernard parish grand jury and, later, a federal grand jury, in neither case was an indictment returned. Mrs. Treadaway's death did not prove to be a rallying point for seafood workers, however. Fishermen did not see her as a symbol of their struggle. District Attorney Leander Perez, with vested political and economic interests in the labor dispute, helped break the strike and the union. His critics accused him not only of intimidating union workers, but of failing to prosecute Mrs. Treadaway's murderer.[14]

13 Thomas Becnel, "A History of the Louisiana Shrimp Industry, 1867–1961," (M.A. thesis, Louisiana State University, 1962), 34–37.
14 Glen Jeansonne, *Leander Perez: Boss of the Delta* (Baton Rouge: Louisiana State University Press, 1977), 88–91.

From time to time the problems of national labor groups caused disputes in Louisiana. Since antebellum days New Orleans longshoremen had tended to join unions and to fight for their economic well-being, but during the lean years of the 1920s a business-sponsored open shop movement decimated both black and white locals of the International Longshoremen's Association (AFL). There were clashes, sometimes, between black and white longshoremen over meager job pickings. When the New Deal created the National Recovery Administration in 1933 and allowed workers to join organizations of their own choosing, steamship associations formed company unions. In 1936 Governor O. K. Allen closed the port at Lake Charles, Louisiana, after three men died in the fighting between ILA members and their company union rivals. After 1935, CIO waterfront unions, such as the International Longshoremen and Warehousemen's Union (ILWU) locals, began to compete with ILA locals affiliated with the AFL. The CIO sent Harry Bridges to New Orleans to organize for the ILWU. City police harassed CIO organizers, and the Louisiana legislature adopted a resolution that called the ILWU communistic and considered the unionization of blacks a threat to white supremacy. In 1937 the ILA in New Orleans defeated the ILWU in a bargaining election.[15]

Labor was occasionally an issue in state politics also. Most disputes in the Louisiana strawberry industry centered around various marketing agreements for selling the early ripening Louisiana berries. Jimmy Morrison of Hammond, who sounded like a Populist, advocating Huey Long-like reforms to aid the little man, was nearly always in the midst of these controversies. Morrison, a Tulane University Law School graduate, was the leader of a strawberry farmers union. He ran for governor in 1940, advocating removal of the tax on gasoline used in fishing boats and a free college education for indigent students. Morrison criticized Governor Leche, a member of the Long faction, for not opposing a sales tax whose burden fell heavily on poor families. He also accused Leche of reneging on a promise to obtain a subsidy from the Louisiana legislature of one dollar per crate to strawberry growers, and during the 1940 gubernatorial campaign, he accused Leche of trying to starve berry farmers. Nonetheless, Leche at least tried to get federal aid for Morrison's constituents, as his many letters to Senator Allen J. Ellender and the Agriculture Department attest. Locally, the best Leche could do was

15 Marshall, *Labor in the South*, 202–10.

pledge to maintain law and order when violence flared in the strawberry belt.[16]

Morrison did not win the 1940 Louisiana gubernatorial election, nor did the Long faction. The campaign was replete with rhetoric in support of organized labor, perhaps because the Long faction considered labor the issue to detract attention from the scandals that wrecked the Leche administration. However, in courting labor, candidates overplayed the importance of the labor movement and of their own labor records. Candidate Earl Long told labor leaders he favored a tax on laborsaving devices that replaced workers. In the campaign, Sam Jones led the anti-Long forces, a faction dedicated to preventing the remnants of Huey's organization from returning to power. Jones considered the recent scandals a main campaign issue, but he did not overlook the labor vote. He told labor leaders that he was willing to be judged on his Lake Charles labor record. Speaking before a state labor convention that had endorsed Earl Long, Jones cautioned the group: "Keep your organization out of politics." Jimmy Morrison criticized both Long and Jones during the campaign. He suggested that Earl Long had not helped strawberry farmers as much as he could have but Earl replied: "Why that man stole from the strawberry farmers." Senator Ellender and the State Federation of Labor endorsed Earl Long, but other union groups, sensing an end to Longism, endorsed Jones, the eventual winner.[17]

During the war, antiunion forces aggressively tried to undermine organized labor and offset rapid union growth. The American Farm Bureau Federation and the Southern States Industrial Council joined the antiunion Christian American Program, consisting mainly of conservative Protestant ministers. Founded in 1936, the Christian American Program was active in Alabama, Arkansas, Florida, Louisiana, and Texas. In 1942 the Christian American Program was circulating antilabor material. E. H. "Lige" Williams of the State Federation of Labor believed Senator W. Lee O'Daniel of Texas to be the sponsor of this antilabor campaign. Williams sent the mimeographed flyer to Senator Ellender, who had denounced any attempt to use the war as an excuse to suppress labor. The flyer outlined the organization's plans to intro-

16 New Orleans *Times-Picayune*, March 10, October 3, November 16, December 4, 1939; Ellender to Jimmy Morrison, December 21, 1937, in "Strawberry Marketing Agreement" folder, Box 321, AEP.

17 Sindler, *Huey Long's Louisiana*, 255; New Orleans *Times-Picayune*, March 15, 1939–January 14, 1940; H. J. Marmande to Ellender, March 14, 1940, in "Agriculture, Sugar Prices" folder, Box 280, AEP.

duce antilabor measures when the Louisiana legislature convened on May 11, 1942. Other objectives included right-to-work legislation, antiviolence statutes, legal restrictions against farm-labor groups, and measures for controlling Communists and radical labor groups. In 1944 Christian American leaders tried to push through the Louisiana legislature a right-to-work bill which would have outlawed the union shop and the closed shop. They also backed a bill that would have imposed sweeping controls over organized labor. Father Jerome Drolet, a controversial, outspoken labor priest, who had clashed with Harry Bridges over Communist influence on the New Orleans waterfront, called the Christian American Program a "sweatshop front" and testified against the bill at hearings.[18] It did not pass.

In the summer of 1946, however, the Louisiana legislature did pass a right-to-work bill. Jimmie H. Davis vetoed the measure, and "Lige" Williams expressed his gratitude by calling Davis "the best governor Louisiana labor ever had." That same year the legislature repealed the Goff Act of 1946 that had outlawed certain strikes and labor practices. In addition, it enacted a law that prohibited transporting strikebreakers into the state and one that raised workmen's compensation benefits.[19]

World War II brought to the United States full industrial productivity, an end to the Great Depression, and an expanding bureaucracy to deal with an acute labor shortage. Union membership increased rapidly as a result of economic recovery and a favorable government attitude toward labor. Determined to prevent strikes and to ease demands for higher wages, Roosevelt established the National Defense Mediation Board in 1941. The board, consisting of representatives from labor, management, and public life, failed in November when CIO members resigned over its refusal to recommend a union shop arrangement. To replace it Roosevelt created a stronger unit in January, 1942, the National War Labor Board, which could determine wages, hours, and working conditions and could even seize plants under certain circumstances. The NWLB encouraged union membership and exacted no-strike, no-lockout pledges from unions and management, using regional boards through-

18 Marshall, *Labor in the South*, 241–42; E. H. Williams to Ellender, April 24, 1942, with *Christian American Program for 1942*, in "Labor, General, 1942" folder, Box 333, AEP.

19 Quoted in Sindler, *Huey Long's Louisiana*, 194–95; Key, *Southern Politics*, 165.

out the country to settle wage disputes and stabilize wages. Unlike the National Labor Relations Board, the NWLB's functions extended beyond conducting elections to choose bargaining representatives; they now included negotiating contracts between labor and management. In the union shop controversy the board compromised with "maintenance of membership" clauses that required senior workers to remain in the union, but did not require new members to join. In the Fourth Regional War Labor Board, whose jurisdiction included the South, unions organized such war plants as Ingalls Shipbuilding Company, Andrew Higgins Company, and Aluminum Company of America.[20]

Congress created the War Food Administration in March, 1943, to establish national priority needs for food. The WFA was also involved with labor relations since it made county agents responsible for mobilizing farm labor and provided funds for state agricultural extension service systems. The United States Employment Service and the Agricultural Extension Service were trying to prevent an exodus of farm workers from southern fields to higher-paying factory jobs. Regulation No. 7 of the War Manpower Commission, created in the fall of 1943, required a specific job reference from the United States Employment Service before a farm worker could transfer to nonfarm employment. Congress had already passed the Tydings Amendment to the Selective Service Act in November, 1942, to allow local boards to defer men classified as essential to local agriculture. After June, 1943, the War Food Administration's Office of Labor imported workers from foreign countries. The WFA also established Farm-Labor Supply Centers that used old Civilian Conservation Corps camps and buildings formerly occupied by the National Youth Administration and the Farm Security Administration. Louisiana Senator Allen J. Ellender, who otherwise generally supported the Farm Security Administration, objected to its wartime policy of transporting Louisiana laborers to other sections of the country.[21]

20 U.S. Department of Labor, *Brief History of the American Labor Movement* (Washington: U.S. Government Printing Office, 1976), 27–33; Marshall, *Labor in the South*, 225–27.

21 War Food Administration, *Food Program for 1944* (U.S. Government Printing Office, 1943), 52–54, in "War Food Administration # 2" folder, Box 445, *Final Report of the War Food Administration 1945* (U.S. Government Printing Office, 1945), 28–29, in "Agriculture, General, 1945" folder, Box 27, Ellender to R. W. Collier, April 21, 1943, in "Pace Bill" folder, Box 77, all in AEP.

Senator Allen Ellender arrived in Washington in 1937 when organized labor was expanding dramatically and sugarcane producers were demanding a permanent comprehensive program to regulate the production and importation of sugar. As a member of senate committees on agriculture and labor, he helped draft legislation affecting both farmer and industrial workers. A product of the Long organization and heir to political support from organized labor in Louisiana, he came to detest CIO president John L. Lewis, whom he considered irresponsible and unpatriotic. In time, his animosity toward Lewis led to his estrangement from the entire labor movement. Within a decade Ellender underwent a metamorphosis that changed him from a supporter of the prolabor Wagner Act to cosponsor of the antiunion Taft-Hartley Act of 1947.

In the power struggle after Long's assassination in September, 1935, Ellender had emerged as the Long faction's choice for Long's seat in the U.S. Senate. Ellender won the election after a heated fight. He found the Washington legislative format different from Louisiana's. "When Huey was living he took matters in his own hands and appeared in person before his committees," Ellender wrote in 1937. "Up here the wishes of the President are put through by various department heads who act as his agents." Ellender adjusted quickly, however, and became a New Deal supporter. In a 1940 speech he cited FDR's recognition of labor's right to organize as one reason he backed Roosevelt. He often expressed his belief that the president's program improved chances for maximum wartime production. He opposed Senator Harry Byrd's antistrike legislation and suspected antiunion forces of encouraging persistent calls for new labor laws. During his early years in Washington, he won the respect of liberal reformers and labor leaders alike for these antiestablishment, pro–little man views. Paternalistically, he advised "Lige" Williams to run his union honestly, without corruption or unreasonable fees, and said most antiunion legislation would die a natural death.[22]

Ellender's labor support was somewhat undermined when Sam Jones was elected governor. He confronted "Lige" Williams directly about the State Federation of Labor's drift from the Long organization into

22 Ellender to Harry Wilson, January 15, 1937, in "FSA, Farm Tenancy" folder, Box 321, "Why Elect Roosevelt," in "Miscellaneous Presidential Campaign —1940" folder, Box 50, Sam Sibley to Ellender, February 26, 1942, Ellender to Sibley, March 7, 1942, David Brown to Ellender, March 23, 1942, E. H. Williams to Ellender, April 24, 1942, Ellender to Williams, May 4, 1942, all in "Labor, General, 1942" folder, Box 333, all in AEP.

Jones's. "As you know," he wrote a labor leader, in disbelief at being mistrusted, "I have a 100% labor record in Washington which shows that I have been doing all in my power to help organized labor." Nevertheless, State Federation leaders, no doubt thinking that the Long era in Louisiana had come to an end, heeded Jones's warning against maintaining political ties to Longism. "The labor situation is awful," a political supporter of Ellender reported, "Jones and Noe and their representatives are in control." Jimmy Morrison, the voice for strawberry farmers, who acted as spokesman for Ellender, asked W. Horace Williams, the prime contractor at a military base in the state, Camp Polk, to place someone friendly to Senator Ellender in the camp's personnel office. Later, obviously pleased, Morrison informed Ellender that Williams had fired Speedy Rhodes, a personnel officer who backed Jones and discriminated against workers who supported the Long faction.[23]

John L. Lewis, the dynamic and forceful leader of the CIO, was a catalyst in Allen Ellender's change of attitude toward organized labor. As early as the 1937 sit-down strikes, Ellender called Lewis a "Mussolini of the mines," and during World War II, while he denounced antilabor forces with vigor, he criticized John L. Lewis even more. In May, 1943, Lewis' United Mine Workers demanded wage increases in excess of the fifteen percent provided in the Roosevelt administration's "Little Steel Formula." Congress reacted the following month by overriding President Roosevelt's veto to pass the Smith-Connally (War Labor Disputes) Act. The law authorized presidential seizure of war plants on strike. Ellender criticized the UMW action and supported passage of the act. He asked for legislation to set a new national labor policy "that will curb the power of would-be labor dictators like Lewis." No longer reluctant to support antilabor bills, he wrote: "I am actively supporting the [Harry] Byrd Amendment to prevent labor unions from exacting tribute from management."[24]

23 Ellender to Paul Fink, October 16, 1941, Ellender to E. H. Williams, March 27, 1941, in "War National Defense, General # 2" folder, Box 50, Robert McGehee to Ellender, February 22, 1941, Jimmy Morrison to Ellender, February 11, 1941, Ellender to W. Horace Williams, February 7, 1941, Ellender to W. Horace Williams, February 10, 1941, Morrison to Ellender, February 14, 1941, in "General Somervell Investigation" folder, Box 198, all in AEP.

24 Unidentified clipping, in "Labor Situation (July 1, 1937)" folder, Box 92, Ellender speeches, May 4, 1946, in "Education and Labor Committee, Case Bill" folder, Ellender to Dallas A. Picou, November 2, 1945, in "Education and Labor, Minimum Wage Bill, # 1" folder, Ellender to O. J. Hood, May 15, 1946, Ellender to W. Scott Heywood, May 18, 1946, both in "Education and Labor Committee, Case Bill" folder, Box 211, all in AEP.

By the end of World War II, AFL president William Green, after examining congressional voting records, considered both Ellender and Louisiana's senior senator, John Overton, opponents of labor. Overton was a Longite, like Ellender, who spoke eloquently about the plight of the masses but never endeared himself to workers or became popular with them. Senator Ellender still believed himself to be prolabor; it was the corrupt labor leaders he opposed. "I have always done everything I could for the laboring man," he observed in 1948, "and I am in favor of labor unions, if they are administered properly, but many labor unions have been victimized by these racketeers." Indeed, during congressional debate on the Taft-Hartley Bill in 1947, he opposed punitive amendments to the bill, emphasizing that thirty percent of all industries operated under a closed shop arrangement and adding: "Industry as a whole has made huge profits since the war." Nonetheless, the Louisiana Federation of Labor placed him on its "enemies" list and planned to campaign against him at the polls.[25]

Ellender believed that the Wagner Act gave labor an unfair edge over management, and through the years, he supported a number of schemes designed to correct the imbalance. He wanted to modify the act to give independent unions more autonomy and to convince NLRB officials that company unions were indeed real unions. It was Ellender who helped guide the Taft-Hartley Bill through Congress and over President Truman's veto, in 1947, but the Taft-Hartley Act hurt organized labor in several significant ways. It removed antiunion citizens' committees from NLRB jurisdiction by changing the definition of *employer*. It outlawed secondary boycotts and prevented strong unions from helping weak ones. It permitted charges of unfair labor practices against unions to drag on for long periods before being settled. It denied men on strike the right to vote in representation elections. It permitted states to pass right-to-work laws and outlawed the closed shop. It required unions to submit financial reports that made their weaknesses known to industry. And, generally, the Taft-Hartley Act, by guaranteeing the rights of nonunion workers, helped create the impression that workers did not need unions.[26]

25 William Green to John Overton, April 15, 1946, in "Education and Labor, Minimum Wage Bill" folder, Box 211, Ellender to C. C. Sheppard, April 23, 1948, in "S. 2386, Minimum Wage Legislation" folder, Ellender to Harvey Peltier, March 22, 1947, in "Labor, 1947" folder, Box 463, New Orleans *Times-Picayune*, August 25, 1947, in "Miscellaneous 'B'" folder, Box 408, all in AEP; Williams, *Huey Long*, 269.

26 Ellender to George Hutchins, March 20, 1940, in "National Labor Relations

Most of the Louisiana congressional delegation joined Ellender and Overton in supporting the Taft-Hartley Act; the two exceptions were not surprising. Hale Boggs, the liberal New Orleans–born Democrat and Tulane Law School graduate, voted against final passage of the Taft-Hartley Bill. Jimmy Morrison, formerly a close political ally of Ellender and a supporter of strawberry farmer unions, did not vote on the bill. The six other congressmen—F. Edward Hebert, Otto Passman, Overton Brooks, A. Leonard Allen, James Domengeaux, and Harry Larcade, Jr.—voted for the measure.[27]

At a strategy meeting of the Long faction in New Orleans in September, 1943, Earl Long announced his intention to seek the governorship. Ellender, who was willing to run only if all Longites declined in deference to him, blamed labor racketeers for encouraging Earl Long to run. He said that labor criticized members of Congress who voted for the Smith-Connally Act, which curtailed arbitrary actions by labor leaders. Even so, Ellender, refusing to concede the labor vote, wrote in 1943: "I cannot make up my mind that the bulk of labor is against me." But one of the senator's strong supporters, viewing his position more realistically, cautioned him: "Your position with labor is not nearly so strong as it was." Another political ally indicated other kinds of political support for the senator: "In your case it was the members of the Chamber of Commerce, AAA Committeemen who were counted on for you." Neither Ellender nor Earl Long received the nomination in 1944, but the man who did, Lewis Morgan, chose E. J. Bourg, treasurer of the Louisiana Federation of Labor, as the Long faction's candidate for auditor.[28] Jimmie H. Davis, an anti-Long Democrat, won the election.

In the 1948 gubernatorial election the State Federation of Labor again endorsed Earl Long for governor, and when he won, labor realized several minor legislative gains. (By 1949, though, Long was not on speaking terms with Federation president "Lige" Williams.[29]) Labor

Act, To Amend, S. 2123" folder, Box 92, AEP; Marshall, *Labor in the South*, 324–25.

27 *Congressional Record*, 80th Cong., 1st Sess., 1947, Vol. 93, Part 3, pp. 3670–71.

28 "Gubernatorial Campaign—1944" folder, *passim*, Ellender to Fred Benton, October 5, 1943, J. L. McInnis to Ellender, October 4, 1943, L. Austin Fontenot to Ellender, September 7, 1944, all in "Senator John H. Overton" folder, Box 408, all in AEP.

29 I. Lee Parker to H. L. Mitchell, October 4, 1949, Box 63, Folder 1214 of the Southern Tenant Farmers Union Papers, housed in the Southern Collection

leaders failed to oust several members of the congressional delegation who had voted for the antilabor Taft-Hartley Act the previous year. They opposed Ellender in his reelection campaign, but the veteran lawmaker won again.

The Dixiecrat revolt of 1948 had direct repercussions for organized labor in Louisiana. Louisiana Dixiecrat leaders supported Strom Thurmond of South Carolina against the incumbent Democratic nominee, Harry S. Truman, who had vetoed the Taft-Hartley Bill. John U. Barr and Leander Perez, leaders of the Louisiana Dixiecrats, both expressed strong antilabor sentiments. Barr was a major supporter of right-to-work legislation and had been a leader of the Louisiana Citizens' Committee. Perez, who had asked voters to repudiate labor leaders Dave Dubinsky and Walter Reuther, had instructed the sheriff of Plaquemines Parish to arrest labor leaders who came into his bailiwick. When Dixiecrats gave the rooster, the traditional Democratic party symbol in Louisiana, to the Dixiecrat faction rather than to the Democrats, organized labor protested.[30]

DeLesseps S. Morrison, mayor of New Orleans, had an indifferent labor attitude. Both he and his predecessor, Robert Maestri, learned to make concessions to organized labor, but Morrison never gained the confidence of most legitimate labor leaders. His friendship with Clarence "Chink" Henry, black president of General Longshore Workers' Local 1419, was a gesture of racial-political accommodation rather than a genuine prolabor proclivity. The political arm of Henry's local, The Crescent City Independent Voters League, supported Morrison in exchange for political funds with no strings attached from the Morrison-dominated Crescent City Democratic Organization. When sanitation workers struck in 1946 during his first year in office, Morrison's response to their demands for higher wages and shorter hours alerted union leaders to the new mayor's position. Morrison considered the strike illegal, an attack against city government, and called on volunteers to collect garbage. Regular sanitation workers returned after city engineers redrew garbage routes and replaced mule-drawn wagons with modern sanitation equipment. In 1948, however, when sanitation workers threat-

(and photoduplicated by the Microfilm Corporation of America in 60 rolls), University of North Carolina, Chapel Hill, hereinafter cited as STFU, with box and folder number or roll number.

30 Sindler, *Huey Long's Louisiana*, 220–22; Robert Sherrill, *Gothic Politics in the Deep South: Stars of the New Confederacy* (New York: Grossman, 1968), 25, 19.

ened to strike again, Morrison, who had relented somewhat, agreed to a new contract and found $30,000 for salary increases. That same year the mayor asserted the right of National Airlines workers to picket peacefully. Because Morrison's attitude toward labor had improved and because his political opponents had labor records worse than his own, Morrison received labor support in his 1949 mayoral campaign and his 1960 campaign for governor. But important labor leaders such as Fred Cassibry, a popular CIO lawyer later active in city government, continued to oppose the man whose efforts reflected only an image of reform.[31]

During the first half of the twentieth century, organized labor in Louisiana posed no serious threat to the economic and political status quo. By mid-century Louisiana laborers, like workingmen throughout the United States, had gained a legal status by virtue of New Deal labor legislation. Agricultural and rural Louisiana still had large numbers of seasonal and casual workers, however, who did not qualify for the protections enjoyed by industrial laborers. Furthermore, the labor movement in the state lacked a unified voice and a steady political ally, especially after the 1939 scandals decimated the Long ranks. But even Huey Long had never attempted a frontal attack against the bulwark of antiunion forces; instead, he had tried to help workingmen by pushing programs designed to bring free textbooks, better roads and bridges, state-operated hospitals, and other needed reforms to the masses. Jimmy Morrison came closest to being a prolabor politician, openly vying for labor support, but he was primarily identified with strawberry farmers, agrarians who had problems with complicated marketing agreements. In his early years in Washington, Senator Ellender supported organized labor, but he later became antagonistic toward organized labor. DeLesseps Morrison at least responded to worker needs when political expediency demanded it. Earl Long, like his brother Huey, received support from organized labor because he sponsored legislative programs beneficial to the masses, not because he introduced labor laws per se.

31 Edward Haas, *DeLesseps S. Morrison and the Image of Reform: New Orleans Politics, 1946–1961* (Baton Rouge: Louisiana State University Press, 1974), 251, 23–24, 56–57, 94–95, 247, 176.

Chapter 2

The Union: From Cotton Patch to Cane Field

Agricultural unions sprang up again after New Deal agricultural programs backfired, and distressed sharecroppers took matters into their own hands. Encouraged by the success of big national unions such as the recently formed CIO in 1935 and protected—they thought—from unfair labor practices by the National Labor Relations (Wagner) Act, tenant farmer unions first protested against Agricultural Adjustment Act policies and then, in 1935 and 1936, struck, especially in the cotton fields of Alabama and Arkansas. Some unions joined together in loose organizations, which could be quickly dissolved. The Alabama Sharecroppers' Union, merged with the Louisiana Farmers' Union and Alabama Farmers' Union to form the Sharecroppers' Union (SCU). The Southern Tenant Farmers Union (STFU), led for many years by H. L. Mitchell, was active in Arkansas, Missouri, Oklahoma, and Louisiana. In 1937 both the STFU and the SCU joined the CIO's radical United Cannery, Agricultural, Packing and Allied Workers of America (UCAPAWA), which planned to organize laborers and tenants. UCAPAWA agreed that farm owners would be enrolled by the National Farmers' Union.[1]

Many agricultural unions, including the Sharecroppers' Union and the CIO's UCAPAWA, espoused radical political and economic ideology. In the Lafayette area of Louisiana in the 1930s charges by antiunion forces of Communist collaboration undermined the efforts of Father Wilton Labbé, a Catholic priest, to form a laborers' union that would

1 F. Ray Marshall, *Labor in the South* (Cambridge: Harvard University Press, 1967), 156–57; George Brown Tindall, *Emergence of the New South, 1913–1945* (Baton Rouge: Louisiana State University Press, 1967), 428.

work with the Farmers' Union. In 1936, on a tour of Louisiana to search for new members, Alabama Farmers' Union leader, W. C. Irby, a lawyer, former Socialist, and writer for the *Farmers' Weekly*, stated his belief in government ownership of essential industries. Government conscription of labor for railroads or steel mills, he said, is no worse than the drafting of men for military service. Donald Henderson, president of UCAPAWA and reputedly a Communist, was accused of using the Missouri Roadside Demonstrations of 1939 for Communist propaganda purposes. Extremely active during World War II, UCAPAWA, after undergoing a name change, was expelled from the CIO in 1949 as a Communist-dominated union.[2]

To study the agricultural labor movement in America from the Great Depression to the 1950s is to trace the itinerary of the ubiquitous champion of farm labor, H. L. Mitchell, who, with sixteen others, founded the racially mixed Southern Tenant Farmers Union in 1934. From 1934 to 1974 he participated in almost every phase of the agrarian protest throughout the United States. Sharecroppers in Arkansas, sugarcane plantation laborers in Louisiana, small farmers here and there, braceros in the West—Mitchell, with his colleagues, worked among them all. His union was not known for orthodoxy nor for resounding success, compared to trade unions at least. It rallied to the cause of those whom no industrial union would have wanted, changing its name several times as Mitchell moved along lines that reflected changing agricultural problems. When tenancy declined, he turned to farm laborers, to migrant workers, and to those who had no spokesman. In the process he dealt with the famous and near famous, including Lyndon Johnson, Richard Nixon, Spiro Agnew, Norman Thomas, Eleanor Roosevelt, CIO organizer Gardner Jackson, agricultural experts Aubrey Williams, Clarence

2 Vincent O'Connell, interview, April 4, 1972, with Bishop Joseph Vath and Monsignor Charles J. Plauché, hereinafter cited as VPO interview. *Southern Farm Leader*, October, 1936, roll 58 of the Southern Tenant Farmers Union Papers, housed in the Southern Collection (and photoduplicated by the Microfilm Corporation of America in 60 rolls), University of North Carolina, Chapel Hill, hereinafter cited as STFU, with box and folder or roll number; Louis Cantor, "A Prologue to the Protest Movement: The Missouri Sharecroppers Roadside Demonstration of 1939," *Journal of American History*, LV (March, 1969), 804–822; Marshall, *Labor in the South*, 237; F. S. O'Brien, "The 'Communist-Dominated' Unions in the United States Since 1950," *Labor History*, IX (Spring, 1968), 184–209.

Senior, and Will Alexander, labor leaders such as George Meany, Ernesto Galarza, Cesar Chavez, and Howard Kester.[3]

As a youngster in a sharecropper family and as a cropper himself, Mitchell learned firsthand of the hardships tenant farmers endured during the 1920s and 1930s. When the policies of the New Deal Agriculture Adjustment Act led planters to evict their tenants rather than share benefit payments with them, Mitchell and his followers banded together to try to stop the evictions by petitioning the Department of Agriculture for corrective action. They organized the Southern Tenant Farmers Union in a little one-room schoolhouse called Sunnyside on the Norcross plantation near Tyronza, Arkansas, on July 26, 1934. Perhaps because Mitchell and his cohorts knew the extent of discontent among laborers, black and white, and because they were grounded in the tradition of agrarian protest, the STFU proved to be the most durable and tenacious—and historically fascinating—of all the farm labor unions that sprang up in the 1930s. Its formation and growth were strongly influenced by Socialists and their ideology. Mitchell was himself a Socialist, and, after meeting Norman Thomas, he organized Socialist locals in the Tyronza area, which later became the nucleus for STFU locals.[4]

In 1935, and again in 1936, the STFU struck for higher wages in the cotton fields. Some planters reacted with violence to intimidate union members, sometimes even in the rural churches where they were meeting. Though the strikes usually failed, the publicity generated by the planters' harsh antiunion methods brought the STFU new members and financial and political support from many sections of the country. By 1937 the union, operating from Memphis, where the STFU had fled to avoid the planter violence—dubbed the "reign of terror" in union news releases—boasted 30,000 members in seven states.

The Sharecroppers' Union and the National Farmers' Union often made overtures to the STFU. Both groups became involved with the farm union movement in Louisiana and tried to persuade the STFU to strike if growers did not agree to the one dollar both groups demanded for picking one hundred pounds of cotton. In 1936 the SCU invited STFU leaders to attend its New Orleans convention. But Mitchell's union ex-

3 H. L. Mitchell, *Workers in Our Fields: The Story of a Union That Would Not Die*, (n.p.: National Agricultural Workers Union, 25th Anniversary Publication, 1959), *passim*.

4 David E. Conrad, *The Forgotten Farmers: The Story of Sharecroppers in the New Deal* (Chapel Hill: The University of North Carolina Press, 1971), *passim*.

pressed concern that some of the conferences were plots to destroy the STFU; it responded politely to most suggestions but made no commitment. When Gordon McIntire of the Farmers' Union wrote to Mitchell in 1937, however, about the prospects of organizing the sugar industry in Louisiana, the STFU paid more attention than it had to earlier SCU proposals. McIntire said his group planned to move into sugar organizing soon and wondered if Mitchell was interested in joining him. Mitchell replied that McIntire's members, "small farmers and all," were eligible to join the STFU, but emphasized that the CIO, which the STFU had joined, expected membership dues—and results. McIntire then outlined his plans for Louisiana, where the AFL, by organizing only the sugarcane factory workers, neglected 6,000 cane-field workers within a forty-mile square of the cane country. He felt that the AFL had botched things by organizing only mill workers rather than the whole sugarcane industry, as the CIO would have done. McIntire asked for local French-speaking organizers to unionize not only the cane fields and the refineries but also the shrimp and oyster canneries and the cottonseed oil plants. He said that, by itself, Godchaux Sugars, a corporation with extensive holdings in south Louisiana, hired 3,500 workers for its fields and factories during the grinding season.[5]

Sugar growers received New Deal help in the form of a comprehensive sugar program, begun when Congress in 1934 passed the Jones-Costigan Act, an amendment to the Agricultural Adjustment Act of 1933, to provide adequate supplies of sugar to American consumers at reasonable prices, to protect domestic producers and workers, and to maintain trade relations with friendly nations. Not until the passage of this law, which became the basis for the modern sugar program, did the sugar industry demonstrate any measure of stability. The act divided the market among domestic and foreign producers, allocated quotas among various processors, adjusted production in accordance with quotas, levied a processing tax on sugar, and ensured equitable division of returns to sugar growers and to farm workers. In 1936 the processing tax used to finance payments to growers for limiting production under the Agricultural Adjustment Act was declared unconstitutional by the Supreme Court in

5 Albert Jackson to J. R. Butler, July 4, 1935, Clyde Johnson to Butler, July 19, [1936], Mitchell to Johnson, September 3, 1936, Gordon McIntire to Mitchell, September 7, 1937, Mitchell to McIntire, September 8, 1937, McIntire to Mitchell, September 14, 1937, McIntire to First Annual Convention, District 4 of UCAPAWA, September 24, 1937, Rolls 1, 3, 5, all in STFU.

the *Butler* case. Congress then passed the Sugar Act in 1937, which circumvented the discriminatory processing tax by imposing an excise tax only indirectly related to government payments to growers. Other provisions of the act were similar to those of the Jones-Costigan Act. Congress has extended the life of the Sugar Act by amending it in 1948, 1951, 1956, 1961, 1965, and 1971.[6]

Congress authorized the secretary of agriculture to implement the Sugar Act giving him the power to regulate many aspects of the sugar industry. The secretary began establishing minimum wage rates at hearings conducted annually in the sugarcane-growing areas. He protected the interest of cane-field workers by requiring that growers comply with wage and child-labor regulations and with acreage reduction contracts in order to qualify for their benefit payments. The secretary also conducted hearings to determine the size of benefit payments and the price growers received at the mill for a ton of cane. The USDA usually based the price on raw sugar prices in Cuba, but when raw sugar producers in Louisiana found the margin between what they paid for a ton of sugarcane and what they received for raw (brown) sugar too thin, they sought relief from the Sugar Division of the Department of Agriculture. The secretary, by lowering domestic consumption estimates, could reduce the amount of raw sugar imported and cause raw sugar prices to advance, thereby aiding Louisiana mill owners. Any rise in raw sugar prices, however, would raise costs for eastern seaboard refiners, who sold white granulated sugar several cents per pound above the raw sugar price. The refiners would pass their increased prices on to consumers, another group whose interests the secretary could not overlook. What benefited one sector of the industry often hurt another, and the secretary controlled the delicate balance of interest. When factionalism developed in the industry, no one who had grappled with the intricacies of the Sugar Act was surprised.[7]

Agricultural labor unions looked to Title III, Section 301, of the Sugar Act as the best safeguard for protecting workers in the sugar industry. The title clearly listed wage rates that were "fair and reasonable" for different categories of plantation jobs, outlined penalties for violations, restricted child labor, and listed perquisites, such as garden plots

6 U.S. Department of Agriculture, *The United States Sugar Program* (Washington: U.S. Government Printing Office, 1971), 33–36.

7 The Allen J. Ellender Papers, Division of Archives, Nicholls State University, Thibodaux, La., hereinafter cited as AEP, are replete with agonizing over the impact of various sections of the law.

and houses, which growers had to provide at no cost to workers. The annual hearings conducted by the Department of Agriculture afforded agricultural union leaders an opportunity to present a case for cane-field workers.

Many of these spokesmen came to champion the cause of sugarcane plantation workers in the 1938 wage hearings of the Department of Agriculture in New Orleans. Clyde Johnson of UCAPAWA advocated higher wages than the USDA recommendation, paid in cash, and an end to the commissary system. He asserted that workers were afraid to attend the annual hearings and demanded overtime pay, free housing, medical care, and garden space for workers, and prosecution of landowners who mistreated their employees. Union leaders complained that growers produced dishonest "Uncle Tom" witnesses to express satisfaction with the system. Cane planters, asking for a wage scale lower than the one the USDA was recommending, were fearful that many labor representatives would appear and therefore objected to having the hearings in New Orleans. Other planters said that they could not pay higher rates and denied having commissary stores that used scrip. One Houma, Louisiana, grower announced that the USDA representatives should "stay in Washington and leave us alone to work out our business problems." Dillard University professor, L. D. Reddick, testified that planters actually could afford to pay higher wages.[8]

The most thorough and sensible efforts in behalf of workers, however, were made by the Louisiana Farmers' Union leader, Gordon McIntire, whose judicious reports no doubt influenced later approaches used by Mitchell and his union. Because many Farmers' Union cotton tenants also cut cane during the harvest season, McIntire contended that his union had a stake in the sugarcane proceedings. He was not convinced that plantation owners actually planned to pay the rates agreed upon at the hearings, even though they risked losing large subsidies. McIntire prepared a simple questionnaire for workers to indicate how they were being paid, what deductions came from their pay, and whether they had been fired by the WPA and, in effect, forced to cut cane. Referring to pressure tactics used to break up a union meeting, McIntire said: "We

8 New Orleans *Times-Picayune*, August 6, 1938; *Louisiana Farmers' Union News*, March 1, 1938, Roll 58, STFU; Donald Holley, "Old and New Worlds in the New Deal Resettlement Program: Two Louisiana Projects," *Louisiana History*, XI (Spring, 1970), 137–65.

fought and risked our lives to get the wage raised. Now let's see that it is paid."⁹ Unemotionally and without rancor he discussed the ramifications of the methods by which workers were paid for hoeing or cutting cane, citing glaring inequities, such as the practice of paying "water boys" (usually old men or cripples) about thirty-five cents per day. Growers, he said, should pay wages in cash and maintain duplicate sets of records so workers would know what they were entitled to. McIntire complained of many problems not the responsibility of cane growers. He spoke of short school terms, a shortage of buses, and an absence of mandatory school attendance policies. He concluded his statement by asking for minimum pay of $1.50 per day, a ten-hour workday, and the removal of loopholes in the wage system. "Translate all these so-called 'free' paternalistic concessions," he said, "into tangible, cash terms."¹⁰

At the 1939 wage hearings Gordon McIntire called for a wage increase from $1.50 for a ten-hour day to $2 for a nine-hour day. He reported that some planters, claiming they could not afford it, were still paying less than the prevailing wage of $1.50 a day. Not content with mere wage increases, though, McIntire again emphasized such social problems as the quality of schools and the need for members on parish agricultural committees to represent small growers and tenants. Growers questioned his right to testify and demanded to know the names of the workers he claimed to represent.

The same year, Joseph Francis Rummel, the social activist Archbishop of New Orleans, had asked Raymond Witte, a professor at Loyola University in New Orleans, to testify in behalf of field workers at the hearings. On one occasion Witte arrived in Thibodaux late for the hearings and found a large crowd of blacks standing outside the Grand movie theater, site of the proceedings. Witte assured them the theater's policy of social segregation did not apply to governmental functions and led them into the meeting.¹¹ Obviously, the workers needed someone to speak for them.

McIntire had implied, correctly, that vested interest groups in agriculture induced Works Progress Administration officials to lay off workers during rice and sugarcane harvest seasons, but he could not prevent the

9 *Louisiana Farmers' Union News*, March 1, 1938, Roll 58, STFU; New Orleans *Times-Picayune*, August 6, 1938.

10 *Louisiana Farmers' Union News*, March 1, 1938, Roll 58, STFU.

11 Raymond Witte, interview, February 20, 1974; New Orleans *Times-Picayune*, June 15, 17, 1939.

pressure groups from having their way. The WPA had adopted a plan to provide manpower when the sugarcane harvest was threatened by cold weather in November, 1937. The plan, which became WPA policy, had been prepared by officials of the American Sugar Cane League; J. W. Bateman of the Agricultural Extension Service at Louisiana State University; officials from the Louisiana State Employment Service; WPA personnel; and the adjutant general of Louisiana, Raymond Fleming, who was to provide transportation for workers to the cane fields. James Crutcher, a WPA administrator, wrote to Senator Ellender: "If necessary, we will close down sufficient projects and influence the workers, as far as possible, to accept temporary employment in the canefields. . . . The workers will be told that their jobs on W.P.A. will be waiting for them as soon as they return from harvesting the cane crop." At least the workers who accepted employment cutting cane received the Sugar Act wage of $1.50 per day in 1938 rather than the $1.35 WPA rate. By 1942 Crutcher and various federal and state agencies had formalized a policy with the United States Employment Service for using WPA workers in agricultural jobs. Ellender told an executive of a large sugar corporation to notify his parish welfare director if he needed more field workers. "I had several released to my farms in that manner," Ellender wrote.[12]

Allen Ellender, proud of his association with small farmers, tried to improve the plight of tenants being evicted by landlords unwilling to share Sugar Act benefit payments with them. In 1936, a year before taking his United States Senate seat, Ellender had considered asking government officials to direct the Federal Land Bank, which held considerable farm acreage, to subdivide large tracts and "give the poor farmers a chance." The next year he discovered that assigning a quota to a tenant, rather than to a landowner, could solve a tenant-eviction problem on sugarcane plantations by allowing an evicted tenant to produce his quota on a new tract of land. In 1938 he explained to Department of Agriculture officials the advantage wealthy individuals and corporations had over landless farmers. "If the sale of the property can put an end to the tenant system," he wrote, "you can readily understand how wash sales could be made, and anyone in this fashion get rid of his tenants." Articulate correspondents undoubtedly influenced Ellender's views on

12 James Crutcher to Ellender, November 24, 1937, J. B. Hutson to Ellender, February 18, 1938, both in "Sugar" folder, Box 321, Crutcher to Ellender, February 26, 1942, Ellender to C. F. Dahlberg, May 9, 1942, both in "Farm Labor" folder, Box 333, all in AEP.

tenants. Mrs. M. G. Smith, who trained farmers in St. Charles Parish for the Resettlement Administration, wrote her views forcefully and clearly in 1937: "Small diversified farms are not wanted by the sugarcane interest. They want cheap labor, and to be cheap it must be poor, and the poorer it is the better they like it." She protested because greedy planters deprived tenants of their land and put it back into day wage crops like sugarcane. "Grasping local politicians . . . seek to exploit these illiterate, ignorant farmers, who are not farmers, but ex–day-laborers off of sugar plantations, that I am trying to train as farmers."[13]

Many of Senator Ellender's constituents did not share his concern for tenants or his overall optimism about the future of the sugar industry after passage of the Sugar Act in 1937. Harry D. Wilson, commissioner of the Louisiana Department of Agriculture and Immigration, considered tenants "lazy and very unreliable" and blamed city women welfare workers and Communists for stirring them up. G. J. Durbin complained that the Farm Security Administration permitted tenants to rent land from the Federal Land Bank and use checks from the Reconstruction Finance Corporation to guarantee payment. He considered the practice unfair to businessmen. Nevertheless, Harvey Peltier, a Longite politician and businessman, who saw economic prospects in sugar wrote to Ellender that "sugar seems to be back" and asked about placement (rather than removal) of tenants on land he hoped to put into sugarcane production.[14]

Although Ellender worried about small farmers and tenants, he seemed to doubt the integrity of some large sugarcane operators. Tenants often complained to him about Realty Operators, a large land-owning corporation whose managers Ellender mistrusted. In 1937 when Realty Operators tried to evict Ernest and Charles Martine from Clark Plantation, where they had been tenants since 1925, the Martines' attorneys asked Senator Ellender for help. He forwarded their complaint to the Sugar Division of the USDA, which informed him that Realty Operators could neither evict the Martines nor force them to stop selling their

13 Ellender to H. E. Delafosse, August 1, 1936, in "Farm S A, Farm Tenancy" folder, Ellender to Henry A. Wallace, September 10, 1937, in "Sugar" folder, Ellender to J. B. Hutson, January 22, 1938, in "AAA" folder, Mrs. M. G. Smith to Ellender, January 23, 1937, in "Farm Security Administration, Farm Tenancy" folder, all in Box 321, AEP.

14 Harry D. Wilson to Ellender, January 12, 1937, in "FSA, Farm Tenancy" folder, Box 321, G. J. Durbin to Ellender, December 9, 1941, in "Reconstruction Finance Corporation" folder, Box 39, Harvey Peltier to Ellender, September 7, 1937, in "Sugar" folder, Box 321, all in AEP.

cane crop to nearby Helvetia Sugar Corporation, a competitor of Realty Operators, because the Sugar Act prohibited landowners from interfering with contracts for the sale of cane. Later, however, after authorities had removed the quotas on cane to increase sugar production during World War II, Realty Operators sold the land rented by the Martine brothers. Regretfully, Ellender informed their attorney that in such a case, the Sugar Act did not protect the tenant. The quota, when restored, would remain with the land.[15]

In 1938 Ellender checked with the county agent of Terrebonne Parish, a government employee who helped local farmers implement agricultural policies, to verify complaints against South Coast, another large sugar corporation. Apparently, South Coast was buying additional land to increase its total acreage so that it could maintain the same number of acres in sugarcane as in previous years while appearing to reduce its sugarcane acreage. "In other words with a high past history record of say 70% of one's land in cane, all that was necessary was to increase the cultivable acreage to utilize that past history record," Senator Ellender complained. Mervin Polmer, a friend of the senator's who operated a plantation store in Terrebone Parish, often wrote letters to Ellender which, however poorly written, were clear enough about tactics employed by big sugar interests. "The [American] Sugar [Cane] League does not properly represent the small tenant cane grower in matters of this kind," Polmer wrote, "so It's up to you to take care of the Underdog small Cane farmer and see if you Can't help them." Polmer told the senator that Realty Operators was deducting part of the benefit payments for cane delivered after the Commodity Credit Corporation increased these payments in 1943 to compensate the growers for increased labor costs. Ellender inquired about sending benefit payments directly to growers, but the Sugar Division replied that making payments through the processor simplified matters even though, at times, it created problems.[16]

15 Ellender to Mrs. L. J. Barrios, January 23, 1939, in "Miscellaneous B" folder, Box 322, refers to "their manipulations." J. B. Hutson to Ellender, October 20, 1937, in "Realty Operators, Inc." folder, Box 321, Walter Lemann to Ellender, January 31, 1944, Ellender to Lemann, February 2, 1944, both in "Agriculture, Sugar, Quotas" folder, Box 280, all in AEP.

16 C. C. Couvillion to Ellender, October 14, 1938, C. A. Duplantis, Jr. to Ellender, September 25, 1938, both in "Sugar-Acreages, 1938" folder, Box 409, Mervin Polmer to Ellender, December 7, 1943, February 4, 1944, Ellender to Polmer, December 10, 1943, all in "Commodity Credit Corporation, General, 1945-'46" folder, Box 446, all in AEP.

Allen Ellender's concern for small sugar growers did not go unnoticed by corporate sugar leaders. They reacted promptly to the senator's public statements about the domestic sugarcane allotment controversy, giving him their version of the problem. J. J. Munson of South Coast, a veteran Cane League member, asked Ellender about his statement charging large growers with usurping the quotas of small growers, "going to the extent of renting land in order to do so." Ellender said he meant that all growers, big and small, should suffer some acreage cutback. He reassured Munson, who feared losing acreage to new producers entering the field, that he did not want to see longtime producers suffer the brunt of acreage cuts. Ellender, having changed his thinking, wrote: "I believe that the best course for us to pursue . . . is for us to be able to show the large number of people that will be favorably affected by an increase in quota."[17]

Senator Ellender received many letters from farmers and farm lobby groups seeking larger benefit payments for themselves and lower wages for their laborers, but in 1938 Ellender spelled out to Clarence Bourg, the American Sugar Cane League's principal lobbyist, his basic philosophy regarding agricultural aid programs: "I have asked for better prices so that those who employ can be in a position to pay better wages." Even after the senator had expressed his faith in wage-and-hour legislation and his determination to allow field workers to share in increased benefits provided by the Sugar Act of 1937, though, sugar growers sent him countless schemes for lowering the wages of plantation workers. One planter complained of wage increases wiping out the gains growers expected from passage of the Sugar Act. Another planter claimed that, because migrant workers failed to leave forwarding addresses, it was impossible for him to comply with Department of Agriculture rulings that wage increases be paid retroactively to the beginning of the harvest season. One grower complained that he could not afford to pay older workers full wages and wanted permission to pay them at lower rates rather than dismiss them. (The Sugar Division approved compensating such workers on a piece-rate basis.) Another wanted to pay his workers 50 cents per ton, rather than the required 75 cents per ton, for cutting cane that had been stripped of leaves by burning.[18]

17 J. J. Munson to Ellender, December 23, 1938, Ellender to Munson, January 11, 1939, in "Agriculture, Department of, Sugar-Acreage, 1939" folder, Box 409, AEP.

18 Ellender to Clarence Bourg, August 22, 1938, in "AAA" folder, F. W. Spencer to Ellender, telegram, November 18, 1937, Stephen Munson to Ellender,

If Ellender gained favor with labor leaders early in his senatorial career for his stand on antilabor legislation, he lost ground for his views on child labor in agriculture. Here his position coincided with typical southern congressional opinion and marked a departure from his early prolabor stance. His amendments to the Sugar Act of 1937 reduced the severe penalties for violation of child-labor provisions, and critics in the national press blasted them. Gordon McIntire of the Louisiana Farmers' Union said that an Ellender amendment that allowed growers to receive benefit payments despite child-labor violations encouraged growers to "give up social responsibility" for their actions. In July, 1939, Justice Department investigators looked into possible threats in Louisiana cane fields against workers who testified to child-labor violations. On the Senate floor Ellender explained that his amendment did not condone child labor, but imposed a sensible fine of ten dollars a day per violation rather than hold back a grower's entire benefit payment. He did not support an amendment by Louisiana Congressman James Domengeaux which would have removed all child-labor provisions from the Sugar Act. Downplaying criticism of his own bill, Ellender wrote: "Some opposition to my bills has developed from various organizations who are violently opposed to any form of child labor, but I do not believe it will amount to much." Clarence Fleming, a black leader from Thibodaux, who sought improvement of black schools, accused Ellender of proposing legislation detrimental to youths incapable of fighting back. A Washington newspaper reported that Louisiana's congressional delegation voted for extension of certain trade agreement bills in exchange for favorable action on Ellender's amendments to the Sugar Act. Later Ellender took time to inform several large cane producers, whose benefit payments had been delayed pending settlement of child-labor violations, that Agriculture Department officials had released 1938 benefit payments.[19]

November 20, 1937, Ellender to Stephen Munson, December 1, 1937, Frank Barker to Ellender, November 14, 1937, all in "Sugar" folder, Box 321, all in AEP.

19 New Orleans *Times-Picayune*, July 19, 1939, February 9, 1940; Ellender to Harriet G. Johnson, October 27, 1942; Ellender to Clarence J. Savoie, March 4, 1940, Clarence Fleming open letter to citizens of Lafourche Parish and Town of Thibodaux, undated, Fleming to Ellender, February 9, 1940, all in "Sugar Act of 1937, To Amend—S. 3237 and S. 3236—Child Labor" folder, Box 251, John O'Donnell and Doris Fleeson, "Capitol Stuff," [New York?] *Times-Herald*, May 27, 1940, in "Sugar Child Labor Am" folder, Box 301, all in AEP; *Congressional Record*, 76th Cong., 3rd Sess., 1940, Vol. 84, Part 4, p. 6496.

Several agricultural unions flirted with farm operations in Louisiana in the 1930s, but none of them conducted concentrated organizational campaigns of real significance. Factional rivalries contributed to their problems, but the lack of institutionalized local support of some kind was an even bigger disadvantage. Even a small minority group, if tightly organized and unified, would have provided invaluable assistance to agricultural unionists.

The group that eventually undertook the task of organizing agricultural workers in Louisiana, the Southern Tenant Farmers Union, separated from the CIO's United Cannery, Packing, and Allied Workers of America in 1939 and had problems as a result. "After our break with C.I.O., we did not have much of a union left," H. L. Mitchell said. Mitchell completely lost faith in the trade union movement after the AFL refused to grant the STFU a charter in 1940. "There is no basis," he said, "for trade unionism in southern agriculture with conditions such as prevail." Referring to earlier trade union tactics, Mitchell told delegates at the STFU's 1941 convention in Little Rock, Arkansas: "We were paupers trying to bargain with paupers."[20]

Despite these setbacks, the STFU found a niche in agricultural circles as World War II created problems different from those faced in the 1930s. Altering his tactics, Mitchell began to specialize in labor recruiting to meet the seasonal demands of East Coast food-processing plants such as Seabrook Farms in New Jersey. In 1943, Leon Schachter, organizer for the Amalgamated Meat Cutters and Butcher Workmen of North America, was afraid that United States canneries would use German prisoners of war in their union plants and asked Mitchell to supply southern workers instead. The STFU provided workers who enjoyed conditions comparable to those negotiated by Local 56 of the Butcher Workmen in New Jersey. The STFU worked successfully, through agreements with the Farm Security Administration and the United States Employment Service, to supply union workers in various areas, but as the wartime labor shortages became acute in southern agriculture, congressmen and farm lobby groups took steps that prevented the STFU from shipping workers outside the South. Ellender, who had supported the controversial Farm Security Administration, opposed the prospect of the FSA serving as a clearinghouse for the STFU. Mitchell's operations ended with gas and tire rationing and changes in rules to require permission from county agents before southern workers could be shipped to outside

20 H. L. Mitchell, *Workers in Our Fields*, 14–15.

areas. Even then the STFU was able, for a while, to conduct an "underground railroad" from its Memphis headquarters, circumventing the regulations designed, Mitchell said, to keep a large labor supply in the South.[21]

To better reflect its new role in agricultural labor, the STFU changed its name to the National Farm Labor Union (NFLU) in 1946 and applied to the AFL again for a charter. William Green, AFL president, agreed to charter the NFLU on the recommendations of Leon Schachter and Patrick Gorman of the Butcher Workmen of North America, with whom the STFU had worked harmoniously during the war. After Mitchell further assured Teamster boss Dan Tobin that his group did not plan to organize dairy plants under Teamster jurisdiction, the NFLU received its charter on August 25, 1946.[22]

The NFLU held its first convention in Washington, D.C. in January, 1947, amid considerable publicity, generated primarily by Mitchell's skillfully written news releases. The NFLU intended to organize the nation's agricultural workers, and Mitchell and his associates were kept busy planning campaigns for various sections of the country. At the convention Mitchell met Ernesto Galarza, a trained historian and the chief of the Labor and Information Division of the Pan-American Union, who was touring the country in 1947 lecturing on the problems of laborers in Latin America. The following year Galarza joined the NFLU as its education and research director.

A naturalized American citizen, Galarza was born in Tepic, Mexico, the son of migratory farm workers who came to the United States when he was eleven years old. He attended the public schools of Sacramento, California, and earned his B.A. degree from Occidental College. He took his M.A. at Stanford and his Ph.D. in history at Columbia University. With this academic background he was able to produce in-depth studies of labor-related problems, giving the NFLU a sophisticated research and publicity capability that was the envy of many larger industrial unions.[23]

Bolstered by a grant from the AFL and assisted by Henry Hasiwar, a

21 Marshall, *Labor in the South,* 164–65; Mitchell, *Workers in Our Fields,* 15–16; Mitchell, interview, March 6, 1971; Ellender to R. W. Collier, April 21, 1943, in "Pace Bill" folder, Box 77, AEP.

22 Mitchell, *Workers in Our Fields,* 15–16; Mitchell, interview, March 6, 1971.

23 *Farm Labor News,* March, 1948, Roll 58, STFU; Ernesto Galarza, *Merchants of Labor: The Mexican Bracero Story* (San Jose, Ca.: The Rosicrucian

recent addition to the NFLU, Galarza and his associates challenged a California agribusiness giant, the DiGiorgio Fruit Corporation, in a recognition strike in 1947. By 1948 the union leaders realized that they had become hopelessly deadlocked—and their delay became an ally of the big corporation. Meanwhile the NFLU had shifted its headquarters from Memphis to Washington, D.C., the center of the agricultural bureaucracy. Early in 1949, Mitchell was grappling with a number of reorganization plans, including one for reassigning California personnel to the sugar country of Louisiana.[24]

When Mitchell and his colleagues discussed personnel reassignments, they usually thought of the aggressive organizer Henry Hasiwar, who had joined the NFLU in 1947 and had impressed its leaders with his ability and drive. Hasiwar, like Mitchell, had early links with Socialists and was a friend and admirer of Norman Thomas. Hank, as he was usually called, completed high school in New York and attended Columbia University for two years. Before joining the army in 1943, he had served as a union organizer for CIO auto workers, and during the postwar occupation of Japan, he helped to revitalize the labor unions there. The labor priest, Vincent O'Connell, S.M., remembered him as an idealist, tough when challenged but "soft as butter" when confronted with a soft story. He made personal sacrifices for the union and occasionally faced danger. Though he was "as honest a fellow as I ever met," O'Connell remembered, "Hank was not really a religious guy."[25]

Perhaps remembering Gordon McIntire's reports on opportunities for organizing sugarcane plantation workers or possibly responding to requests from Catholic church leaders, H. L. Mitchell attended his first sugar wage hearing in 1947. He found extensive poverty in the cane-producing area and suggested that if the people there had been living outside the United States, the government would have organized rescue parties to save them. Concerning the 1948 wages of $3.65 for tractor drivers and $2.90 for unskilled workers for a nine-hour day, he said: "The Secretary of Agriculture, Mr. Clinton P. Anderson, should hang his head in shame because his Department approved a wage rate that

Press, 1964), dust jacket blurb; Joan London and Henry Anderson, *So Shall Ye Reap* (New York: Thomas Y. Crowell Company, 1970), Chap. 6.

24 *Farm Labor News*, March, 1948, Roll 58, STFU.

25 Vincent O'Connell, interview, September 11, 1970; Mitchell, memorandum, n.d. [1957]. Roll 40, STFU; Mitchell, interview, June 23, 1970.

amounts to slow starvation for men, women, and children in Louisiana's sugar cane fields." These wages had climbed gradually since the early days of the Sugar Act. In 1943 tractor drivers had received only $2.15 and laborers $1.75 for a nine-hour day. Cane cutters received $2.45 and tractor drivers $3.10 in 1946. When the minimum wage increased to seventy-five cents per hour in 1949, sugar growers realized they would have to pay more or risk losing their workers to higher paying jobs.[26]

In March, 1948, H. L. Mitchell hired a former United States Sugar Corporation employee, I. Lee Parker, ostensibly to help the National Farm Labor Union place workers in canning factories. Parker attended the 1948 sugarcane wage hearings in Thibodaux, Louisiana, and labeled the proceedings a farce since 500 cane growers showed up, including officials of the American Sugar Cane League and the Louisiana Farm Bureau, but no one spoke for the workers. Some growers suggested setting wages as low as thirty-nine cents per hour. Parker recommended seventy-five cents. When questioned about the cost of producing a ton of sugarcane, Parker evaded the question, instead noting that cane growers received subsidies and additional benefits when they experienced difficulties while workers received nothing extra.[27]

Because dues-paying dairy farmers in Louisiana and other states who had joined the union were vital to NFLU finances, Mitchell struggled to keep them in his jurisdiction even though he realized that the dairy locals probably belonged with the Farmers' Union, which now dealt with small farmers and not agricultural workers. James G. Patton of the National Farmers' Union complained to AFL President William Green in 1950 about Mitchell's encroachment. When Green asked Mitchell for an explanation, the NFLU leader stretched the truth a bit and replied that his union was mainly interested in laborers on large industrial farms but that "now and then a small farmer joins." Dissatisfied with Mitchell's evasiveness, Patton complained to Green again, implied that he would fight the incursion of labor into farmer organizations, and requested a meeting of the AFL, the FU, and the NFLU. Moreover he labeled Mitchell's dairy farmer venture an "ill-conceived drive," likening it to John L. Lewis's unsuccessful attempt to organize dairy unions. Weary of explaining to Green his reluctance to surrender the financially

26 *Farm Labor News*, March, 1948, Roll 58, STFU; USDA newsletter, "Dear Grower," June 16, 1943, in "Agricultural Adjustment Administration, 1943–'44" folder, Box 77, Marcel J. Voorhies to Ellender, November 24, 1949, in "Agriculture, Sugar, 1949" folder, Box 9, both in AEP.

27 *Farm Labor News*, March, June, August–September, 1948, Roll 58, STFU.

important dairy farmers, Mitchell asked if he could drop in for a talk before responding to Patton.[28] Eventually, most dairy farmers abandoned the NFLU when they realized how little influence Mitchell's union exerted.

NFLU financial records substantiate Mitchell's contention that his union did not possess the wealth of big industrial unions. In 1948 the union's total income was $67,000 and expenditures were $57,000. In 1949, however, total income was only $46,000 of which $32,000 came from contributions and only $14,000 from dues. Expenditures for that year mostly for salaries and organizing expenses, totaled $49,000. In 1950, NFLU income totaled $49,000, of which $35,000 came from contributions; expenses amounted to $51,000. The AFL paid the salaries of four of its organizers working with the NFLU, plus travel expenses for Mitchell and one other person. The union depended on AFL subsidies, in fact, for survival.[29]

The main contributor to the NFLU besides the AFL was the National Sharecroppers Fund (NSF), a New York–based philanthropic organization that had become the major beneficiary of NSF campaigns for funds to aid the rural poor. Rarely was Mitchell hard-pressed to come up with dramatic statistics of privation or injustice in rural America—evidence on which the Sharecroppers Fund could base an appeal for contributions. Persuading the AFL to continue grants to the NFLU that Mitchell hoped would soon be self-sustaining posed a more difficult problem. In an attempt to remain solvent, the NFLU developed a life insurance program designed primarily to encourage members to pay dues regularly. After a member paid three months of dues, he was entitled to a $250 insurance policy that would remain in force as long as he stayed in good standing.[30]

No contributions or stratagems ever relieved Mitchell of the chronic problem of making the NFLU self-supporting. His health reflected the union's ailing financial condition, and he admitted in 1949 that the situation "has been that way for nearly 15 years, hence I have ulcers and just can't get rid of them." In 1950, after financial problems forced the

28 See Roll 33 and Boxes 63 and 64, STFU, for numerous exchanges among Mitchell, William Green, and James Patton during 1949 and 1950.

29 Audit by A. G. Hall and Co. of Blytheville, Arkansas, December 16, 1949, 63:1219, Mitchell to Patrick Gorman, February 13, 1950, 63:1235, both in STFU.

30 Mitchell to Beth Biderman, September 29, 1950, 64:1252, Green to Mitchell, December 21, 1950, Mitchell to Green, December 29, 1950, 64:1256, Mitchell to Lee Arnold, September 1, 1949, 63:1210, all in STFU.

union to reduce its office force, Mitchell went on a baby-food diet, presumably because of recurring problems with ulcers. His health improved the following year after vitamin and hormone treatments in New York, but his financial problems remained. When money matters became especially pressing, as they often were, Mitchell would suggest economizing. When he proposed a budget of $62,000 for 1951, he exhorted his colleagues in the NFLU: "Put everything you have in getting dues paying membership. Your job and mine is to organize workers." Urging greater personal economy, Mitchell insisted that one man could get by on five dollars a day. "At least I do here in Washington," he added.[31]

By the 1950s Mitchell's union, originally the Southern Tenant Farmers' Union (STFU), had changed its name again from the National Farm Labor Union (NFLU) to the National Agricultural Workers Union (NAWU). The NAWU, financially strapped and politically disadvantaged, was not the same organization that had dabbled in Louisiana sugarcane operations in the late 1930s. It seemed even less likely to succeed in the 1950s with the onset of McCarthyism and the alienation of Senator Allen Ellender, former Longite and friend of organized labor. Even though idealistic Catholic social activists in Louisiana encouraged the NAWU's organizational efforts in the cane country of south Louisiana, the Louisiana congressional delegation, the American Sugar Cane League, and other influential spokesmen for the sugar industry would rally to support antiunion sugar growers.

31 Mitchell to Galarza, March 17, 1949, Roll 34, Dorothy Dowe to Churchill, November 29, 1950, 64:1255, and January 23, 31, 1951, Mitchell to All Vice Presidents of the NFLU, January 26, 1951, 65:1263, Mitchell to Churchill, undated, 64:1259, and May 17, 1950, 64:1244, all in STFU.

Chapter 3
The Church

A scholarly study of Catholic church support for anything as controversial as the labor movement requires a clear explanation of two factors. One is a specific definition of church support; the other is an understanding of the nature and structure of the Catholic church in America. Even though American bishops are nearly autonomous in their own dioceses, their economic and political policies are not necessarily binding on American Catholics, despite a common belief to the contrary among Protestants. Rank-and-file Catholic clergy and laymen usually distinguish between religious and secular worlds in deciding whether to support social action policies when they are brought to a test, and few bishops dare to alienate their communities with strong stands on political issues. The doctrine of papal infallibility is narrowly applied by American Catholics and poses no unreasonable restrictions. Although Archbishop John Ireland of St. Paul, Minnesota, expressed the view of many Catholics when he said, "The Church is supreme in one order of things; the state is supreme in another order," it is not clear, even today, where the demarcation should be drawn between the two orders.[1]

Defenders of the Catholic church disagree with critics who view their church as authoritative, domineering, and ultraconservative. They contend that what some observers consider docility on the part of Catholics in evaluating doctrine actually entails a different concept of arriving at religious truth. Protestants approve doctrine only when each sees for himself that it agrees with Scripture. Catholics, on the other hand, feel that man's duty is not to judge the divine message but to receive it. Since a Catholic receives the word of God from a living church that explains holy teachings to him, he judges the whole rather than each

1 Quoted in Robert D. Cross, *The Emergence of Liberal Catholicism in America* (Cambridge: Harvard University Press, 1958), 74, 79, 81.

part. Furthermore, church teachings are not limited to papal encyclicals, but also include the interpretations of the bishops, the liturgy, works by men of the church "under divine inspiration," Scripture, and common beliefs and practices of Catholics through the ages.[2]

A major problem for scholars attempting to evaluate the role of the Catholic church in America has always been that of definition. Some observers consider the term *American Catholic church* itself illusory because there is no central controlling church body—American bishops do not answer to each other. The terms *liberal* and *conservative* can also be misleading, especially since a church leader could be a liberal on doctrinal matters and a conservative on economic or political issues. Even in the secular world, a label such as "liberal" does not predict a man's response to any given issue, and the church is no exception. Nor should *liberal* and *conservative* be equated with *good* and *bad*. A liberal priest might favor labor unions, a conservative stress charity, and a moderate emphasize building schools and hospitals.[3]

Catholic social doctrine, liberal or otherwise, did not follow a straight line of progression and growth. In colonial America, Catholics were a minority struggling to win converts and acceptance by their Protestant neighbors. Later, in the nineteenth century, Irish immigrants settled in cities, making America's small Catholic population predominantly urban. At the Second Plenary Council held in Baltimore in 1866, American bishops recommended charitable works as a means of competing with Protestants in winning souls. Periodic depressions proved, however, that charity alone could not cope with chronic poverty. Some Catholics turned to labor unions or stressed state socialism. In the 1870s New Orleans jurist, T. Wharton Collens, founder of a Christian labor union, suggested that Christians isolate themselves from the world. He called his plans for establishing Christian communes "colonization." His critics labeled him a Catholic Communist.[4]

2 Gustave Weigel, "The Significance of Papal Pronouncements," in Anne Fremantle (ed.), *The Papal Encyclicals in Their Historical Context,* (New York: G. P. Putnam's Sons, 1956), 17–18, 10–11.

3 The author is indebted to the Reverend Charles O'Neill, S.J., an authority on religion in colonial Louisiana, for his advice on the simplistic notion that labels such as liberal or conservative can be equated with right or wrong, good or evil.

4 Aaron I. Abel, *American Catholicism and Social Action: A Search for Social Justice, 1865–1950* (Garden City, N.Y.: Hanover House, 1960), 12, 16, 24, 29–30, 48–49.

It became less radical to support labor unions, such as the Knights of Labor, during the 1880s as church and lay leaders came to recognize the validity of union emphasis on arbitration and on the concept of a living wage. Catholic social action shifted from charity and rural colonization to aid for labor unions.

Two factors troubled church leaders about labor unions: the secret oaths associated with them (especially with the K of L) and the concern that unions endorsed the government ownership of basic industries—socialism. Even after K of L president Terence Powderly, a Catholic, agreed to eliminate secret rituals introduced by the masonic founder of the Knights, Archbishop Elzear Taschereau of Quebec asked for and received in 1884 a ban by the Vatican against the Knights in Canada. American bishops James Gibbons, John Ireland, and John Keane wrote to Rome and asked the Vatican not to ban the union in American dioceses. Gibbons recommended lifting the ban in Canada also and explained that in the United States the K of L had few secrets but many Catholic members.[5]

Pope Leo XIII took a stand on the condition of labor when he issued the encyclical *Rerum Novarum* in May, 1891. The pope viewed social justice as mediation between economic liberalism and socialism, and so pleased neither extreme with his decree. Socialists thought the encyclical favored the capitalist class; businessmen considered it prolabor in tone. It stressed the inviolability of private property and emphasized the role of organized religion in bringing labor and capital together. Feeling that workers should not be forced to work for less than they needed to support themselves, Leo XIII endorsed the idea of a "living" wage.[6]

Rerum Novarum, although criticized by Catholics unwilling to make sweeping concessions to the working class, nevertheless set several new trends for Catholic social thinking. It demonstrated a new desire on the part of church leaders to win support from the masses rather than from the upper class. It also voiced a Christian expectation of industrial peace. But most importantly, it helped develop a concept of justice combined with charity—the notion that man has a right to equality. Some bishops expressed misgivings about the encyclical, and Bishop John L. Spalding of Peoria, Illinois, thought it committed the Church to a mission of

5 *Ibid.*, 67–68; Cross, *The Emergence of Liberal Catholicism*, 116, 119; John Tracy Ellis, *The Life of James Cardinal Gibbons*, ed. Francis L. Broderick (Milwaukee: Bruce Publishing Company, 1963), 88, 90, 460.

6 Abell, *American Catholicism and Social Action*, 73–75.

saving society as well as souls. Some leaders expected that the encyclical's emphasis on negotiation would lead to compulsory arbitration.[7]

Because his support for the Knights of Labor and his tolerant attitude toward Freemasons, Fenians, and other secret societies, Cardinal Gibbons gained a reputation as a liberal and a progressive. Actually, he was more an appeaser and a diplomat. Gibbons' fellow bishops sometimes chided him for his failure to start ambitious projects or to take a stand on issues. Most church historians, including Gibbons's biographer, classified the influential prelate as a moderate in most instances. He encouraged workingmen to organize for their protection and benefit, at the same time demanding that the Knights of Labor discourage violence.[8]

As Archbishop of Baltimore, Cardinal Gibbons held an extremely influential and prestigious position in the United States. Many Catholics considered him the nominal leader of the American church. Even though he was on friendly terms with important political leaders, such as President Rutherford B. Hayes and Alexander Stephens of Georgia, former vice-president of the Confederate States of America, Gibbons maintained informal relations with the pastors of his archdiocese, who often dropped in unannounced to talk. He handled delicate church relations concerning Guam, the Philippines, Puerto Rico, and Cuba with presidents William Taft and Theodore Roosevelt and often spoke out against attempts to tax church property in America.[9]

Gibbons relished his position as liaison between the American church and the Vatican, and, like Bishop John Keane, felt that having an American to represent Rome was preferable to having a foreign apostolic delegate in the United States. Both leaders dreaded the impact of the anti-Catholic, antiforeign American Protective Association in stirring anti-Catholic feelings, and they feared that appointment of a papal nuncio to the United States during a new wave of know-nothingism would make defending the position of the American church more difficult. It was against their advice that Pope Leo XIII in 1893 sent Archbishop Francesco Satolli to the United States to clarify issues and, later, to head a papal delegation. Although viewed by Protestants as evidence of foreign domination of Americans, the Satolli mission actually provided home rule of sorts for American bishops, who could work out policies with Satolli without appealing to Rome for approval.[10]

7 *Ibid.*, 76–77, 79, 82.
8 *Ibid.*, 106; Ellis, *James Gibbons,* 62, 87, 213.
9 Ellis, *James Gibbons,* 33, 170–75.
10 *Ibid.*, 130–32; Abell, *American Catholicism and Social Action,* 96.

Even more than Cardinal Gibbons, Monsignor John A. Ryan, face-tiously called "the Right Reverend New Dealer" by critics, symbolized the growing involvement of the Catholic church in social action in the twentieth century. Monsignor Ryan thought of himself more as a pro-fessor of moral theology than as a New Deal advisor, social reformer, or liberal bureaucrat.[11] He was born in 1869 near St. Paul, Minnesota, where populism later flourished. Ryan, although he often ignored the efforts of other social activists, such as the leaders of the Jesuit labor schools, the liturgical movement, and the Catholic Worker Movement, was nevertheless closely associated with reforms in and out of the church.[12] He served on the faculty at Catholic University and on the board of directors of the American Civil Liberties Union, wrote labor laws with John Commons, and enjoyed a great deal of priestly indepen-dence under the protective wings of such broad-minded bishops as John Ireland and Michael Curley.

Ryan believed that his book, *A Living Wage*, was validated by *Rerum Novarum*. He disagreed with Herbert Hoover and Father Charles Coughlin, but he endorsed the concept of the CIO and staunchly de-fended Franklin Roosevelt's administration. Strongly influenced by his Minnesota Populist background—his father had been active in the Na-tional Farmers Alliance—Ryan came to support not only farm-labor beliefs but also a wide spectrum of ideas espoused by Henry George, the single taxer. Among them were minimum wage legislation; an eight-hour work day; unemployment insurance; municipal housing; women's and children's rights legislation; laws to protect the right to picket; pub-lic ownership of utilities, mines, and forests; regulation of monopolies; a graduated income tax; a tax on future increases in land value; and an end to stock market speculation.[13]

For the most part American bishops were slow to acknowledge their social responsibilties and develop a program of action. In 1919, mem-bers of the Catholic War Council petitioned the Pope for permission to create a permanent organization to replace the War Council. They asked

11 Here *liberal bureaucrat* is used generally to mean one able to accept eco-nomic, political, and social changes even though they may challenge establishment procedures.

12 Francis Broderick, *Right Reverend New Dealer: John A. Ryan* (New York: Collier-Macmillan, 1963), 58, 242.

13 *Ibid.*, 80–81, 278, 57, 59; Abell, *American Catholicism and Social Action*, 88; Andrew M. Greeley, *The Catholic Experience: An Interpretation of the His-tory of American Catholicism* (Garden City, N.Y.: Image Books, 1969), 227–28, 233, 237.

Monsignor Ryan to write a brief program stating their aims. The program he wrote became the widely acclaimed Bishops' Program for Social Reconstruction which called for establishment of a United States Employment Service, continuation of the War Labor Board, formation of a placement service for veterans, and the setting of a minimum wage. Predictably, the National Association of Manufacturers denounced the program. Raymond Graham Swing of *Nation* called it a "Catholic Miracle" because it seemed to him so unlike usual Catholic policy. The Bishops' Program had no formal legislative impact, but the absence of opposition to it among the bishops signified the approval by the hierarchy.[14]

The National Catholic War Council changed its name in 1922 to the National Catholic Welfare Council, retaining the already familiar NCWC initials and began organizing committees to work in specialized problem areas. The Social Action Department had broad jurisdiction, and, under Ryan's influence, campaigned against the open-shop crusade. The Catholic Conference on Industrial Problems dealt with wages, worker-ownership plans, and collective bargaining contracts. More than any other agency, it acquainted the American public with Catholic social doctrine. The National Catholic Rural Life Conference, another branch of the NCWC, considered problems from the farm front and assisted the sporadic but ubiquitous agricultural unions that sprang up in the twenties and thirties.

Even before the stock market crash in 1929 the Social Action Department of the NCWC had criticized the low earnings of workers during a period of high productivity, and the Great Depression heightened Catholic church commitment to social justice. Pope Pius XI, on the fortieth anniversary of *Rerum Novarum* in 1931, issued the encyclical *Quadragesimo Anno*, which encouraged the formation of labor unions and the concept of government economic planning. Many Catholics agreed with Ryan's view that the New Deal's National Recovery Administration fell within the scope of the economic planning described in *Quadragesimo Anno*. Ryan thought that Franklin Roosevelt's speeches during the 1932 presidential campaign reflected familiarity with Catholic encyclicals. Some Catholics outdid the labor leaders with their radicalism on labor issues. Bishop R. E. Lucey of Amarillo, Texas, complained to labor leader John L. Lewis that unions did not

14 Broderick, *Right Reverend New Dealer*, 104–08; Abell, *American Catholicism and Social Action*, 189, 201, 224.

heed *Quadragesimo Anno*'s advice about sharing in the management of industry. Somewhat taken aback, Lewis replied that to suggest such a move at that time was to strengthen allegations that Communists ran the CIO. Monsignor John O'Grady of the Catholic Rural Life Conference, a branch of the NCWC, stood almost alone in his support of the controversial Farm Security Administration when it came under attack by the farm lobby after World War II.[15]

Until the United States Supreme Court struck down the National Recovery Administration in the *Schechter* case in 1935, Ryan had received an annual salary of $6,000 as a member of the NRA Industry Appeals Board, which heard complaints by small manufacturers against NRA codes. Later, Roosevelt appointed him to the Advisory Council of the United States Employment Service. No doubt political expediency prompted Roosevelt to reward Ryan for his support of the New Deal and his opposition to Father Charles Coughlin, the anti–New Deal radio priest. Although he did not relish an open clash with a fellow priest and was no match for Coughlin's oratorical skills, Ryan nonetheless spoke on radio to counter Coughlin's opposition to the New Deal, making it clear that Coughlin did not speak for the American Catholic church. At about the same time, the University of Notre Dame granted an honorary degree to President Roosevelt in an effort, no doubt, to refute Coughlin's ranking in public opinion as the leading Catholic spokesman of the day.[16]

Father Peter E. Dietz, a priest who had become involved in the labor movement, working mainly in Ohio and Wisconsin, formed a group called the Militia of Christ for Social Service in 1910. Later, he served as secretary of a Social Service Commission that included in its membership Charles I. Denechaud, Jr., a prominent New Orleanian. Many priests heeded Dietz's advice and became active in labor matters in the thirties by attending labor schools in Cleveland, Milwaukee, San Francisco, Los Angeles, Pittsburgh, New York, and Baltimore, while Catholic labor leaders in New York formed the Association of Catholic Trade Unionists (ACTU) in 1937.[17]

15 Abell, *American Catholicism and Social Action*, 215–19, 223, 237–38, 253, 257; George Q. Flynn, *American Catholics and the Roosevelt Presidency, 1932–1936* (Lexington: University of Kentucky Press, 1968), 19; Grant McConnell, *The Decline of Agrarian Democracy* (Berkeley: University of California Press, 1959), 97, 105–16.

16 Flynn, *Catholics and the Roosevelt Presidency*, 53; Broderick, *Right Reverend New Dealer*, 217–18, 224–27.

17 Abell, *American Catholicism and Social Action*, 259–61, 177–79.

In mid–twentieth-century Louisiana roughly one-third of the population is Roman Catholic; but in the southern sugarcane parishes, where French and Spanish colonial traditions linger, over two-thirds of the population is Catholic. One observant priest thought that the French influence caused Louisiana Catholics to be less liberal and less interested in social thought than American Catholics in general. Comparing Louisiana practices to the French skepticism and heresies of the past, he wrote that Louisiana Catholics had inherited Voltaire's world devoid of spiritual features and Jansen's spiritual life that was isolated from the real world. "In consequence," he concluded, "politics is politics, business is business, social customs are social customs, and Sunday mass and sermon have slight connection with Monday morning deals."[18]

The labor priest Vincent O'Connell, S.M., views the same problem from a slightly different perspective. He notes that critics have faulted Catholics for failing to live up to the lofty ideals expressed in Catholic position papers, not for failing to say the right things about labor relations, civil rights, or race relations. During Reconstruction, for example, most Catholics shared a common southern prejudice toward blacks, according to Joe Gray Taylor. O'Connell asserts that although Catholics have worked courageously among people afflicted with dreaded diseases like leprosy, the Catholic community generally has not challenged the political, social, and economic power structure in order to solve social problems. Instead, it has accepted a "kind of cop-out," merely going through the motions without effecting real change.[19]

Yet writers have viewed Louisiana Catholics as members of a highly centralized church that they follow in blind obedience. Roger Shugg suggested that St. Louis Cathedral meant more than the state capitol to antebellum Catholics in New Orleans. When the Grange spread to the South in the 1870s, a bishop in Mississippi ruled that Catholics could not become members because of the Grange's ties to Freemasonry. Although New Orleans Archbishop Napoleon Perche did not prohibit members of his flock from joining, south Louisiana Catholics, mostly Acadians, had a deep mistrust of Anglo-Saxon Protestants. Because they were afraid that Baptists—especially those who were Freemasons—dominated the farm protest movement, they refrained from wholehearted endorse-

18 J. B. Gremillion, *The Journal of a Southern Pastor* (Chicago: Fides Publishers Association, 1957), 284–85.

19 Vincent O'Connell, interview, October 19, 1973, and November 25, 1973; Joe Gray Taylor, *Louisiana Reconstructed, 1863–1877* (Baton Rouge: Louisiana State University Press, 1974), 451.

ment of several political groups. William I. Hair believes that this factor contributed to lukewarm support from south Louisiana not only for the Grange but for the Populist party as well. Another observer attributed socialist presidential candidate Eugene Debs's smaller-than-expected vote in south Louisiana to Catholic opposition.[20]

If any Louisiana clergymen exemplified the efforts of such social action leaders as Gibbons, Ryan, or Ireland in the early years of the twentieth century, it was Peter M. H. Wynhoven. A secular priest in the Archdiocese of New Orleans, Wynhoven initiated many social action programs. He wrote for the archdiocesan newspaper, the *Morning Star*, and edited the new *Catholic Action*, the rather conservative official journal of the archdiocese which appeared in 1932. Father Wynhoven pioneered in establishing centers for vagrants and drifters and, in 1922, he founded Hope Haven in Marrero, Louisiana, a home for orphaned, wayward, and underprivileged boys twelve to seventeen years of age. Later, he built nearby Madonna Manor for boys five to twelve years old. In the thirties Wynhoven served as chairman of one of twelve regional National Labor Boards, and he was a member of the National Labor Relations Board.[21]

But the most significant church leader in Louisiana in modern times was Archbishop Joseph Francis Rummel. He was born in Baden, Germany, and came to the United States as a child. After he was consecrated in Rome, he was assigned to the Archdiocese of New York where he served until appointed bishop of Omaha in 1929. Then, in 1935, he succeeded John W. Shaw as archbishop of New Orleans in a dramatic ceremony that included a parade of decorated boats on the Mississippi River to the foot of Canal Street, and from there, a motorized procession to Saint Louis Cathedral for the installation. Later he received local officials and friends at a reception in Municipal Auditorium.

During the early years of his administration, Archbishop Rummel was

20 Roger Shugg, *Origins of the Class Struggle in Louisiana* (Baton Rouge: Louisiana State University Press, 1939), 62–63; Patrick E. McLear, "The Agrarian Revolt in the South: A Historiographical Essay," *Louisiana Studies*, XII (Summer, 1973), 446; William Ivy Hair, *Bourbonism and Agrarian Protest: Louisiana Politics, 1877–1900* (Baton Rouge: Louisiana State University Press, 1969), 244–45, 67, 154; Perry Howard, *Political Tendencies in Louisiana, 1812–1952* (Baton Rouge: Louisiana State University Press, 1971), 245.

21 Roger Baudier, *The Catholic Church in Louisiana* (New Orleans: Louisiana Library Association, 1972), 422, 524, 534, 575; J. E. Burgoyne, "Hope Haven Boys' Home Celebrating Its 50th Anniversary," New Orleans *Times-Picayune*, November 23, 1975; Flynn, *Catholics and the Roosevelt Presidency*, 99.

not overly involved with social action programs. Perhaps conservative advisors and high-ranking diocesan officials exerted a moderating influence. He continued the practice of establishing Negro church parishes, dedicating Our Lady of Grace Church for blacks in Reserve, Louisiana, in 1937. He appointed as pastor Father R. A. Auclair, S.S.J., who had worked with blacks in Josephite missions in the rice-growing area of southwest Louisiana. By the early 1950s, though, Rummel had established himself as an innovator in the field of social justice, demonstrating strong leadership in matters of race and labor relations.

Catholic church support for social action in Louisiana during the 1930s was sporadic and isolated, not planned archdiocesan policy. In the Lafayette area, the Reverend Wilton Labbé organized a short-lived union for potato growers, which failed when the group became associated with the Farmers' Union, which was suspected of Communist influence. In the parishes along the Mississippi River north of New Orleans, the Reverend Joseph Coulombe, who had served in cane country since 1922, openly criticized the sugar industry, something considered extremely unwise and unpopular in those days. Older parishioners and area residents recall that Coulombe called Etienne Caire, a prominent grower and a Knight of Saint Gregory, "public enemy number one."[22] One of Coulombe's parishioners, F. A. Graugnard, who was prominent in the sugar industry, complained about Coulombe's public statements to Archbishop Rummel, but Rummel refused to remove him.[23]

The Roman Catholic faith in the South was influential only in the Catholic population centers of Miami, Charleston, Washington, D.C., south Louisiana, and Kentucky. Wilbur Cash found anti-Semitism and anti-Catholicism widespread among southern Protestants. The Catholic Committee of the South was organized in 1939 by clergy and lay leaders to further Catholic social doctrine. The committee pledged to investigate the problems of labor-management relations, race relations, youth, Christian understanding, and social reform.[24]

22 Baudier, *Catholic Church in Louisiana*, 55, 525, 540, 549, 556, 578, 583; Mrs. E. Becnel, Jr., interview, April 2, 1972; Roger Baudier (comp.), *The Eighth National Eucharistic Congress, New Orleans, Louisiana, October 17, 18, 19 and 20, 1938* (Marrero, La.: The Hope Haven Press, 1941), 25.

23 Joseph Vath, interview, April 4, 1972, with Monsignor Charles Plauché and the Reverend Vincent O'Connell, hereinafter cited as VPO interview.

24 Wilbur Cash, *The Mind of the South* (New York: Vintage Books, 1941), 342; Charles Roland, *The Improbable Era: The South Since World War II* (Lex-

In 1940 Archbishop Rummel became an active leader of the Catholic Committee of the South. Thirteen bishops served on an episcopal committee consisting of two laymen for every cleric. The bishops were, thus, a minority and although they exerted considerable spiritual influence, they did not dominate committee proceedings. The two outstanding liberal spokesmen on the committee in the mid-fifties, Rummel and Bishop Gerald P. O'Hara of Savannah-Atlanta, failed to persuade their more conservative colleagues to take a bold and imaginative stand against racism. Bishop O'Hara later said that the committee, in following public opinion instead of taking a forceful stand against racial segregation, had missed an opportunity to assert Catholic leadership on an important social issue. Instead of being completely honest and poor, O'Hara said, the committee had decided to be relatively honest and fairly affluent. In the 1940s, however, labor problems evoked even more spirited response from politicians and businessmen than did racial matters.[25]

By 1942, although Rummel sent the membership dues for the Archdiocese of New Orleans, he wondered about continued participation in the Catholic Committee of the South. Rummel felt that the CCS had lost its effectiveness, wasting its energies on conventions, secretarial duties, and other bureaucratic rituals. "It is my opinion," he wrote, "that the c.c.s. has overreached the original intention of its foundation." He favored attaching the CCS to the executive department of the National Catholic Welfare Council as a distinct division.[26]

Sometimes Archbishop Rummel's social action programs spilled over into the political arena. There were rumors in 1939 that he was being investigated for illegal oil activity. Rummel issued a statement denying any links between the Archdiocese of New Orleans and illegal "hot oil" operations. The archbishop claimed that he did not own a single share of oil stock and welcomed an investigation. There were persistent attempts to entangle Rummel in the heated 1940 gubernatorial campaign, but the archbishop refused to take sides. Anti-Long forces, hoping to

ington: The University Press of Kentucky, 1975), 122; Stephen Ryan, "The Church and the New South," *Catholic World*, September, 1953, pp. 417, 419.

25 O'Connell, VPO interview.

26 Joseph Francis Rummel to Gerald O'Hara, October 20, 1942, in "CCS 1942" folder, Minutes of Meeting of Bishops of the South, January 29, 1941, in "CCS 1941" folder, both in Catholic Committee of the South Papers, Amistad Research Center, Dillard University, New Orleans, Louisiana, hereinafter cited as CCS Papers.

capitalize on scandal in the administration of Governor Richard Leche, a Long follower, quoted Rummel's denunciation of corruption and implied that the prelate had endorsed Sam Jones, the anti-Long candidate. The Long organization reprinted Rummel's statement from *Catholic Action* and emphasized that the prelate had endorsed no candidate. Meanwhile, Monsignor Peter Wynhoven urged both camps to think less about politics and more about workingmen.[27]

At a national Catholic gathering in December, 1939, Archbishop Rummel had expressed his concern that labor-management problems could weaken the social, moral, and spiritual well-being of a community. He hoped leaders would find fair ways of settling industrial disputes. In 1940 he appointed Monsignor Wynhoven chairman and the Reverend John X. Wegmann vice chairman of a Catholic conference on industrial problems, which he convened in New Orleans to publicize a program of social justice. Wynhoven, explaining that moral law justified strikes under certain conditions, said that workers should join unions and should receive wages commensurate with their abilities. Monsignor John Ryan, who attended the convention even though he was in poor health, told the delegates that unemployment resulted from failure to spend a sufficient portion of national income. Fred Pieper of the CIO and Charles Logan also appeared on the program. In a closing session of the conference, Archbishop Rummel cited *Rerum Novarum* and *Quadragesimo Anno* to show the right and responsibility of churchmen to express their views on social and economic matters. In a followup seminar, he urged priests to become aware of the principles of social justice and to educate their parishioners.[28]

To implement the policies formulated at the conference on industrial problems and to serve as a liaison between the church and industry, Rummel created the Archdiocesan Social Action Committee. He searched the New Orleans area for priests with suitable temperament and training to serve on the committee, settling on the Reverend Vincent O'Connell to chair the committee. He also appointed, as members, the Reverend Jerome Drolet and the Reverend Charles C. Chapman, S.J., a member of the history faculty of Loyola University of New Orleans.

27 New Orleans *Times-Picayune*, August 14, 1939, February 19, 20, 1940, January 23, 1940; Charles Logan, interview, September 26, 1974.
28 New Orleans *Times-Picayune*, December 5, 1939, March 20, 1940, April 9–11, 1940; Broderick, *Right Reverend New Dealer*, 249; Rummel to Gerald O'Hara, May 24, 1940, in "CCS, 1940" folder, CCS Papers.

All three of these young activists were to play important roles in labor relations for many years.[29]

Among Father O'Connell's earliest recollections are those of heated labor-management disputes between his mother, the daughter of a Philadelphia dock worker killed in a labor dispute before she was born, and his father, a Massachusetts hosiery manufacturer. The elder O'Connell, a man with kindly paternalistic instincts, never understood why workers found it necessary to join unions or to strike. In Europe, where Father O'Connell studied social philosophy in the thirties, he observed at close range the Spanish Civil War, the Abyssinian War, and the rise of fascism in Italy, Austria, and Germany. When he left Europe he was assigned to the Archdiocese of New Orleans, and, shortly thereafter, assumed Social Action Committee chairmanship.

The Social Action Committee met with representatives of labor and management on several occasions but experienced no major success. Several times the Reverend William H. Reintjes, C.S.S.R. of Saint Alphonsus Church in the Irish Channel section of New Orleans hosted meetings that evidenced a willingness on the part of businessmen to recognize company unions but not national or international unions. The committee enjoyed some success in organizing garbage workers, domestics, carpenters, and communications workers.[30]

At times O'Connell's activities led him on a confrontation course with pillars of the Catholic community, but despite their complaints, Archbishop Rummel seldom interfered with O'Connell's social action programs. The sting of O'Connell's committee was felt by Charles I. Denechaud, Sr., Knight of Saint Gregory, early member of a national Catholic Social Service Committee, lay representative during World War I on the National Catholic War Council, and important member of the 1921 committee that raised money to construct Notre Dame Seminary in the archdiocese. As attorney for the Archdiocese, Denechaud asked O'Connell in the late 1940s to stop organizing workers employed by the church at the Pere Marquette Building in downtown New Orleans. The priest replied that only a direct order from his superior would cause him to halt his efforts. Instead of winning his point by appealing to the archbishop, however, Denechaud soon found himself explaining to

29 O'Connell, VPO interview; New Orleans *Item*, January 31, 1945.
30 O'Connell, interview, September 11, 1970 and VPO interview.

Rummel why the employees were being paid so little. Shortly thereafter the employees received a raise.[31]

One of the chief publicists for the Catholic Committee of the South and the Archdiocesan Social Action Committee was A. Jackson, a bearded, eccentric narcotic addict, former newspaperman, and member of the Third Order of Saint Francis. Because he pledged his colleagues to secrecy, little is known about his early career. The scion of a prominent St. Paul, Minnesota, family, he was blacklisted as a newspaperman for his leadership in a strike against the Hearst newspaper chain. He afterward assumed the name A. Jackson and lived in the French Quarter of New Orleans. When his funds would run short, Jackson would assume a stage name and strike out on the roadshow circuit, performing his magic act until he had accumulated enough money to return to his life in New Orleans. Sometimes he performed magic tricks in Jackson Square to attract crowds for the Catholic Evidence Guild talks that priests gave in the forties. Mostly, though, he wrote radio scripts and news releases for O'Connell's committee, also collaborating with O'Connell on the "Our Stand" column in *Catholic Action*.[32]

Later Jackson moved to Hammond, Louisiana, and edited the *Union Farmer*, the journal published by the strawberry local affiliated with H. L. Mitchell's agricultural union. He wrote feature stories explaining that prior to the formation of the strawberry local, big handlers were conducting rigged auctions that shortchanged small berry farmers. Jackson died in early May, 1953, and after an elaborate funeral conducted by Monsignor Charles J. Plauché at Saint Louis Cathedral, his body, clad in his Franciscan habit and lashed to a plain wooden plank, was carried to the grave.[33]

In 1942, while on temporary duty assisting at Saint Peter's Church in Reserve, Louisiana, Father O'Connell heard from Monsignor Jean Eyraud, the pastor, of worker discontent at the nearby Godchaux sugar refinery. Edward Godchaux had given money to renovate Saint Peter's

31 Greeley, *The Catholic Experience*, 225; Baudier, *Catholic Church in Louisiana*, ,524, 560, 588; O'Connell, VPO interview.

32 O'Connell, interview, September 11, 1970 and VPO interview; "Our Stand" excerpts, in "CCS, 1950–1952" folder, CCS Papers.

33 A. Jackson, *The Union Farmer*, February, 1953, Microfilm Roll 58, Southern Tenant Farmers Union Papers, housed in the Southern Collection (and photo-duplicated by the Microfilm Corporation of America in 60 rolls), University of North Carolina, Chapel Hill, hereinafter cited as STFU, with box and folder or roll number; Plauché, VPO interview.

in 1922, and his company had sold land to the church for a school, and therefore, as Eyraud wrote: "Courage was needed to execute the program of Catholic Action ordered by Archbishop Rummel." After O'Connell learned from E. H. "Lige" Williams, Louisiana Federation of Labor president, that the AFL had no one to organize sugar mills and refineries, he helped the workers to get a union contract as a local independent union (LIU) of the CIO. Later, with the assistance of CIO District Director Fred Pieper and organizer Bob Stearns, the CIO formed sugar workers LIUs in Chalmette (No. 1101), Reserve (No. 1124), Gramercy (No. 1167), Mathews (No. 1420), Labadieville (No. 1422), and Raceland (No. 1474).[34]

During World War II, Father O'Connell served as chaplain to several German prisoner-of-war camps in the cane country. His visits to Valentine Sugars on Bayou Lafourche below Lockport provoked a confrontation with Frank L. Barker, Sr., a prominent Catholic layman who managed the Valentine plant and was also chairman of the American Sugar Cane League's labor committee. Barker had served with Charles Denechaud, Sr., on the seminary fund-raising drive in the Archdiocese of New Orleans in 1921, and, like Denechaud, was a Knight of Saint Gregory. At a meeting on the front porch of the Holy Savior Church rectory in Lockport at the end of World War II, O'Connell told Barker that agricultural workers would become unionized just as many others had throughout the country. The usually calm Barker became excited and pointed his finger first at O'Connell and then at nearby Bayou Lafourche; "Before that happens," he said, "the bayou will run red with blood—some of it yours."[35] The intensity of the clash between the liberal priest and one of his prominent parishioners surprised Father Dominic Perino, pastor of Holy Savior, who had witnessed the beginning of a controversy in which he, too, would become deeply involved.

O'Connell's colleague on the Social Action Committee, the Reverend Jerome Drolet, soon made his presence felt in archdiocesan labor rela-

34 Jean Eyraud and Donald Millet (comps. and eds.), *A History of St. John the Baptist Parish with Biographical Sketches* (Marrero, La.: The Hope Haven Press, 1939), 35, 37; O'Connell, interview, September 11, 1970; Henry Pelet, interview, February 29, 1972.

35 O'Connell, interview, November 25, 1973; Joseph T. Butler, Jr., "Prisoner of War Labor in the Sugar Cane Fields of Lafourche Parish, Louisiana, 1943–1944," *Louisiana History*, XIV (Summer, 1973), 283–96; Baudier, *Catholic Church in Louisiana*, 524, 588; O'Connell, VPO interview and November 25, 1973, and September 11, 1970.

tions. He plunged into the issue of Communist influence in labor unions with a characteristic gusto and a single-mindedness that later ranked him with such labor priests as Charles Rice in Pittsburgh, William Smith in Brooklyn, and George Higgins in Washington, D.C. Drolet, who had studied under Bishop Francis J. Haas at Catholic University before coming the leader of the New Orleans Association of Catholic Trade Unionists, was called the "CIO Padre" in a *Business Week* article.[36]

Jerome Drolet grew up in Kankakee, Illinois, where he knew Father John Maguire, one of the first priests to be involved with the labor movement. Inspired by Maguire's example, after he was ordained by Archbishop Rummel on June 16, 1936, Drolet lost little time becoming a labor activist, too. In 1937 he actively supported the Lane Mill Hosiery strike on Tchoupitoulas Street in New Orleans. The next year he opposed a proposed Louisiana law banning sit-down strikes, and he made headlines by supporting Willie Dorsey, black leader of Local 207 of the International Longshoremen and Warehousemen's Union (ILWU), against J. R. Robertson of the ILWU, who charged Dorsey with misusing union funds. Drolet said that the ILWU had attempted to impose the Communist line on Local 207, and when Dorsey refused to go along, it brought the charges to discredit him. Negro newspapers in New Orleans supported Drolet and Dorsey, whom the courts later exonerated. Even during World War II, when the United States was allied with the Soviet Union against Germany and Italy, Drolet maintained the view that Communists were no better than Fascists. He openly criticized Harry Bridges, a suspected Communist, who supported the ouster of Willie Dorsey. Bridges complained to CIO President Philip Murray that Drolet was supporting Dorsey against the national organization, which was spending $1,500 a month to subsidize the New Orleans *News Digest* which ran Drolet's weekly column.[37]

Eager to solve social problems, Father Drolet often used bombastic language and advocated an immediate frontal assault on anyone or anything that stood in the way. He read antisegregation material from the pulpit; assisted seamen, textile workers, shrimpers, and oyster fisher-

36 *Look*, [March 1, 1949]; "The C.I.O. Padre," *Business Week*, July 1, 1944, both in Jerome Drolet Scrapbook, lent to the author.

37 F. Ray Marshall, *Labor in the South* (Cambridge: Harvard University Press, 1967), 206, 209–210; Murray Kempton, "The Beginning," New York *Post*, September 25, 1954, several unidentified newspaper clippings, November, 1947, Harry Bridges to Philip Murray, June 17, 1943, all in Drolet Scrapbook.

men to organize; worked on arbitration and prevention of union disputes; campaigned to prevent Communists from taking over labor
unions; and helped to kill a right-to-work bill in the Louisiana legislature in 1944. He even made a public challenge of Senator Allen Ellender's antilynch bill filibuster from the pulpit of Saint Francis de Sales
Church in the senator's hometown of Houma. Although he was quiet
and shy by nature, his writing was fiery and uncompromising. On several occasions Archbishop Rummel had to restrain Drolet from making
shocking yet injudicious disclosure of conditions in New Orleans.[38]

In 1944 Father Drolet distributed a mimeographed sheet to textile
workers, prospective members of the union he was attempting to organize. Quoting Bishop Francis J. Haas on the God-given right of workers
to join unions, Drolet pointed out that the Wagner Act protected the
worker's right to organize. He promised personally to relay union application blanks of those too timid to hand them in. New Orleans
Association of Commerce leaders, apparently thinking that Archbishop
Rummel would want to take disciplinary action, sent him copies of the
material Drolet had distributed. The archbishop replied with a letter
that left no doubt about his feelings. He acknoweldged that Drolet had
been "unusually zealous, but who will deny him the right to present to
them the benefits and advantages of such organization? . . . surely there
can be no objection to the presentation of the right and even the duty
of employees in industry to safeguard their common interests through
legitimate organization."[39]

Because industrialists in the New Orleans area took advantage of the
rivalry between the AFL and the CIO, playing one union against the
other, labor priests, such as O'Connell and Drolet, had to maintain strict
neutrality in their dealings with the rival unions to avoid alienating
either group. Occasionally, however, the presence of a common foe produced a unified labor front of surprising vitality. The right-to-work bill
proposed by the Louisiana legislature in 1944 served as such a rallying
point. Father Drolet took the lead in uniting Catholic, Protestant, and
Jewish religious leaders, as well as AFL and CIO representatives, to fight
the bill. The Christian American Association, which Drolet had labeled
a "sweatshop front," bent on outlawing union shop agreements in the
state, opposed the clergymen and labor leaders. Despite efforts to keep

38 Drolet to J. Don Davis, undated, in Drolet Scrapbook; O'Connell, interview, September 11, 1970; Raymond Witte, interview, February 20, 1974.
39 George H. Gardner to Rummel, March 21, 1944, Rummel to Gardner,
April 6, 1944, file copies in Drolet Scrapbook.

Drolet "from mixing labor and religion," he persisted. The legislature acquiesced to the strong church-labor opposition and rejected the measure that year.[40]

In time, the liberalism espoused by Archbishop Rummel and his activist advisors evolved into overt support for labor union activity in Louisiana agriculture. Although Catholic laymen in the cane country who disagreed with their church's support for agricultural unions often complained to Archbishop Rummel, he consistently supported his outspoken priests, refusing to be pressured into changing his policies. At one time or another, church leaders differed to some degree not only with leaders of the American Sugar Cane League, the Louisiana Farm Bureau, and the biggest sugar corporations in the state, but also with many influential Catholic laymen.

In sensitive areas concerning Catholic social doctrine, Senator Allen Ellender was one layman who did not always agree with church leaders. In his labor files he kept an English translation of *Rerum Novarum*, with passages underlined in red ink. He seemed keenly sensitive to federal and Louisiana constitutional strictures regarding separation of church and state. When Archbishop Rummel objected to lunch programs that prohibited the use of federal funds to buy equipment for nonpublic schools, Ellender wrote a three-page letter to explain his view. He opposed amending the Ellender-Russell School Lunch Bill of 1946 because it contained the old Huey Long–inspired provision that lunches and other benefits go to school children and not to educational institutions. Therefore, Ellender believed that denying nonpublic schools money for equipment was an accurate First Amendment interpretation and he told the Archbishop so. To an Ursuline nun who criticized racial segregation policies in schools, Ellender in 1949 wrote bluntly: "I wonder how long you would maintain the Ursuline College in New Orleans if you were to admit colored girls to go to the same class and occupy the same dormitories, if any you have, with the white girls."[41]

40 O'Connell, interview, September 11, 1970; *CIO Oil Facts*, April 16, 1945, in Drolet Scrapbook.

41 *Rerum Novarum* copy in "Labor, 1948" folder, Box 463, Rummel to Allen Ellender, February 15, March 11, 1946, Ellender to Rummel, February 28, March 11, 1946, both in "School Lunch and Milk Program" folder, Box 211, M. Columba, O.S.U. to Ellender, April 20, 1949, Ellender to Columba, April 28, 1949, both in "Civil Rights, 1949" folder, Box 306, all in Allen J. Ellender Papers, Division of Archives, Nicholls State University, Thibodaux, Louisiana, hereinafter cited as AEP.

The church was concerned with every facet of union activity, down
to the smallest detail. Besides looking into the broad area of collective
bargaining, clergymen studied a union oath for concepts contrary to
Catholic doctrine, provided church halls for union meetings, supplied
information on forming cooperatives, translated union programs for
French-speaking Acadian farmers, assisted workers who had been fired,
conducted a strike vote prior to the 1953 sugarcane field workers strike,
appealed to big unions in behalf of small agricultural unions, and even
suggested a name change for a union to make before its organizational
campaign in Louisiana. Under Rummel's leadership, the activist priests
were thoroughly committed to improving the laborers' lot, and their
activism was soon to be tested.

Chapter 4

Allen Ellender and the Agricultural Establishment

The agricultural establishment, which includes the United States Department of Agriculture, the American Farm Bureau, land-grant colleges, and the Extension Service—Frank Freidel called them components of the "great national empire of the Farm Bureau"—is greatly different from the Populist movement of the late nineteenth century. Populism represented sharecroppers, small farmers, and urban workers, but the agricultural establishment evolved during the 1920s into a voice for large-scale agriculture. Just after the turn of the century, the Farmers' Union, the lobby of small farm owners, rather than tenants, laid the foundation for modern power structure in agriculture.[1]

In twentieth century American agriculture the Farmers' Union represented small farmers; the Farm Bureau looked out for large farmers. The Farmers' Union, which sprang up in Texas in 1902 and soon became a conservative voice for small farmers, stood midway between agricultural labor unions and agribusiness, the two groups it battled for dominance. Newt Gresham, its founder, brought together landowners, rather than sharecroppers, under a variety of cooperatives, acreage-reduction proposals, and crop-holding plans that failed during the 1920s. John A. Simpson of Oklahoma, with programs designed to guarantee to farmers the "cost of production," attempted to reactivate remnants of the organization in the 1930s. The Farm Bureau, however, which catered to affluent farmers, had no problem deciding whether it would be an organization of farm owners or farm laborers. Founded during the 1920s as an outgrowth of the county agent system, the Farm Bureau never became a mass movement because its high dues excluded sub-

---

1 Frank Freidel, *FDR: Launching the New Deal* (Boston: Little Brown and Company, 1973), 252; Grant McConnell, *The Decline of Agrarian Democracy* (Berkeley: University of California Press, 1959), 1–2, 19–20.

sistence farmers. Agricultural experts, such as Seaman Knapp, who brought new farming technology to Louisiana from the Midwest, established demonstration farms and hired agents to teach improved farming techniques. Later, agricultural colleges established "extension" sections to direct county agents. In order to "foster the illusion" that colleges were the controlling power in the movement, Farm Bureau leaders perpetuated the myth that college extension administrators directed county agents in the states. Actually the Farm Bureau gained almost exclusive control over the services of county agents.[2]

Agricultural labor unions were anathema to the agricultural establishment, which resisted them wherever they threatened farm operations. The farm lobby succeeded in denying to agricultural laborers the guarantees won by industrial unions in 1935 under the National Labor Relations (Wagner) Act. If the management of an industrial plant refused to recognize a workers' union as a bargaining agent, workers could appeal to the National Labor Relations Board for an election to determine who would represent them. Agricultural workers, because they were employed in jobs not considered to be interstate commerce, did not have this protection unless they lived in a state that had passed a "little Wagner" act. For years, members of the U.S. Senate Committee on Appropriations stipulated when they allocated funds for the National Labor Relations Board, that agricultural workers did not come under NLRB jurisdiction. In 1949, C. J. Bourg of the American Sugar Cane League, obviously concerned, wrote Allen Ellender: "This year the NLRB is trying to eliminate this provision. We are opposed to such elimination because we do not want any labor union interfering with our agricultural labor." The farm lobby also sought to maintain the exemptions to the Fair Labor Standards Act of 1938 that agricultural producers enjoyed. Section 7 (c) exempted agricultural processors from overtime pay; Section 7 (b) (3) exempted seasonal overtime pay; and Section 13 (a) (6) exempted farm workers from provisions of the Act relating to minimum wages.[3]

2 George Brown Tindall, *The Emergence of the New South, 1913–1945* (Baton Rouge: Louisiana State University Press, 1967), 130–31, 392; Murray R. Benedict, *Farm Policies of the United States, 1790–1950: A Study of Their Origins and Development* (New York: Octagon Books, 1966), 190.

3 C. J. Bourg to Allen Ellender, June 30, 1949, in "Appropriations Deficiencies and Army Civil Functions, 1949" folder, Box 69, "Legislation, Labor, 1965" folder, Box 116, "Wage Hour Division, Autin Packing Company, Inc." folder, Box 53, all in Allen J. Ellender Papers, Division of Archives, Nicholls State University, Thibodaux, Louisiana, hereinafter cited as AEP.

In south Louisiana, the American Sugar Cane League overshadowed the
Farm Bureau in its lobbying activities. The sugar industry's need for
tariff protection distinguished it from southern agriculture in general.
It, therefore, grew along lines different from those of other agricultural
staples; developing a lobby of its own which took its place beside the
Farm Bureau in the agricultural establishment in Louisiana.

Raw sugar producers had to contend with refiners bent on buying
raw sugar at low prices. The monopolistic Havemeyer sugar trust controlled sugar refining in the United States from 1888 until early in the
twentieth century. Even though the trust did not set prices directly, its
control of processing amounted to price-fixing. Although Louisiana
grew its own cane and had many raw sugar mills, it had few refineries.
Louisiana sugar refiners at first competed with the trust; but later, they
were forced to join it in order to survive. The Planters Sugar Refining
Company and the Louisiana Sugar Refining Company shared a portion
of the trust's market, but most refineries associated with the trust were
in the East, Midwest, and West Coast and depended on imported raw
sugar, which they refined into high-grade white granulated sugar.
Raw sugar producers often complained that the trust contrived to keep
raw sugar prices down by supporting legislation that taxed refined sugar
imported into the United States, but allowed raw sugar to enter virtually
duty free. Then, during grinding season in Louisiana, trust refineries
would sell raw sugar among themselves at abnormally low prices in
order to set a low price for Louisiana raw sugar. Raw sugar producers
argued that such practices would destroy the local industry and allow the
trust a free hand in controlling supplies and prices.[4]

The Havemeyer trust's power declined early in the twentieth century
because of many factors, among which were successful antitrust suits,
Henry Havemeyer's death in 1907, and new regulations that were
prompted by the shortages caused by World War I, which made it impossible to continue such a monopoly. As problems from the sugar
trust declined, however, natural disasters befell the Louisiana sugar industry. Cold weather, mosaic disease, and cane borers reduced the yield
of sugarcane per acre. Insecticides and hardy new varieties of cane
helped, but they raised production costs. Many marginal cane farmers
went out of business during the era, and their holdings were concen-

4 Alfred S. Eichner, *The Emergence of Oligopoly: Sugar Refining As a Case
Study* (Baltimore: The Johns Hopkins University Press, 1969), 78–79, 81–82,
105; J. Carlyle Sitterson, *Sugar Country: The Cane Sugar Industry in the South,
1753–1950* (Lexington: University of Kentucky Press, 1953), 300–301, 329, 349.

trated among fewer producers. Large-scale producers comprised a minority of Louisiana sugarcane growers, but they accounted for 75 percent of total production. In 1922, after several disastrous crop failures that threatened the existence of the southern sugar industry, several organizations representing the big growers met in New Orleans. Some of these—the Louisiana Sugar Planters' Association, the American Cane Growers' Association, and the Producers' and Manufacturers' Protective Association—decided to work collectively to save the sugar industry centered in Louisiana, Florida, and Texas. They formed the American Sugar Cane League. Raw sugar mill directors were the dominant force in the League; they chaired important committees and held most of the top positions.[5]

The American Sugar Cane League did not always present a successful case for tariff protection of the sugar industry during its early years. Secretary of Agriculture Henry A. Wallace called sugar an "inefficient industry" that should face "the winds of world competition." The historian George Tindall agreed that the cane industry "survived only because of tariff protection." World production of sugar exceeded demand by 1925, and chaotic price fluctuations characterized world trade in sugar. The Republican tariffs of the 1920s and early 1930s raised the rates on imported sugar, but did not solve the problem of oversupply. After about 1927 the Louisiana sugar industry experienced a recovery. New cane varieties proved resistant to disease, and sugar cooperatives rebuilt factories with credit from the Federal Intermediate Credit Bank in New Orleans. In 1932 the world price of sugar fell to about one cent per pound, and the next year agricultural experts considered limiting supplies rather than raising tariff duties. Both the Jones-Costigan Act of 1934 and the Sugar Act of 1937 included aspects of this line of thinking.[6]

Of rural agricultural background and disposition, Senator Allen Ellender considered himself a farmer and liked to reminisce about his youth

5 Sitterson, *Sugar Country*, 344–45, 306–307, 388, 356–57; Rudolph Carroll Hammack, "The New Deal and Louisiana Agriculture," (microfilm-xerography facsimile, 1975, of Ph.D. dissertation, Tulane University, 1973), 149; American Sugar Cane League, Minutes of Executive Committee Meeting, Nicholls State University Library, Thibodaux, Louisiana.

6 Wallace was quoted in Tindall, *Emergence of the New South*, 397–98; U.S. Department of Agriculture, *The United States Sugar Program* (Washington: U.S. Government Printing Office, 1971), 30–34; Sitterson, *Sugar Country*, 382–83, 392.

on a small sugar plantation. When Senate Majority Leader Joseph Robinson of Arkansas asked freshman Senator Ellender to list his first three preferences for committee assignments in 1937, the Louisianian wrote: first, agriculture; second, agriculture; third, agriculture. Robinson assigned him to the Committee on Agriculture and Forestry, which he later chaired. American Sugar Cane League officials and the agricultural establishment in Louisiana applauded Ellender for his part in the passage of the Sugar Act of 1937. They considered it an improvement over the Jones-Costigan Act of 1934 because the new law allocated domestic production quotas on an acreage basis rather than on total tons of sugarcane. This, in effect, raised the quotas for Louisiana farmers, who fertilized more generously and produced more sugarcane on fewer acres. In 1937 they grew 460,000 tons, a substantial increase over the 260,000 tons produced in 1934.[7]

No member of the Louisiana congressional delegation was ever able to exert as much influence on sugar legislation as Senator Ellender. As chairman of the Senate Committee on Agriculture and Forestry, he oversaw all farm legislation, on which he had become a leading authority, but sugar legislation did not go to Ellender's committee. Because the Sugar Act dealt with tariffs and taxes, the bills for its renewal always went to the Senate Finance Committee, chaired for many years by Senator Harry Byrd of Virginia. Byrd always deferred to Ellender's expertise in these matters and reported the bills favorably, no doubt in exchange for Ellender's support for other projects. Congressman Edwin Willis, whose district included much of the Louisiana cane country, played an active part in directing sugar legislation, but failing health limited his usefulness late in his career. John Overton, senior senator from Louisiana, did not possess the agricultural expertise nor the political skills of Ellender, and although his successor, Huey Long's son, Russell, eventually became chairman of the Senate Finance Committee, which handled sugar legislation, the Sugar Act expired in 1974 despite his efforts. Those close to Ellender believe that he alone could have pushed through a renewal amendment as he had done for thirty years prior to his death in 1972.

When World War II started abroad in 1939, USDA officials, fearing a severe sugar shortage, suspended the Sugar Act quotas on raw sugar. Later that year the Sugar Division restored the quota provisions, but in

7 "Agriculture" folder, *passim,* Box 409, Ellender speech, November 17, 1950, in "Speeches, 1950" folder, Box 105, *The Sugar Bulletin,* XVI (August, 1938), 1–8, in "Sugar" folder, Box 321, all in AEP.

the meantime, some growers had planted sugarcane in excess of 1940 quotas. R. C. Hammack, who studied the origins of early sugar legislation, wrote: "In reality they gambled on their political connections rescuing them from the [Agriculture] Secretary's decrees." Large growers complained bitterly when the sugar branch decided that they would have to plow under portions of the 1939 crop which was already growing. Louisiana farmers reported plowing under forty thousand acres of cane in April and May in order to quaify for conditional benefit payments. Since these unpopular measures were taken just one year before the expiration date of the Sugar Act, some planters expressed a hope that the act would not be renewed. New Orleans journalists described the Sugar Act as a repressive measure. Nevertheless the Louisiana industry expanded and grew prosperous under the stabilizing influence of the government sugar program.[8]

Ellender resented charges and insinuations by sugar growers that he had not prevented the 1939 cutbacks in production. Aware of rapidly shifting political fortunes, he reminded one critic: "When I returned to Louisiana in 1937, I was hailed as a hero for having had the Sugar Bill signed."And, while promising to obtain relief for his constituents, he pointed out to them that Louisiana growers had actually increased productivity on fewer acres. The Sugar Act established a quota of less than 400,000 tons of sugar for Louisiana and Florida together, he told an irate grower, but "Louisiana farmers alone have produced 490,000 tons of sugar last year [1938] and they received benefits on the entire amount." Despite Ellender's belief in the inevitability of acreage cuts in 1939, he suggested giving a portion of the Cuban import quotas to Louisiana and Florida growers. American Sugar Cane League officials endorsed this view. They attempted to discover evidence of connections between eastern seaboard refiners and Cuban sugar producers and of Japanese and German influences in other countries that sold sugar to the United States. Ellender wrote a constituent: "I have data to show that 56% of the Cuban sugar production is controlled by New York, Boston, and Chicago, and that all of Mr. [Cordell] Hull's efforts to help the poor Cubans are useless, because most of the benefits flow back into the pockets of the big corporations located in the above named cities." In September, as farmers prepared to harvest their crops and

8 Hammack, "The New Deal and Louisiana Agriculture," 256, 263; Ellender to C. A. Duplantis, Jr., September 12, 1938, in "Sugar" folder, Box 321, AEP; Meigs Frost, New Orleans *Times-Picayune*, April 25, 28, May 27, October 15, 1939.

plant seed cane for the next year, they received good news from Washington. President Roosevelt, using emergency powers because war had broken out in Europe, suspended domestic sugar quotas and restored a tariff of $1.50 per hundredweight on Cuban sugar. He ended grower concern about cutbacks but reminded growers that they should not expect unlimited production in the future.[9]

In 1940 Louisiana sugar growers used political leverage to increase their domestic quotas. Early that year Ellender had tried unsuccessfully to attach to an appropriation bill a rider prohibiting the USDA from holding back benefit payments to farmers who produced sugarcane in excess of their quotas. Later he introduced Senate Joint Resolution 225, which provided that a farmer could harvest 100 percent of his domestic quota plus twenty-five acres without suffering a cut in benefit payments. After Resolution 225 had passed, sugar growers, who had withheld their endorsement, once again became enthusiastic Roosevelt supporters. The adjustment did not establish a permanent exemption from quota restrictions, though. In 1941 Ellender's aide cautioned Clarence Savoie that if he sold over-quota cane he could lose his entire benefit payment.[10]

Aware that the sugar lobby had emphasized only the negative, restrictive aspects of the Sugar Act, Department of Agriculture officials released information emphasizing the beneficial features of the sugar program. They pointed out that Cane League proposals would benefit large growers, not small farmers. Ellender's plan to reduce quotas of foreign sugar-producing areas would hurt Puerto Rico, Hawaii, and the Virgin Islands while benefiting few in Louisiana according to President Roosevelt. Henry Wallace disliked Ellender's amendments that would

9 Ellender to Duplantis, February 21, 1939, in "Agriculture, Department of, Sugar-Quotas" folder, Box 409, Ellender to Cordell Hull, June 3, 1942, Hull to Ellender, June 13, 1942, both in "Agriculture, Sugar, 1942" folder, Box 286, Charles A. Farwell to Ellender, November 17, 1941, F. Evans Farwell to Ellender, November 28, 1941, both in "Agri.—Sugar—General, '40 & '41" folder, Box 39, Ellender to Ernest A. Gurguieres, March 4, 1940, in "Sugar Division, Legislation" folder, Box 409, Franklin Roosevelt proclamation (mimeographed), September 11, 1939, in "Sugar Act, 1940" folder, Box 301, Ellender to Amedee L. Brou, September 15, 1939, in "Sugar Division Quotas (Factory and Producer)" folder, Box 409, all in AEP; New Orleans *Times-Picayune*, January 14, September 12, 1939.

10 Frank Wurzlow, Jr. to Clarence Savoie, August 12, 1941, in "Agr., Sugar Acreage" folder, Box 39, AEP; Hammack, "New Deal and Louisiana Agriculture," 257–260.

have prevented the USDA from making acreage reduction a condition for receiving benefit payments under the Sugar Act. "It should be understood, of course," Wallace added, "that there is no restriction on the production of sugarcane by any grower who does not desire to apply for such government payments." The secretary went on to mention large growers in Louisiana, "some of whom now receive relatively large payments." Senator Harry Byrd of Virginia, who agreed that sugar growers received excessive payments, failed in an attempt to pass legislation limiting maximum payments to any one grower to $5,000 per year. Later he failed twice to limit payments, even after raising the maximum to $10,000 and finally to $50,000. Fearful of such amendments to limit payments, Ellender in 1941 acknowledged that "many Senators would vote to decrease those payments and I would hesitate to present the matter before the Senate at this time." News releases from Henry Wallace's office emphasized that acreage reduction did not apply to farms of ten acres or less. The USDA also stressed protection to cane growers in "the 'visible' form of direct conditional payments, and in the 'invisible' form of the maintenance of a price differential over the world market."[11]

The most effective response to Ellender and the Cane League came when the USDA published the names of growers who had received benefit payments of more than $10,000 for the crop in 1937 or that in 1939. The list substantiated Wallace's contention that Ellender's amendments to the Sugar Act favored large growers and showed that big planters were already benefiting substantially from the Act. Some of the Cane League officials who had been most critical of agricultural policy were on the list. Included among the large mainland recipients in 1939 were the United States Sugar Corporation ($470,000), Godchaux Sugars ($97,000), Realty Operators [Southdown] ($121,000), South Coast ($181,000), Sterling Sugars ($48,000), Miliken and Farwell ($65,000), Valentine Sugars ($16,000), Clarence Savoie ($16,000), and Caire and Graugnard ($22,000). During World War II sugar growers received additional assistance from the War Food Administration when it paid sugar planters thirty-four cents per ton of sugarcane in 1943 and eighty-five cents per ton in 1944.[12]

11 New Orleans *Times-Picayune*, April 9, March 15, 1939, March 23, 1940; Henry A. Wallace to E. D. Smith, March 10, 1939, in "Cotton, 1939" folder, Box, 301, Ellender to Charles Farwell, November 15, 1941, in "Agri.—Sugar— General, '40 & '41" folder, Box 39, all in AEP.
12 United States Department of Agriculture, "Sugar Payments of $10,000 and

As Ellender adjusted to his duties and matured as a member of the U.S. Senate Committee on Agriculture and Forestry, he sought support increasingly often from the agricultural establishment of which he had become a part. His jousts with Secretary Wallace and the USDA over reducing acreage and limiting benefit payments drew him closer to the American Sugar Cane League, which provided him technical assistance in his continuing clashes with the sugar branch. Often the Cane League would send Ellender a "suggested letter" that the senator could forward to the Department of Agriculture, sometimes without alteration. At times the senator would quibble with the USDA over interpretation of the Sugar Act. To an Extension Service director he voiced disapproval of obstinate sugar branch officials, saying he hoped "to find other jobs for these two gentlemen." A constituent complained that sugar branch personnel had classified his three different plantations in three different parishes as one "farm." The senator himself wondered if his own benefit payment would be held up in 1939 because he took over-quota cane from one of his tracts of land and used it for seed cane on another tract. This constituted a violation since the USDA classified the two tracts as "a farm." Ellender wrote to Dr. Joshua Bernhardt of the Sugar Division: "Now Doctor, I am asking that you be practical."[13]

No interest group, including the Louisiana Farm Bureau, had a closer working relationship with Allen Ellender than the American Sugar Cane League. In 1937 when an Agricultural Extension Service director recommended using Farm Bureau personnel to serve on local agricultural committees, Ellender suggested, instead, that county agents select representatives to serve on committees and testify at various USDA hearings. Long before the Sugar Act was due to expire, Cane League officials sought his advice on planning a lobby campaign to insure extension of the act. In 1940 a Cane League lobbyist, realizing that the sugar indus-

---

Over Announced," July 9, 1941, in "Agriculture, Sugar Acreage" folder, Box 39, C. J. Bourg to Ellender, September 2, 1943, in "War Department, Prisoner-of-War Labor, 1943–'44" folder, Box 18, both in AEP; New Orleans *Times-Picayune*, March 15, 1939.

13 C. J. Bourg to Wurzlow, June 28, 1937, Ellender to Wallace, June 29, 1937, both in "Sugarcane Contracts" folder, Box 321, "Agriculture, Sugar 1945–46" folder, Box 446, Ellender to J. W. Bateman, May 2, 1938, in "Agr., Dept. of, Potatoes" folder, Box 464, F. Evans Farwell to Ellender, December 1, 1941, in "Agr.—Sugar—General, '40 & '41" folder, Box 39, Ellender to Joshua Bernhardt, November 9, 1939, in "Ellender, A. J. # 1 (Personal)" folder, Box 322, all in AEP.

try could not accomplish all its legislative goals, listed its priorities to the senator: first, additional quotas for growers; second, higher sugar prices; and third, administrative changes in the agricultural bureaucracy.[14]

Senator Ellender's legislative technique stressed conciliation and compromise, not confrontation and rhetoric. He had little patience with rambunctious, heavy-handed lobby techniques. During the controversy over acreage reduction in 1939, he criticized Governor Richard Leche and New Orleans Mayor Robert Maestri for sending a telegram to Washington blasting President Roosevelt and Secretary of Agriculture Henry Wallace. "We need both the President and the Secretary of Agriculture in this crisis," he wrote, "and we can't afford to use such tactics as were suggested in the telegram." He told Maestri to tell Leche "not to permit some of those over-enthusiastic sugar planters to barge in and make our fight harder in Washington." Several growers called off a protest meeting and cancelled a march on Washington when Ellender suggested they save their energy for a campaign to amend the Sugar Act. A sugar industry spokesman asked Ellender to make a speech in the Senate to complain about the soft drink industry's pleas for low sugar prices. "Puffing off" from the Senate floor, Ellender replied, did very little good. "I have been keeping in touch with Clarence Bourg [head lobbyist for the American Sugar Cane League] regarding developments in the sugar industry, and have taken the steps suggested by Clarence." Clarence Bourg's recommendations ranged from "suggested letters" to a written script, or scenario of sorts, for Ellender's use in outlining points to the USDA.[15]

To determine the amount of sugar needed to supplement U.S. production, which amounted to less than half the sugar consumed domestically each year, the Secretary of Agriculture estimated annual domestic

14 J. W. Bateman to Ellender, August 25, 1937, Ellender to Bateman, August 27, 1937, both in "Sugar" folder, Box 321, Charles Farwell to Ellender, April 15, 1939, in "Sugar, S. 69 and S. Res. 10" folder, Box 251, Ellender to Michael Bakalar, July 15, 1950, in "B, 1950" folder, Box 105, W. F. Giles to Ellender, August 10, 1940, in "Agr.—Sugar—General, '40 & '41" folder, Box 39, all in AEP.

15 Ellender to Robert Maestri, March 24, 1939, in "Sugar, S. 69 and S. Res. 10" folder, Box 251, Frank Barker to Ellender, April 24, 1939, telegram, in "Agriculture, Department of, Sugar—General, 1939–'41, # 2" folder, Box 409, Stephen Munson to Ellender, August 11, 1950, Ellender to Munson, August 14, 1950, both in "Agriculture, Sugar, 1950" folder, Box 162, [Bourg] to Ellender, September 16, 1949, in "Agriculture, Sugar, 1949" folder, Box 9, all in AEP.

needs. A low estimate would lead to smaller raw sugar imports, short supplies in the United States, and higher sugar prices, and, whenever prices declined, the sugar lobby demanded lower domestic estimates in hopes that prices would advance. The Sugar Division feared that a lower-than-realistic estimate would bring excessive prices and possibly leave the United States in an embarrassing position if domestic production fell short of expectation and Cuba had sold her raw sugar on the open market. Nor would the Secretary of Agriculture overlook the need to protect American consumers from high prices nor the necessity of maintaining stability among allied sugar exporting nations. In order to protect domestic sugar producers, the USDA, using an adjustment formula, based the price of sugarcane on the world market price of sugar. In the late 1940s the price a farmer received for a ton of sugarcane at the grinding mill amounted to $1.03 for each cent of the world sugar market price per pound.[16]

Government officials often balked at demands for increasing direct and indirect benefits to the sugar industry. In 1937 Henry Wallace criticized sugar benefit payments, saying that "farmers did nothing to earn them, that the program is a racket, and that expenditures on the program should be drastically curtailed." In 1942 Leon Henderson, director of the Office of Price Administration, complained that raising sugar prices to aid domestic producers, as Ellender requested, would cost the American consumer $85 million. Ellender saw an opportunity to increase prices during World War II when shipping difficulties delayed Hawaiian sugar and Cuban producers held back supplies in anticipation of a price increase. "My idea would be to let the price go up and our argument for more quotas will be better understood by the American people," Ellender told Charles Farwell, a veteran Cane League officer. "If we can get the American people to fight with us, I have no doubt that we will get a good sugar bill if and when we make the attempt."[17]

Some members of the American Sugar Cane League thought that greedy sugar refiners conspired to hurt American raw sugar manufac-

16 Memo to Ellender, October 19, 1951, in "Agriculture, Sugar, 1951" folder, Box 109, AEP. Thus, if raw sugar sold on the world market at five cents per pound, growers would receive $5.15 per standard ton of cane.

17 Wallace to Ellender, June 11, 1937, in "Agr. Conservation Program—add. 10%" folder, Box 321, Leon Henderson to Ellender, October 28, 1942, in "Agriculture, Sugar Prices" folder, Box 289, Ellender to Charles Farwell, November 15, 1941, in "Agr.—Sugar—General, '40 & '41" folder, Box 39, all in AEP.

turers. Traditionally sugar refiners on the eastern seaboard found ways to import low-priced raw sugar, which they melted and refined into white granulated table sugar. They relied on high import duties to block imports of granulated sugar. Louisiana raw sugar producers, already faced with stiff competition from Cuba, the Philippines, and other areas, had to contend with refiners bent on keeping raw sugar prices low. Clarence Bourg believed that refiners conspired to depress raw sugar prices during the grinding season in Louisiana, but he was unsure how they accomplished this objective. Jules Godchaux, whose family owned refineries, cane fields, and raw sugar mills, processed Louisiana brown sugar during the grinding season and melted raw sugars from abroad during the rest of the year. He explained to Senator Ellender that unless the price of granulated sugar exceeded the raw sugar price by 2.25 cents per pound, refiners could not make a profit. Ellender checked with Bourg, who reminded the senator that Godchaux spoke first and foremost as a refiner, and that refiners always tried to depress raw sugar prices. The Cane League executive considered a 2.25 cents per pound margin above the raw sugar price for granulated sugar excessive since refiners had once survived on a 1.85-cent margin. Ellender then informed Godchaux that he considered a margin of 2.05 cents per pound for sugar refiners reasonable.[18]

In 1951 Senator Ellender became chairman of the Senate Committee on Agriculture and Forestry, which meant greater prestige and influence for the senior senator from Louisiana. The year was disastrous for the sugar industry. The sugar lobby complained bitterly of low sugar prices and also of a drought and a freeze and, consequently, smaller-than-expected cane production. In April, when housewives were paying 8.25 cents per pound for refined sugar, raw sugar prices dropped almost to 5.0 cents per pound. Ellender forwarded to the USDA a letter drafted by Bourg suggesting that, in view of granulated sugar prices, the USDA help boost raw sugar to 6.0 cents per pound. Raising the price of raw sugar to 6.0 cents would maintain a margin of 2.25 cents between raw and refined sugar.[19]

18 Bourg to Ellender, November 2, 1951, Jules Godchaux to Ellender, April 13, 1951, Ellender to Godchaux, May 5, 1951, all in "Agriculture, Sugar, 1951" folder, Box 109, AEP.

19 Bourg called Ellender " 'first friend of the domestic sugar industry', particularly since you have become the Chairman of the Agriculture and Forestry [Committee] in the U.S. Senate," Bourg to Ellender, October 22, 1951, Malcolm Dougherty to Ellender, October 18, 1951, F. Evans Farwell to Lawrence Myers,

Although Ellender became a major congressional protector of the sugar industry, he unhesitatingly rejected or ignored capricious or unreasonable requests from his constituents. In 1947 he used his influence to delay the removal of price ceiling and rationing controls on sugar until the end of October when Louisiana raw sugar reached the market. He knew that prices would advance when wartime agencies removed controls, and he wanted his Louisiana constituents to share in the prosperity. But when a prominent grower on Bayou Lafourche asked him to use his influence to close a state-supported trade school for blacks during sugarcane harvesting season, the senator did nothing. Since he had received letters of support for technical training schools from veterans' organizations and civic groups, he probably felt relieved to tell the grower to confer with the state superintendent of education about the facility.[20] Clearly, although he favored racial segregation of public institutions, Ellender did not support blatant attempts to provide a subservient black labor force during the grinding season.

During World War II, the American Sugar Cane League took advantage of opportunities and became a highly successful force in promoting its members' interests. It capitalized on feelings of patriotism and a sense of emergency in planning to increase sugarcane production without losing benefit payments. War quickly shifted the emphasis from acreage restriction and benefit payment curtailment to maintaining production of a scarce commodity. As early as September, 1939, consumers, fearful that supplies would be curtailed because of the war, were hoarding sugar and had depleted the reserves in stores. Louisiana raw sugar producers feared that hastily eliminating the quota system would permit importers to dump excess sugar on hand in Cuba, Puerto Rico, the Philippines, Hawaii, and Latin America on the United States market, thus drastically lowering prices. Depressed raw sugar prices, coupled with the loss of benefit payments of ninety cents per ton, would have been disastrous to Louisiana growers. Domestic growers hoped instead that shortages would lead to unlimited production without loss of ben-

December 7, 1951, Ellender to sugar branch, April 6, 1951, all in "Agriculture, Sugar, 1951" folder, Box 109, AEP.

20 Ellender to Mrs. L. S. Howell, April 3, 1947, George Billeaud to Ellender, April 3, 1947, both in "Dept. of Agriculture, Sugar, 1947" folder, Box 42, Savoie to Ellender, August 19, 1948, Ellender to Savoie, August 27, 1948, both in "Veterans Administration, General, 1948" folder, Box 447, all in AEP.

efit payments. "Our sugar friends in the House . . . ," Ellender wrote in
1941, "let a rider slip through that would have cut benefit payments if
quotas were lifted."[21] No riders of this type eluded the careful scrutiny
of Ellender or the sugarcane lobby. After the United States entered
World War II, the United States Department of Agriculture allowed
unlimited production and continuation of subsidy payments.

Scarcity of materials and manpower during World War II posed
serious problems for the sugarcane industry. The Sugar Cane League's
labor committee blamed the labor shortage on the military draft, competition from new industries, the WPA, and the unemployment program.
To solve its labor problem the League carefully explored possible domestic and foreign sources of manpower. It consulted Ellender about
using nisei, some of whom were housed in camps in Arkansas, but
these plans were never realized. In July, 1943, the League discussed
possible use of German prisoners of war in the cane fields, but Ellender
discouraged the idea. He said military regulations prohibited locating
a POW camp within 150 miles of the coast and required among other
things, that camps have electricity and hot and cold running water.
Aware of the difficulty of circumventing military regulations, Ellender
wrote: "Personally I would not advise employment of German prisoners."[22]

Confronted with a labor crisis, however, the Cane League pressed on
for a solution. In August Frank Barker of Lockport, chairman of the
League's labor committee, met with military, educational, Selective Service, and various other wartime agency representatives at Thibodaux
High School to discuss possible manpower measures. Besides the nisei,
the group considered importing laborers from Mexico, Jamaica, and the
British West Indies. Here they ran into racial problems. Because of
segregation in the South, the Jamaican government did not allow its
nationals to work south of the Mason-Dixon line. Ellender attempted
unsuccessfully to have this ban lifted. Cane League members also discussed ways of transforming loiterers into productive workers. Barker
proposed reducing the hourly pay rates of those who worked less than

21 New Orleans *Times-Picayune*, September 9, 11, 1939; Ellender to Barker,
September 12, 1940, in "Sugar, 1940" folder, Box 301, Ellender to Leon J. Landry, April 18, 1941, in "Agr., Sugar Acreage" folder, Box 39, both in AEP.

22 American Sugar Cane League, Minutes of Executive Committee Meeting,
February 25, 1942, pp. 1–2, August 7, 1942, p. 5, August 25, 1943, p. 5, July
27, 1943, p. 3; Ellender to R. H. Chadwick, August 3, 1943, in "War Department, Prisoner-of-War Labor, 1943–'44" folder, Box 18, AEP.

five days a week. Others favored various types of bonuses. One spokesman suggested granting furloughs to black American soldiers during the grinding season so they could help harvest the crop. Despite the many military obstacles, however, the most practical solution considered involved using German prisoner-of-war labor in the cane fields.[23]

The Cane League refused to admit defeat merely because growers could not comply with military rules regulating use of POW labor. Instead it launched a major campaign to obtain waivers and exemptions from existing rules. Congressmen, mayors, elected state officials, state legislators, police jurors, Extension Service personnel, county agents, local newspaper editors, local businessmen, educators, farmers, and Cane League members wrote letters, signed petitions, sent telegrams, drafted resolutions, wrote editorials, and used their influence to persuade military and governmental officials to permit POWs to work in Louisiana's coastal rice and sugarcane fields. Ellender served as spokesman for the agricultural establishment before various governmental agencies, departments, and bureaus. Apparently the barrage succeeded, for after August, 1943, the War Department encouraged increased use of prisoners of war. It provided information to employers, opened more jobs to POWs, constructed more side camps in lieu of regular prison camps, and generally worked closely with the United States Employment Service. A major breakthrough for cane growers came when the Army reclassified some POW jobs and cleared the way for using more POWs for agricultural work. Seven or eight prison camps sprang up in the cane country less than fifty miles from the Gulf of Mexico. In October, 1943, Ellender informed the state director of the Agricultural Extension Service, H. C. Sanders, that the commanding general in charge of POWs could use his own judgment about housing POWs in abandoned Civilian Conservation Corps camps. A week later the senator attempted to obtain from military authorities a waiver of a ruling that a tent housing POWs must have a wooden floor. In March, 1944, he reported to his constituents that the Extension Service could apply directly to the War Department for POWs without having to go through the War Manpower Commission. This ruling gave the agricultural establishment a direct role in administering the POW program. The Eighth Service Command apportioned POWs on the recommendation of

23 Florence LeCompte to Joseph Lallande, August 18, 1943, in "War Department, Prisoner-of-War Labor, 1943–'44" folder, Box 18, AEP; Cane League, Minutes of Executive Committee Meeting, August 25, 1943, pp. 3–4.

H. C. Sanders of the Extension Service, according to a news release from Senator Overton's office in August. During the entire period farmers bombarded officials with requests for more prisoners to perform agricultural tasks.[24]

Charles A. Farwell, a veteran League member with extensive holdings in West Baton Rouge Parish, supervised the industry's end of the POW program and worked closely with Brigadier General L. F. Guerre, director of Security and Intelligence, Eighth Service Command of the United States Army, who was in charge of the POWs. By January, 1944, before the program had operated a full year, the Louisiana sugar industry had employed 4,634 war prisoners who had performed 231,700 man-days of labor. League member Murphy Foster of St. Mary Parish called the POW contribution a "life saver." In July, 1944, Major General Richard Donovan promised Senator Ellender additional camps at Reserve, Montegut, Houma, and Thibodaux by November 1. He listed existing camps at Franklin (237 prisoners), Woodlawn (242), Port Allen (254), Lockport (126), Mathews (138), Donaldsonville (346), Jeanerette (240), and Youngsville (102).[25]

Once the sugar lobby had obtained POW labor for use in the cane fields, it tried to convince military authorities that substandard POW labor should be paid at less than the usual rate. The military based its pay scale for POWs on the pay of an Army private—twenty-one dollars per month, or eighty cents per day. But Army regulations, which specified that POW labor should not compete with free labor, stated that prisoners should receive pay for services "in accordance with the minimum rates for similar labor in the locality or area." In 1939 the USDA wage hearings had established a rate of $1.50 for a nine-hour day for cultivating and harvesting sugarcane in Louisiana. By 1944 the rate had risen to $2.70. The chairman of the Cane League's labor committee informed Ellender in 1945 that abandonment of a War Manpower Commission policy now permitted paying POWs less than fifty cents per

24 George G. Lewis and John Mewha, *History of Prisoner of War Utilization by the United States Army, 1776–1945* (Washington: U.S. Government Printing Office, 1955), 110, 104; Ellender to H. C. Sanders, October 15, 1943, Harvey Peltier to Ellender, October 20, 1943, Ellender to Peltier, October 23, 1943, Ellender to V. C. Rives, March 23, 1944, John Overton release (mimeographed), August 8, 1944, all in "War Department, Prisoner-of-War Labor, 1943–'44" folder, Box 18, AEP.

25 Cane League, Minutes of Executive Committee Meeting, October 27, 1943, p. 5, January 26, 1944, pp. 2–3; Richard Donovan to Ellender, July 24, 1944, in "Sugar, Prisoner File" folder, Box 445, AEP.

hour as previously required. The labor committee attempted to persuade the Army to accept sixty per cent of the regular pay for POW labor because "the German prisoner cannot perform anything like the amount of work that free labor does." The Army rejected the wage reduction proposal for prison labor. Unabashed, the League formally requested more POWs for the 1945 harvest and suggested using Italian prisoners incarcerated at Camp Plauché in New Orleans. Organized labor complained about these repeated requests for more "slave labor," but the League was undeterred. Hoping to agree on a common piece rate schedule to propose to the Army as an alternative to an hourly rate of pay, the League gathered factual data from its members. Military commanders of POWs were no less confused than agricultural union leaders by the complicated piece rate and task rate pay schedules for cutting various sizes and varieties of sugarcane. Colonel Tom B. Martin of the Eighth Service Command announced at a meeting with cane growers in Thibodaux in August, 1945, that no prisoner would cut large-barrel cane varieties for less than ninety-six cents per ton nor small-barrel types for less than $1.05 per ton. This angered cane growers, who claimed the officer did not understand the industry and its problems. They bombarded Secretary of Agriculture Clinton Anderson with a form letter apparently prepared by the Sugar Cane League.[26]

In addition to solving a major labor problem in Louisiana's sugar country, German POW labor made planters less dependent on Negro laborers, whose bargaining position had improved somewhat as wartime shortages became acute. In August, 1943, Ellender instructed his administrative assistant, "without giving the matter any publicity at all, which as you know has been our usual course, try to find out what can be done toward securing a lot of the colored soldiers who are now encamped in various parts of the South." In September Frank Barker reported that the Cane League sought furloughs for black soldiers who could be sent more expeditiously than POWs to small growers each day. Larger plantations could house the soldiers. By December a Cane League director felt that POW labor performed well and in addition exerted a positive influence on black workers: "I am also told that the presence of the prisoners has served to wake up the negroes to some

26 Lewis and Mewha, *Prisoner of War Utilization*, 77, 101–102; Sitterson, *Sugar Country*, 391–94; Cane League, Minutes of Executive Committee Meeting, March 29, 1944, pp. 2–3, July 26, 1944, p. 2, August 30, 1944, p. 2; Barker to Ellender, March 2, 1945, in "War Department Prisoner-of-War Labor, 1945–'46" folder, Box 18, AEP.

concern about more prisoners being brought in to take over their jobs entirely. As a result the negroes are working better and are staying on the job throughout the week."[27]

Even after World War II ended, some growers hoped to continue using POWs, but President Harry Truman wanted all war prisoners returned by June, 1946. By then, he reckoned, returning GIs would be looking for jobs, and civilian labor would also be available. When the POW population in Louisiana declined, the Cane League worked out arrangements for Jamaican and Mexican laborers to come to the United States. By the time agricultural union activity had begun to stir in Louisiana in the early 1950s, T. M. Barker, Frank Barker's son and his successor as chairman of the Cane League labor committee, had planned to set up a permanent labor-supplying organization under the auspices of the Sugar Cane League.[28]

Requests for additional laborers during the war years, the Cane League soon realized, invited careful scrutiny of wage policies and working and living conditions by government officials, church groups, and labor leaders. Usually the League chose to remain silent, because workers had no spokesmen to represent them. Once during the war, when several League members proposed replying to adverse criticism of the industry, Frank Barker suggested a policy of silence because a public debate would detract from the industry's wartime slogan: "Where would the United States be now if the domestic producers had not produced sugar?" Nevertheless, when East Coast refiners criticized the Louisiana cane industry's labor policy in 1943, the League reacted to the criticism. They informed Ellsworth Bunker, then an official of the National Sugar Refining Company of New York, that the League would not join a proposed sugar research foundation.[29]

Cane League records indicate that members often recognized the va-

27 Ellender memo to Wurzlow, August 11, 1943, Barker to Ellender, September 17, 1943, Bourg to Ellender, December 7, 1943, all in "War Department, Prisoner-of-War Labor, 1943–'44" folder, Box 18, AEP.

28 See Box 18, AEP for letters, telegrams, and resolutions requesting POWs. Lewis and Mewha, *Prisoner of War Utilization*, 173; Cane League, Minutes of Executive Committee Meeting, July 30, 1947, p. 4, January 31, 1951, pp. 3–4, September 25, 1952, p. 6.

29 Cane League, Minutes of Executive Committee Meeting, January 27, 1943, pp. 3–4, February 24, 1943, pp. 3–4.

lidity of the charges leveled against them. It was easier, they knew, to circumvent the military rule against having a POW camp within 150 miles of the coast than to provide POW camps with running water, electricity, heat, and "other provisions for physical comfort." Wallace Kemper, a prominent League member and president of Southdown Sugars, proposed that military authorities house POWs in old Civilian Conservation Corps camps because "the type of house on the plantations would probably be considered unsuitable for their use." This was an open admission from an industry spokesman that housing for sugarcane workers did not meet even the minimum military standards for prisoners of war. League members later worried that Senator Harry Truman's Senate Committee to investigate the National Defense Program might look into conditions in the sugar industry.[30]

The benefit payments that growers and processors received were not related to the economic status of field workers, and the agricultural establishment kept the system that way. During World War II there were proposals to provide wage subsidies directly to workers in the cane industry, but the Cane League rejected them. In October, 1942, it declined the State War Board's offer to recommend a dollar a day in subsidy pay for field workers. Later, growers signed agreements with the War Food Administration that provided subsidies of eighty-five cents a ton for cane to be paid to growers through the processors. The League had developed the useful stratagem of tying wage hikes to increases in the price of sugar, not to increases in subsidies. Therefore, subsidy increases provided sizable gains for processors and growers but only slight benefits to workers. As has been noted, Senator Byrd's attempts to limit the maximum benefit payment to a single grower were all unsuccessful. In 1944 the League discussed at great length how subsidy monies should be paid and spent.[31]

Even though the sugar lobby had persuaded the USDA to sever any direct relationship between subsidy payments to growers and the welfare of plantation workers, members mentioned the plight of workers to justify demands for additional benefit payments. In 1951 the Louisiana Farm Bureau president wrote Allen Ellender: "Sugar prices are so

30 *Ibid.*, July 27, 1943, p. 3, May 26, 1943, p. 5, March 29, 1944, p. 4.

31 *Ibid.*, October 28, 1942, pp. 2–3, January 26, 1944, p. 5, February 14, 1944, pp. 1–23, June 29, 1949, pp. 6–7; Charles Farwell to Ellender, June 23, 1939, in "Agriculture, Department of, Sugar—General, # 3" folder, Box 409, AEP.

low this year, that the cane field labor is only half fed." F. Evans Far-well reported that because of drought and a freeze in 1951 growers had stopped harvesting and workers had no money to buy food. Yet, the Cane League concentrated its efforts at the annual wage hearings on preventing significant wage increases. The League came to rely increasingly on cost studies conducted by agricultural economists at Louisiana State University to justify limiting wage increments. Before the war ended, the League filed complaints, based on cost studies produced by LSU, with Chester Bowles of the Office of Price Administration. Further, the League sent Ellender statistics about the sugar industry from LSU Professor J. N. Efferson.[32]

At the annual wage hearings held by the USDA to implement the Sugar Act growers, of course, would testify that sugar prices were too low, wages too high, citing figures collected by the Sugar Cane League's labor committee. The roster of Cane League officials through the years clearly reveals that big growers and processors dominated the organization, although the League claimed to represent the entire industry. Plantation laborers were hard pressed to counter statements by the League's legal and public relations experts. After agricultural labor leaders appeared at the 1947 hearings, Farwell wanted the League to recommend closed hearings by the USDA. The executive committee did not oppose the idea but decided that such a move would be imprudent. In 1944 the chairman of the labor committee complained that agricultural officials had gathered statistical information from individuals rather than from the Cane League. "I told you at our conference," he wrote an investigator for the Sugar Division, "I felt that individual effort to obtain this type of information would be resented by the Industry unless all of the information secured was made available to the Industry for their study and reaction." He admitted discouraging members from furnishing data on an individual basis and intimated that government officials had been gathering evidence surreptitiously. A USDA official replied that since he had not received the promised man-hour data on the cost of producing a ton of sugarcane, he simply took steps to obtain this information independently. He told the labor committee chairman that he had no objections to sending his statistical data to the Cane League.[33]

32 Dougherty to Ellender, October 18, 1951, F. Evans Farwell to Lawrence Myers, December 7, 1951, both in "Agriculture, Sugar, 1951" folder, Box 109, AEP; Cane League, Minutes of Executive Committee Meeting, April 25, 1945, pp. 5–6, August 31, 1949, p. 6.

33 Cane League, Minutes of Executive Committee Meeting, July 30, 1947, p.

Despite uncertainties about labor problems, acreage reduction, and continued government support of the sugar industry at the end of World War II, Ellender remained optimistic about the future for the sugar industry in Louisiana. He told a friend who wondered about its prospects that he did not expect drastic cutbacks at the end of the war. He felt that "producers will be allowed a more liberal amount of production than in the past," and concluded, "I don't believe you would make a mistake in remodeling your factory."[34]

After more than a decade in Washington battling for sugar legislation, Ellender had good reason to feel optimistic. He had helped guide the industry through and around tough obstacles. With passage of the Sugar Act in 1937 Louisiana growers took advantage of ambiguities in the law and increased production. Reluctantly and begrudgingly they plowed sugarcane under in 1939 in order to comply with agricultural regulations and to qualify for conditional benefit payments. Then, suddenly the outbreak of war in Europe eliminated a problem of overproduction and lifted the cloud of uncertainty that hung over the sugar industry. With usual foreign sources of sugar in doubt, the USDA encouraged domestic cane growers to increase production and, through the efforts of Ellender and other congressional leaders, continued to subsidize growers with benefit payments. The industry survived a severe wartime labor shortage with German prisoner-of-war labor and emergency payments to growers. The postwar industry realized Ellender's importance more than ever when he became chairman of the Senate Committee on Agriculture and Forestry in 1951.

The American Sugar Cane League tried to hold the line on labor costs not because growers sought to impoverish the plantation workers, but because they wanted to stabilize production costs. Raw sugar producers in Louisiana knew that, in turn, the refiners and the soft drink manufacturers were trying to depress raw sugar prices. Like other lobby groups, the League sought a favorable business climate in Washington that could bring lower operating costs and greater returns to growers, and it was highly successful. Its professional staff, backed by a budget

---

4, October 20, 1948, pp. 4–5; Barker to Bourg, August 28, 1944, Barker to Ward Stevenson, August 28, 1944, Stevenson to Barker, August 22, 1944, all in "War Food Administration, 1944–'45" folder, Box 445, AEP.

34 Ellender to Peltier, November 17, 1945, in "Agriculture, Sugar, 1945–'46" folder, Box 446, Ellender to Peltier, May 15, 1947, in "Dept. of Agriculture, Sugar, 1947" folder, Box 42, Ellender to Peltier, June 10, 1948, in "Agriculture, Sugar, 1948" folder, Box 208, all in AEP.

considerably larger than H. L. Mitchell's STFU or its mid-century counterparts,[35] wrote position papers, hounded legislation relating to agriculture, served as an information clearinghouse, and coordinated propaganda beneficial to the industry. The League's use of data provided by
agricultural economists at Louisiana State University to verify cost-of-
production figures added academic respectability to its data-gathering
operation. Clearly the League became a significant part of the agricultural establishment. Although it is true that the League did not attempt
to elevate the economic status of plantation growers, this is not to say
that individual growers did not have second thoughts about the plight
of workers living in quarters once occupied by slaves.

35 Cane League, Minutes of Executive Committee Meeting, March 26, 1952,
p. 4. The League's budget for fiscal 1951 came to $108,227, of which $19,000
was used to run the Washington office; Mitchell's union budget averaged about
$50,000 per year.

Part II

The Confrontation, 1949–1976

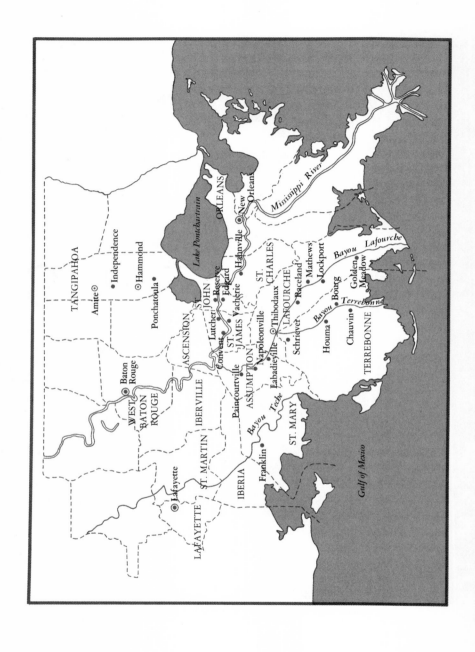

ORLEANS

New Orleans

Mississippi River

Lake Pontchartrain

Hahnville

Bayou Lafourche

TANGIPAHOA

Independence

Hammond

Amite

Ponchatoula

ST. JOHN

Reserve

Edgard

Mathews

Lockport

Golden Meadow

Lutcher

Convent

ST. JAMES Vacherie

ST. CHARLES

Raceland

Bourg

Bayou Terrebonne

ASCENSION

Napoleonville

Thibodaux

LAFOURCHE

Schriever

Houma

Chauvin

TERREBONNE

Baton Rouge

WEST BATON ROUGE

Paincourtville

Labadieville

ASSUMPTION

Bayou Teche

Bayou Lafourche

IBERVILLE

ST. MARTIN

LAFAYETTE

Lafayette

IBERIA

Franklin

ST. MARY

Gulf of Mexico

Chapter 5

The NAWU Comes to Louisiana

Each major group interested in Louisiana agriculture—the NFLU, the American Sugar Cane League, and the Catholic church—played a distinct part in a drama that unfolded in the early 1950s. The NFLU attempted to become the bargaining agent for various agricultural workers, a move opposed by the agricultural establishment, which cited precedents of long standing for denying agricultural workers the rights and privileges of industrial workers, and refused to negotiate with the NFLU.[1] Archbishop Joseph Francis Rummel of New Orleans and his social action priests, undoubtedly more concerned about the workers than either of the other two groups, attempted to bring the union spokesmen and the agricultural establishment together, although even Catholic sugar growers belligerently refused to agree to their prelate's suggestions. The situation was to reach its climax during the sugarcane harvesting season in October, 1953.

The Social Action Committee appointed by Archbishop Rummel in the Archdiocese of New Orleans eventually dealt with labor matters of a global nature as privation in eastern Europe worsened after World War II. Americans, such as Father Luigi Ligutti of the influential National Catholic Rural Life Conference, were concerned about the large number of displaced persons in central and eastern Europe. He recommended sending DPs to work the agricultral lands of the United States rather than allowing them to suffer hardship at home.[2] After displaced persons began arriving in the United States, Archbishop Rummel appointed the

1 See Chapter 1 for handicaps agricultural unions faced.
2 Reverend Vincent O'Connell, interview, April 4, 1972, with Bishop Joseph Vath and Monsignor Charles Plauché, hereinafter cited as VPO interview.

Reverend William Castel and the Reverend Hubert Lerschen to direct the Archdiocesan Resettlement Bureau, a clearinghouse for processing DP laborers' applications.

Authorities in the office of the Displaced Persons Commission in Washington assigned some DPs to sugarcane plantations in Louisiana. Here Polish and Hungarian workers complained about living and working conditions on the plantations. Father Castel came to realize that the economic plight of displaced persons was improved very little—if at all—by sending them to work on the plantations. When the director of the Resettlement Bureau criticized the conditions under which some DPs lived and worked, conservative upper clergy replied that the DPs fared better on plantations than did their countrymen living in camp-like conditions in eastern Europe. Many DPs with relatives and friends in the North left sugar plantations for better-paying northern jobs. Because plantation work at least provided refugees a toehold in the United States, Castel felt the resettlement scheme had not been a complete failure.[3]

The press publicized the failures of resettlement efforts involving displaced persons. The Reverend Joseph B. Koncius, president of the United Lithuanian Relief Fund in America, reported deplorable situations in some sections of the South. At a New Orleans disembarkation point he spoke to Latvians and Lithuanians who did not know what salary they would receive nor that blacks on some plantations had averaged only $890 in income the previous year. DPs, Koncius concluded, deserved something better than jobs nobody else wanted. *Collier's* published a feature depicting the sugarcane areas of Louisiana as less than a promised land.[4]

Roman Catholic Polish DPs in the cane country often appealed to their parish priests about poor living conditions and low pay. Pastors, in turn, consulted the Social Action Committee of the archdiocese for solutions. Father Vincent O'Connell, committee chairman, noting that many non–English speaking Poles had left the plantations on foot, replied that he could do little for them because they were isolated and out of his reach—"behind the Cane Curtain." O'Connell's figurative and obviously provocative expression no doubt angered cane growers, but there evidently was some truth in his metaphor. O'Connell was refer-

3 Plauché, VPO interview.
4 "DP Okies and Sharecroppers," *The Commonweal*, May 27, 1949, pp. 163–64; "Who Said Promised Land? Sugar Land of Louisiana," *Collier's*, July 2, 1949, pp. 19–21+.

ring to the wall of ignorance, segregation, prejudice, and poverty that encircled the isolated and largely disfranchised black plantation workers. He knew from his experiences organizing sugar refinery workers in the late 1930s that the paternalistic plantation system generally reacted vigorously to criticism and to unionization threats. There would be foreclosures for debts carried by the company store, the cutting off of water and natural gas in the company-owned houses, dismissals, and evictions.

As he had done earlier for sugar refinery workers, O'Connell asked E. H. Williams, president of the State Federation of Labor, for assistance. Williams recommended contacting H. L. Mitchell's National Farm Labor Union, which had become affiliated with the American Federation of Labor in 1946. O'Connell then spoke to the former STFU leader, and before long Mitchell sent organizers to contact dairy farmers and strawberry growers, as well as shallot, pepper, and potato growers. Mitchell believed his best chance to breach the Cane Curtain would be to attack it from a base of agricultural locals in other areas.[5]

Mitchell's National Farm Labor Union developed ties not only to Father O'Connell's Social Action Committee, but to Catholic clergymen outside the Archdiocese of New Orleans as well. Whether Catholic church contact with the NFLU influenced the enactment in 1949 of an anti–displaced persons resolution by the NFLU is uncertain. However, just two months after Catholic publications publicized post–World War II conditions for DPs, the NFLU adopted a resolution asking federal authorities to stop placing DPs in depressed agricultural areas like the sugar country of Louisiana. The resolution may have merely reflected the NFLU's opposition to the introduction of foreign labor into American agriculture. In California the union opposed the use of braceros; in Florida the importation of workers from the British West Indies. One thing is certain—influential Catholic leaders who had spoken out on the DP problem continued their close ties with the National Farm Labor Union.[6]

Senator Ellender never enthusiastically supported the Displaced Per-

5 O'Connell, interview, September 11, 1970, and VPO interview.
6 National Farm Labor Union Executive Board Resolution, July 7, 1949, roll 34, Luigi F. Ligutti to H. L. Mitchell, October 6, 1949, 63:1214, George G. Higgins to Mitchell, November 10, 1949, 63:1217, Mitchell report to Federal Advisory Council, Bureau of Employment Security, [1949], 63:1219, all in Southern Tenant Farmers Union Papers, housed in the Southern Collection (and photoduplicated by the Microfilm Corporation of America in 60 rolls), University of North Carolina, Chapel Hill, hereinafter cited as STFU, with box and folder or roll number.

sons Act of 1948, even though he favored importing foreign agricultural labor. He introduced a bill in 1951, for example, to permit the
importation of Mexican laborers, blaming the Korean War for a labor
shortage. When Catholic groups urged him to support more comprehensive DP programs, however, Ellender informed them that he did not
believe that displaced persons faced death or privation if they returned
to their homelands. Besides, war-torn Europe needed skilled DPs—
nurses, doctors, and other professionals. After an exodus of DPs from
sugar plantations, Ellender mentioned their lack of interest in agricultural work. He nonetheless assisted individuals with problems related
to displaced persons, and with Congressman Hale Boggs, tried to persuade the Displaced Persons Commission in Washington to ship DPs
destined for the South through the port of New Orleans rather than
through eastern ports.[7]

H. L. Mitchell's agricultural union first became active in Louisiana by
organizing dairy farmers. In June, 1948, several dairy farmer groups
in Louisiana asked to join the National Farm Labor Union. His union
chartered one local in Amite north of Lake Pontchartrain and formed
the Florida Parishes Milk Producers Union, which became Local 236
of the NFLU on June 12, 1948. Another local at nearby Franklinton
became Southeast Louisiana Dairy Farm Union, Local 237 of the NFLU.
Through an arrangement with the AFL and the Louisiana Federation of
Labor, union members purchased milk from processors who handled
only products of AFL dairy farm members.[8]
    The International Brotherhood of Teamsters had earlier chartered
locals of the United Milk Producers in Franklinton, Amite, Baton
Rouge, Lake Charles, and New Orleans. In 1947, just a year before
Mitchell's union became active, the Teamsters affiliated union had be-

    7 Ellender speech, June 3, 1947 (mimeographed), in "Speeches, 1948" folder,
Box 634, "Immigration, 1949" folder, passim, Box 635, Ellender speech, March
11, 1950, in "Speeches, 1950" folder, Box 105, "Legislation, Immigration, 1953"
folder, passim, Box 4, "Mexican Labor" folder, passim, Box 392, Hale Boggs to
Ellender, October 25, 1948, in "Displaced Persons Commission" folder, Box 374,
all in Allen J. Ellender Papers, Division of Archives, Nicholls State University,
Thibodaux, Louisiana, hereinafter cited as AEP; The American Sugar Cane
League, Minutes of Executive Committee Meeting, September 25, 1952, p. 6,
Nicholls State University Library, Thibodaux, Louisiana.
    8 Farm Labor News, August-September, 1948, Roll 58, Mitchell to Beth
Biderman, April 6, 1950, 64:1240, both in STFU; F. Ray Marshall, Labor in the
South (Cambridge: Harvard University Press, 1967), 288–89.

come involved in a heated dispute and strike when a large New Orleans dairy raised consumer prices and lowered rates paid to milk producers. On March 24, 1947, the Teamsters affiliate shut off the flow of milk in the New Orleans milk shed. At Amite, armed union men stopped an Illinois Central train on March 25, and poured cans of milk into ditches. Later they halted eight tank trucks, each carrying about two thousand gallons of milk, and deflated the tires. In Independence, union men at the St. Charles Dairy dumped seven hundred gallons of milk into the Tangipahoa River. The strike ended after United States marshals arrested twenty-five strikers for interfering with delivery of the United States mail and for theft of milk. One union leader involved in the strike served one year in prison and paid a $5,000 fine. Most others received lighter sentences. The violence of the strike made many dairymen distrustful of unions in general and the Teamsters Union in particular.[9]

Workers in the NFLU Washington office at first doubted the abilities of E. H. "Lige" Williams, who headed the State Federation of Labor, but they soon benefited from his organization's assistance to dairy farmers. The Louisiana Federation not only provided organizers but prestige and political influence as well. It arranged for a delegation from the Florida parishes to meet at the capitol with Governor Earl Long, even though Williams and the governor were not on speaking terms. The dairymen wanted legislation to require Louisiana ice cream producers to use Grade A rather than powdered milk.[10]

Mitchell worked diligently to make the Louisiana dairy organizing venture a success, but economic and legal problems beset the dairy farm locals in Louisiana throughout their operation. As he had done the year before, Mitchell, in the summer of 1951, presented austerity budget proposals to NFLU officials. Pointing out that the union had sufficient funds for operation through August only, Mitchell added: "We must make some changes or find some new sources of revenue to continue thereafter." Money from outside sources for organizing would be hard to find, he said.[11]

9 Marshall, *Labor in the South*, 289; "Justice Department, Re: Milk Strike" folder, *passim*, Box 628, AEP.

10 Dorothy Dowe to I. Lee Parker, September 13, 1949, Parker to Dowe, September 11, 1949, both 63:1211, Parker to Mitchell, October 4, 1949, 63:1214, *Union News,* June 2, 1950, 64:1247, all in STFU.

11 Mitchell to Hazel Whitman, February 16, 1949, Roll 34, Dowe to Churchill, May 28, 1951, 66:1269-B, Aubrey Hirsch to Parker, April 24, 1951, 65:1270-A,

One of the NFLU's leading organizers, Henry Hasiwar, was trans-
ferred from California, arriving in Hammond, the strawberry center of
Louisiana, on February 20, 1951. After he arrived, the newly formed
Louisiana Fruit and Vegetable Producers Union, Local 312, (NFLU-
AFL) rapidly increased its activity. With help from E. H. Williams, the
local planned to picket six strawberry handlers who had not signed
union agreements. Williams helped line up attorneys and picketing
organizations to oppose the Louisiana Farm Bureau, which controlled
two of the handlers' associations that were giving Hasiwar trouble.

For years Louisiana strawberry growers had felt victimized by buyers
and chain stores that they thought were profiting most from the sale of
the perishable specialty. As early as 1898 men in Ponchatoula had
joined together to ship their early berry crop by car lot. By 1908 they
had formed shipping associations that loosely agreed on a minimum
price. But buyers of large quantities of berries outwitted the shipping
associations by agreeing on a maximum price before the bidding started,
thereby dominating the carload auctions that began in 1923. In the
1950s small growers formed a cooperative selling agency that received
assistance from E. H. Williams and the Louisiana Federation of Labor.
Father Vincent O'Connell was the "sparkplug behind the scene" in
organizing the strawberry cooperatives, according to H. L. Mitchell.
Simply by "talking strawberries," O'Connell says, the formerly hostile
Catholics, Baptists, Negroes, Anglo-Saxons, Hungarians, and Italians,
who operated small family farms in the Florida parishes, united and
formed a cooperative. Williams referred the strawberry farmers to the
National Farm Labor Union, which, in August, 1951, reported that
1,691 members of the vegetable and fruit producers local in Hammond
had joined the NFLU.[12]

In 1951 Archbishop Rummel helped to settle a strawberry dispute
that arose because of a strike and a picket line in Ponchatoula, Louisiana. Because local growers, demanding twenty-five cents per pound,
refused a fifteen-cent offer from handlers of frozen berries, a growers'
organization attempted to halt all berry traffic in the area. The state
police, refusing to take sides in the dispute, stood by on the alert.

Mitchell, Memorandum to NFLU officers and organizers, July 3, 1951, 66:1271,
all in STFU.

12 Mitchell, "A Letter to Judge Barnes," June 11, 1953, 68:1327, Dowe to
Churchill, August 28, 1951, 66:1272, all in STFU; Mitchell, interview, June 23,
1970; O'Connell, VPO interview.

Archbishop Rummel appealed to Charles Sinagra, a strawberry cold-pack shipper, to consider the growers who "are for the most part poor people with large family responsibilities." Pointing out that the offer of fifteen cents was ten cents less than the price of berries on the stem the previous year, Rummel surmised that God would be pleased with a sensible settlement. Sinagra replied that with sixty million pounds of frozen berries on hand, he could not offer more than eighteen cents per pound. John Simpson, who dealt only in fresh crated strawberries, informed the prelate confidentially that the packers were offering about as much as they could. Word of this disclosure, he said, could ruin him financially, but he authorized the Archbishop to quote him if doing so would solve the problem. On May 18 growers and frozen pack opera-tors met in the office of Charles Anzalone, state representative of Tangi-pahoa Parish, and compromised at eighteen cents per pound. Arch-bishop Rummel sent congratulatory telegrams to handlers and thanked them for sending word of the settlement to him.[13]

In September, 1951, the NFLU's chronic economic problems reap-peared. In August Mrs. Mitchell had sold her Alexandria, Virginia, house, which she found "too big to keep up," and in late October Mitchell reported: "For the first time in a number of years it appears that we shall not be able to meet our monthly payroll in full." The next month, while awaiting dues from the Hammond local, the NFLU paid part of everyone's salary, but dissension among dairy farmers over man-agement of the milk plant denied the agricultural union its primary source of dues. In January, 1952, the NFLU laid off three employees, ceased printing *Farm Labor News*, and cut its budget to $4,000 per month.[14]

In February the executive board of Fruit and Vegetable Producers Union, Local 312, had again voted to picket the six handlers who had not signed union agreements. Prior to the beginning of the harvest sea-son in March, 1952, Hank Hasiwar devoted himself full-time to straw-

13 New Orleans *Item*, May 18, 1951; New Orleans *Times-Picayune*, May 19, 1951; Joseph Francis Rummel to Charles Sinagra, May 17, 1951, Sinagra to Rummel, telegram, May 18, 1951, John Simpson to Rummel, telegram, May 18, 1951, Rummel to Marion T. Fanally and Sinagra, May 19, 1951, Rummel to Simpson, May 18, 1951, all in "Farmers Union" folder, Joseph Francis Rummel Papers, Archives of Archdiocese of New Orleans, hereinafter cited as JFR Papers.

14 Mitchell to Churchill, September 12, 1951, 66:1273, Dowe to Churchill, August 28, 1951, 66:1272, Mitchell to NFLU staff, October 29, 1951, 66:1274, Dowe to Churchill, November 1, 1951, 66:1275, Mitchell to Executive Council, January 22, 1952, 66:1289, all in STFU.

berry operations in Hammond. The local hoped to stop the movement of berries to nonunion handlers, but in Ponchatoula the association sponsored by the Louisiana Farm Bureau posed a serious challenge to this objective. Feeling more confident with Hasiwar in Louisiana, Mitchell nonetheless cautioned his colleagues against becoming party to any contracts or agreements signed by the local. Hasiwar felt that the union's strategy, to split the opposition of nonunion berry handlers and the association sponsored by the Louisiana Farm Bureau, would work. He urged taking no action against Farm Bureau members: "We can . . . use the Church to move in on them," he said. "The leaders of it are Catholic."[15]

Late in February, Hasiwar won a major victory over the Farm Bureau group in Ponchatoula with the help of Father O'Connell, who had persuaded the group to accept the union arrangement. After the Farm Bureau acquiesced, other handlers of fresh berries also signed agreements with the union. The peaceful nature of the strike and O'Connell's assurances that the NAWU would not tolerate Communists impressed the handlers. Predicting $2,000 per month in dues once the union won over the frozen-pack handlers, Hasiwar told Mitchell: "I hope this makes your ulcer better." The next month Hasiwar was optimistically planning to expand into the strawberry-growing areas of Arkansas and Tennessee.[16]

In November the Justice Department notified the Louisiana Fruit and Vegetable Producers Union, Local 312 of the NFLU, that it would examine its records for alleged violations of antitrust laws. George Forstall, president of Local 312, reported that Federal Bureau of Investigation agents had looked at correspondence, minute books, and contracts in his office, and he wondered if Mitchell could learn the reason for the investigation. Mitchell suspected Senator Ellender of having encouraged the FBI probe. As if to reassure himself, Mitchell said that since the union was a cooperative marketing project which guaranteed producers the right to organize, bargain, and market their products cooperatively within the jurisdiction of the Capper-Volstead Act, nothing

15 Henry Hasiwar to Mitchell, January 7, 1952 and February 22, 1952, 66: 1287, Mitchell to Hasiwar, February 25, 1952, 66:1293, Hasiwar to Mitchell, December 26, 1952, 67:1313, all in STFU.

16 Hasiwar to Mitchell, February 25, 1952, 66:1293, Hasiwar to Churchill, March 2, 1952, 67:1294, both in STFU.

would come of the probe. He added ominously: "It may be necessary however to set up the marketing arrangement as a cooperative association separately." He admitted that the union controlled the auction of strawberries in conjunction with handlers in violation of the antitrust laws and told Forstall to send him copies of the records the FBI had confiscated. Answering this charge, he acknowledged, "could be a tough one for us."[17]

Mitchell did not lose sight of the threat posed by antitrust action against the strawberry local as the NFLU planned campaigns among sugarcane plantation workers and shallot farmers, even though he seemed confident in December, 1952, that the Louisiana strawberry growers qualified for the antitrust exemptions afforded cooperatives under the Capper-Volstead Act. Mitchell believed that a federal marketing order allowed producers to set a minimum price for farm products. However, since Local 312 had both growers and processors on its coordinating committee, lawyers told Mitchell that the authorities might file a suit against the union for conspiring to fix prices. Hasiwar was convinced that Local 312 faced no antitrust convictions, and assured Mitchell that the union did not fix prices but merely set a minimum and that handlers were neither processors nor buyers. Mitchell replied that setting minimum prices could be construed as price-fixing and added: "Neither you, nor I are lawyers so we ought to get some good legal advice."[18]

In January, 1953, Mitchell's lawyers informed him that "the operation now is a price fixing device," and "we may get an injunction stopping the operation once the season gets under way." His attorney friend Daniel Pollitt, after clarifying several points on the Capper-Volstead Act, agreed to make the necessary changes in the strawberry charter for a fee of $600 and transportation expenses to Hammond. Later in the month Mitchell told union members he was going to Hammond to set up a "bona fide co-operative marketing arrangement" for Local 312 so that the union could set minimum prices without fear of prosecution

17 H. G. Morison to Louisiana Fruit and Vegetable Producers Union, March 28, 1952, 67:1302, George Forstall to Mitchell, May 22, 1952, 67:1303, Mitchell to J. L. Rhodes, May 27, Mitchell to Forstall, May 28, 1952, both 67:1294, all in STFU.

18 Mitchell to Hasiwar, December 10, 16, 17, 22, 1952, Hasiwar to Mitchell, December 29, 1952, all in 67:1313, STFU.

under the antitrust laws.[19] It was, perhaps, wishful thinking on the part of the NFLU leader to believe that the problems were solved.

In February, 1953, just one week before the beginning of the strawberry harvesting season, attorney Daniel Pollitt completed a new handlers' agreement, which had been planned since the first threats of antitrust action appeared. Under the new setup the union cooperative hired handlers to act as its agents. The co-op could require these agents to give their exclusive attention to its members and prohibit them from handling strawberries grown by nonunion members. These changes had been made because the state of Louisiana granted charters of incorporation to co-ops, but not to labor unions.[20]

On May 15, 1953, C. Paul Barker of the New Orleans law firm of Dodd, Hirsch, and Barker informed Mitchell that the Justice Department contemplated antitrust action against Local 312. That same week a federal grand jury summoned Hasiwar to appear with all of Local 312's records. Mitchell thought that a jury trial would afford an excellent opportunity to publicize the conspiratorial practices of chain stores and sugar planters. Convinced that the suit resulted from pressures generated by union opponents, Mitchell discussed with Hasiwar plans for a big publicity campaign exposing the antitrust tactics of the Justice Department, which had recently dismissed antitrust suits against big oil companies. Public relations, Mitchell thought, "if handled right could help get a favorable decision."[21]

After learning more about Judge Stanley Barnes of the Antitrust Division, who was handling the case against the strawberry local, Mitchell planned to air the case in public. "If he isn't what he seems to be," Mitchell wrote, "we are ready to blast his division in the newspapers; but we don't want to do it if he is the kind of man who is fair and square." Mitchell checked into ways to pressure the Justice Department and released a story of government prosecution of people with low incomes.[22]

19 Mitchell to Hasiwar, January 14, 1953, Daniel Pollitt to Mitchell, January 19, 1953, both 68:1319, Mitchell to "Dear Sir and Brother," January 23, 1953, 68:1320, all in STFU.

20 Hasiwar to Mitchell, February 11, 1953, Pollitt to Fortsall, February 13, 1953, both 68:1322, *Union Farmer*, March, 1953, Roll 58, all in STFU.

21 C. Paul Barker to Mitchell, May 15, 1953, Mitchell to Ernesto Galarza, May 18, 1953, Mitchell to Hasiwar, May 19, 1953, all in 68:1326c, STFU.

22 Mitchell to James E. Murray, June 11, 1953, Mitchell to Barker, June 12, 1953, both in 68:1327, STFU.

During the summer of 1953, Mitchell thought his charges of undue government pressure would bring relief to strawberry Local 312. He told North Dakota Senator William Langer of the folly of prosecuting such a small group and asked him to try to get Attorney General Herbert Brownell to drop the case. After meeting with a group of Biloxi, Mississippi, fishermen who faced similar antitrust charges, Mitchell asked his attorney to sound out Judge Barnes on the entire matter. Barnes wrote that the Justice Department did not intend to "break up" the NFLU locals as Mitchell had implied. Mitchell also spoke to Louisiana Senator Russell Long, who promised to consult with Congressman James Morrison before taking any action. Later in the month Mitchell, who assumed that his letter to Barnes had had some effect, told an attorney friend that the Justice Department might not indict the union.[23]

But a week later a federal grand jury indicted Local 312, charging its officials, including Henry Hasiwar, with conspiracy to restrain trade and commerce, conspiracy to fix prices, and compulsion and coercion of processors and handlers to enter price- and fee-fixing agreements. Mitchell quickly leveled verbal blasts at the Justice Department as he had originally planned. Labeling the attorney general's actions "union busting," Mitchell said: "Brownell is out to make a record for his Department by persecuting the poor and needy. His first act as Attorney General was to dismiss the antitrust actions against the international oil cartel." Mitchell told Congressmen of Justice Department pressures on small farmers. To Senator Paul Douglas of Illinois he stressed a possible connection between the strawberry indictment and attempts to break up the sugarcane local. Later he reassured Douglas that the NFLU had nothing to do with violence associated with a strawberry strike in 1951, since "we adopted the tactics of Ghandi . . . and adhered to the principles of non-violence."[24]

Despite Mitchell's verbal barrage against government antitrust policies, union attorneys attempted to solve the legal entanglements and

23 Mitchell to William Langer, June 18, 1953, Mitchell to Barker, June 22, 1953, Stanley Barnes to Mitchell, July 1, 1953, Mitchell to Barker, July 3, 1953, all in 68:1329, Mitchell to Pollitt, July 22, 1953, 68:1330a, all in STFU.

24 *United States of America* v. *Louisiana Fruit and Vegetable Producers Union, Local 312; Lester C. Felder, et al.*, Department of Justice mimeographed news release, July 29, 1953, Mitchell, news release, July 30, 1953, Mitchell, identical letters to Paul Douglas, Hubert Humphrey, Russell Long, Wayne Morse, and James Morrison, July 30, 1953, all in 68:1330b, Mitchell to Paul Douglas, August 14, 1953, 68:1332, and September 30, 1953, 68:1334b, all in STFU.

reach an understanding with the Justice Department for future operation of the strawberry local.[25] The impoverished agricultural union's
antitrust difficulties were just beginning.

While awaiting settlement of the antitrust action against Local 312,
Hasiwar used his church contacts to organize other agricultural industries. Catholic priests also participated in organizing activity among
shallot (green onion) farmers in the Acadian country of south Louisiana. Father Roland Boudreaux, pastor of Our Lady of Prompt Succor
Church in Chackbay, a shallot-growing center near Thibodaux, cooperated with farmers interested in banding together for their mutual interest after World War II. Later when Father O'Connell and the NFLU
became active and encouraged growers to market their own shallots, the
Lafourche Parish Farm Bureau and shippers and buyers protested. Some
antiunion parishioners stopped attending services for a while because
the priests were encouraging union membership.[26]

Jac Bokenfohr, a fresh-vegetable shipper from Thibodaux, complained to Archbishop Rummel about Father O'Connell's attempt to
organize the shallot growers. O'Connell had told Chackbay growers
that Thibodaux area shippers and handlers were cheating them, Bokenfohr claimed in a letter to Rummel. Bokenfohr, mentioning his own
Catholic background and education, called O'Connell's actions un-
Christian and said he hoped that at future meetings priests would not
resort to the same propaganda. After waiting almost a month and receiving no response from the Archbishop, Bokenfohr wrote again: "As
a member of your flock, I believe I am entitled to a reply." The Archbishop then checked with O'Connell who told his superior that he had
indeed encouraged farmers to join Mitchell's union at meetings held in
parish halls at the invitation of local pastors. Although shippers and
handlers attended the meetings and heckled the speakers, he said, no
one had called them cheats.[27]

Largely through Father O'Connell's efforts, Local 312 formed the
Lafourche Union Cooperative Growers' Association to market shallots
grown by union members. Leaders planned and worked out arrange-

25 Barker to Mitchell, August 13, 1953, 68:1332, Mitchell to Lester Felder,
September 15, 1953, 69:1334a, Barker to Barnes, undated, 69:1334b, Barnes to
Barker, October 5, 1953, 69:1335, all in STFU.

26 Roland Boudreaux, interview, April 4, 1972.

27 Jac Bokenfohr to Rummel, July 19, 1952, August 11, 1952, O'Connell to
Rummel, August 23, 1951[2], all in "Farmers Union" folder, JFR Papers.

ments for the co-op at organizational meetings at Our Lady of Prompt Succor. In their spare time members constructed a 20-by-104 foot packing shed in Thibodaux, which Auxiliary Bishop L. Abel Caillouet dedicated on October 12, 1952, amid considerable fanfare. Father Jerome Drolet, a member of the Social Action Committee, was the master of ceremonies. He called the occasion the beginning of a new deal for shallot growers. Hank Hasiwar also spoke to the group, and band music was provided by Thibodaux College, a local Catholic high school.[28]

Priests helped spread the co-op idea. In December Father Alexander Sigur of Lafayette conducted a meeting of shallot growers in the Lafayette–St. Martinville area, and Father Boudreaux took a busload of people from Chackbay to a meeting in Cecilia, near Lafayette. The southwest Louisiana shallot farmers joined Local 312 after the meetings. Other priests active in the movement included Marvin Bordelon of Simmesport, Adelard Auclair of Cecilia, John R. Timpany of Arnaudville, and John Coyne of Breaux Bridge. In December, 1952, the priests hammered out an agreement for membership in the biracial cooperative. Also participating were E. H. Williams of the Louisiana Federation of Labor, Hank Hasiwar, members of the Hammond local, and agricultural teachers Roland Bordelon, J. Oubre, and Joe Guidry. Hasiwar tried to hire Joe Guidry, an Acadian who spoke French and seemed to be a natural-born organizer, on a full-time basis.[29]

Hasiwar badly needed a French-speaking organizer among the shallot farmers and asked the AFL to assign one, saying that "these Frenchmen are a little more complicated to deal with than the Hammond group." In publicizing plans for organizing Louisiana, Mitchell, too, stressed the need for French-speaking organizers who would be assisted by "the Catholic priests in the area who are anxious to stop the victimization of the shallot growers." In August, 1952, Hasiwar reported needing organizers badly, especially those who could understand "that bastard French," as he described the Acadian French patois spoken in South Louisiana. "Shallots going slowly," he wrote, "because of language barriers." In December he mentioned meeting cabbage farmers in Breaux Bridge: "These boys jumped at our set up," because buyers had "ganged up on them." In speaking of the Breaux Bridge situation,

28 A. Jackson, unidentified clipping, Drolet Scrapbook, lent to author; *Union Farmer*, October, 1952, Roll 58, STFU.
29 *Catholic Action of the South*, January 8, 1953; *Union Farmer*, January, 1953, Roll 58, Hasiwar to Mitchell, December 26, 1952, 67:1313, Henry Fleischman, news release, March, 1958, Roll 39, all in STFU.

he reported: "We will also have the priests along as the back stops."
Seven priests attended the meetings and helped with French transla-
tions. "Otherwise," Hasiwar wrote, "I would have been lost."[30]

As organizing activities in Louisiana gained momentum, the NFLU's
strike against the DiGiorgio Corporation, a West Coast agribusiness
giant in California, dragged on, neither side able to win a decisive
victory. Union film makers in Hollywood produced *Poverty in the Valley of Plenty*, a documentary showing the deplorable conditions of agri-
cutural workers in California, and DiGiorgio sued the union film makers and the NFLU for misrepresenting living conditions on DiGiorgio
properties. In April, 1950, the union rejected a proposed settlement
that would have ended the strike and have required the NFLU to pay
one dollar in damages to DiGiorgio. The following month, however,
when Mitchell instructed Hasiwar to call off the strike, the NFLU begrudgingly signed an agreement with DiGiorgio that ended the strike
with token damages to DiGiorgio and destruction of all available prints
of *Poverty in the Valley of Plenty*. Since the strike had already failed,
destroying the film proved the bigger loss. Mitchell had shown it as
part of his testimony before the House Labor Committee considering
repeal of the Taft-Hartley Act, and I. Lee Parker had used it for education work among dairy farmers.[31]

After the failure of the DiGiorgio strike, Mitchell and his colleagues
considered concentrating virtually all union activities in Louisiana. "In
six months if I haven't developed something," Ernesto Galarza wrote
from California, "I'll turn in my chips." Mitchell told Arthur Churchill, a Protestant minister and director of the NFLU's mid-south office in
Memphis, to curtail some union operations. If Churchill wanted to help
Parker in Louisiana, Mitchell added, he should refrain from selling or
distributing religious literature. "With the large Catholic element,"

30 Hasiwar to Lew Rhoades [Rhodes], August 20, 1952, 67:1309, Mitchell,
"Agricultural Organization in Louisiana," 69:1343a, Hasiwar to Mitchell, De-
cember 26, 1952, 67:1313, and August 19, December 6, 20, 1952, 67:1309, all in
STFU.

31 Alexander Schullman to Mitchell, April 21, 1950, 64:1214, "Agreement"
between DiGiorgio Fruit Corporation and the National Farm Labor Union and
various film-maker unions, May 8, 1950, 64:1243, Mitchell to Galarza, March 17,
1949, Roll 34, Jim Wolfe to Churchill, August 26, 1949, 63:1209, Mitchell, news
release, May 9, 1950, 64:1243, all in STFU.

Mitchell warned, "we won't want to get some controversy stirred up."[32]

Whatever immediate plans Hasiwar had for joining another union or for returning to California vanished after his exploratory investigation of Louisiana early in 1951. "La. sure looks like the place [where] we can build a base for the union," he wrote. "I am really impressed with the possibilities." His cautiously optimistic report on conditions contrasted sharply with Parker's impression of the sugarcane situation situation a year and a half earlier. Referring to sugarcane as a "sick" industry, Parker had doubted that cane-field workers could support a union. Wage hearings in Thibodaux, which he attended, impressed him as being one-sided since no one testified for workers. Experts from Louisiana State University explained cost studies of producing a ton of cane. Farm Bureau and American Sugar Cane League representatives cited these as justification for not giving wage increases to field workers. Parker complained because one planter proposed amending the Sugar Act by adding a provision for penalizing cane cutters who did not perform their jobs well.[33]

After consulting with members of the Archdiocesan Social Action Committee, Hank Hasiwar decided to conduct an intensive campaign to organize sugarcane plantation workers. E. H. Williams, head of the State Federation of Labor, agreed that Hasiwar should pursue his union's possibilities in the sugar industry. Getting started in the cane fields would be delayed, Hasiwar said, because "the Church is going to need a little more time to finish their operation among the priests." When Hasiwar told Mitchell that the Catholic church needed further preparation of priests before it could begin a major effort to breach the "Cane Curtain," he may have been referring to a conference on industrial problems, scheduled at Loyola University, for Catholic clergymen and industrialists in May, 1951.[34]

At its Memphis convention in 1951, H. L. Mitchell's NFLU changed its name to the National Agricultural Workers Union (NAWU). According to a union resolution, the new name indicated that the union

32 Galarza to Mitchell, June 9, 1950, 64:1246, Mitchell to Churchill, September 29, 1950, 64:1252, both in STFU.

33 Hasiwar to Mitchell, January 18, 1951, 65:1262, Parker to Mitchell, July 18, 1949, Roll 34, both in STFU.

34 Hasiwar to Mitchell, February 21, 28, 1951, 65:1265, STFU; Rummel, pastoral letter, May 1, 1951, in letterbook of Saint Joseph Catholic Church, Thibodaux, Louisiana.

represented more than migratory farm workers. Before approving the name, the American Federation of Labor wanted guarantees that the change did not alter the NFLU's jurisdictional or territorial status. While awaiting AFL approval of the change, Mitchell's organization used its old official title formally and the new name informally. In time the AFL sanctioned the new name, and in August, 1952, the NAWU newspaper, the *Agricultural Unionist*, replaced the old NFLU *Farm Labor News*.[35]

As Hasiwar began his assault on the sugar industry, he remained close to the protective cover of the Catholic church. At a meeting in a Catholic church hall in Reserve on January 6, 1952, 110 cane-field workers joined the union. In February Hasiwar planned to meet Father O'Connell on the "sugar cane deal," and a few days later he added: "Of course, you know the church will be calling the shots in that area." Hasiwar, a Roman Catholic himself, maintained close contacts not only with Father O'Connell but also with Archbishop Rummel and the chancery office. The Chancellor, Monsignor Charles J. Plauché, recalls that Hasiwar often came to his office, and that the vice-chancellor, not easily impressed by labor leaders, had accused him of thinking of Hasiwar as "Saint Hank."[36]

Mitchell sent Hasiwar to represent him at the Louisiana Federation of Labor convention on April 7–10, 1952, in Baton Rouge. Hasiwar addressed the group and discussed the formation of Local 312 in Hammond and the efforts in the cane country. Father O'Connell also spoke at the convention, promising to organize the farm workers in the state.[37]

T. M. Barker of Lockport had succeeded his father, Frank Barker, as manager of Valentine Sugars and as chairman of the important Cane League labor committee. Like his father, T. M. Barker voiced strong opposition to unionism of plantation workers. "Mister Barker does not look favorably upon any attempt to organize his workers," Father O'Connell wrote to Archbishop Rummel in 1951. "In fact, he spoke in

---

35 "Proceedings—17th National convention, NFLU-AFL, Memphis, Tennessee, December 8–9, 1951," 66:1276-A, William Green to Mitchell, February 13, 1952, 66:1291 and May 27, 1952, 67:1303, *Agricultural Unionist*, August, 1952, Roll 58, all in STFU.

36 Hasiwar to Mitchell, January 7, 1952, 66:1287, and February 22, 25, 1952, 66:1293, all in STFU; Monsignor Charles Plauché, interview, March 22, 1972.

37 E. J. Bourg to Mitchell, February 22, 1952, 67:1293, Mitchell to Bourg, March 11, 1952, 67:1294, *Farm Labor News*, June, 1952, Roll 58, Dowe to Churchill, April 14, 1952, Mitchell to William Becker, April 16, 1952, both in 67:1298, all in STFU.

terms of violent opposition." Later, Barker agreed to allow O'Connell and Raymond Witte of Loyola University to address sugar growers, however, and O'Connell asked the union to delay its organizing efforts in the Lockport area in the meantime. Witte recalls that after the talk Barker angrily told him that if they returned to the Lockport area, he could not be responsible for what might happen.[38]

Later, in April, 1952, Barker appeared before a committee of the Sugar Cane League's executive board and presented O'Connell's promise to the AFL convention in Baton Rouge to organize the farm workers of Louisiana. Barker then read a statement drafted by his labor committee in response to O'Connell's declaration. Wallace C. Kemper, veteran member of the organization, urged avoiding a war of words with the articulate and aggressive O'Connell prior to the wage hearing scheduled for July. His observations indicate the type of assistance that Louisiana State University agricultural economist J. Norman Efferson rendered, as well as some League members' lack of confidence in their wage policies:

> We do not have a good case. If I thought we had a good case I would love to go in and swing and make our case public. Our case is bad. If you answer them again very definitely you have invited an attack, whereas, at the minute, in the absence of an answer, it is dead. At the meeting it was discussed how it was best to answer and with the advice of Dr. Efferson who hopes to give us some figures on labor costs and other facts we hope to have a good case to present at the hearing in July.

Even after Barker had won a 9-to-7 vote of approval for his proposal, he had misgivings because so many members had doubts about responding to O'Connell and thereby giving him another chance to fire verbal blasts at the League. Barker agreed to postpone responding to the priest.[39]

Barker said, twenty years later, that he could remember no fiery exchanges with O'Connell or Witte, but he recalled disagreements over labor matters with Father Drolet and with Father Roy Patterson, Monsignor Dominic Perino's young assistant at Holy Savior Catholic Church in Lockport. Barker respected the young assistant for his dedication and idealism but felt that he did not understand the sugar industry. Some

38 O'Connell to Rummel, April 6, 1952, in "Farmers Union" folder, JFR Papers; Raymond Witte, interview, February 20, 1974.
39 Cane League, Minutes of Executive Committee Meeting, April 30, 1952, pp. 3–6.

growers, he says, stopped going to church because of Patterson's pro-labor sermons and Barker himself probably dodged the young priest's comments by attending mass at a different hour. Holy Savior parishioners generally believed that Father Patterson left the parish soon afterward because of his differences of opinion with the pastor and with sugar planters, some of whom defiantly walked out of church during his sermons.

On one occasion Drolet was threatened by members of his congregation. Lewis Edwards and Casel Jones, the burly Baptist sergeants-at-arms of Local 312, came over with their shotguns to guard the CIO padre at his rectory. Drolet felt that reports of this intimidation had been exaggerated, that at most "O'Connell's boys" spent a night watching over the area, and that one of his parishioners spent about a week guarding at the rectory with him. However, Dan Mack, Sheriff Charles Barker's driver, remembers that on one occasion the sheriff had to escort Drolet through a noisy crowd gathered at the rectory and drive him to safety in New Orleans.[40]

Barker thought that the presence of a union at Valentine Sugars was proof that he had not resisted unionization. His father, Frank Barker, had helped organize the Valentine Independent Union, a company union, in December, 1945, when the CIO petitioned the National Labor Relations Board to become the bargaining unit for the Valentine sugar plant. The company union won the NLRB election, but because CIO leaders were aware that the NLRB often refused to recognize company unions, they tried again in 1947 to claim that they represented workers at Valentine Sugars. When Frank Barker asked the CIO to produce evidence of their strength at the plant, though, the CIO withdrew its petition. Barker disliked the maintenance-of-membership agreements, a wartime labor measure that CIO unions were negotiating with nearby sugar refineries, which provided that a worker would lose his job if he resigned from the union.[41]

Injuries that Hasiwar had received in an automobile accident on his way home from the Federation of Labor convention in April, 1952, delayed the union's Louisiana operation and led to consideration of

40 O'Connell, interview, September 11, 1970; Drolet, interview, March 20, 1972; Dan Mack, interview, December 2, 1976.

41 T. M. Barker, interview, May 10, 1972; Ellender to Emile Godchaux, April 17, 1939, in "Godchaux Sugars, Inc." folder, Box 94, Frank Barker to Ellender, March 19, 1947, in "Labor Dept., 1947" folder, Box 371, all in AEP.

alternative proposals by Mitchell and his two most trusted lieutenants, Galarza and Hasiwar. By the end of April Hasiwar was recovering from his injuries, but he was behind schedule in organizing sugar workers. In view of union financial problems, NAWU leaders toyed with the idea of leaving the AFL and asking Walter Reuther of the CIO for money to continue operations in the Imperial Valley in California. Finally, the NAWU triumvirate decided that Galarza should join Hasiwar in Louisiana for a big union drive to organize sugarcane plantation workers.[42]

In August, 1952, the agricultural labor movement in Louisiana suffered another major setback when Father O'Connell left for a new assignment in St. Paul, Minnesota. His leaving, Hasiwar wrote, would "severely cramp our organizational pattern for the plantation workers in the sugarcane industry. . . . Actually, I feel that without the active support of the Church in sugar cane, it makes it almost impossible to go ahead with our plans in the sugar industry. Father O'Connell was our all important anchorman in this drive." Convinced that Dixiecrat and antiunion opposition to his labor activity had forced O'Connell's reassignment, Hasiwar wanted to fight back, but did not know how. Equally sure that O'Connell had been "kicked upstairs," Mitchell spoke to Monsignor George Higgins, who told him that any interference by the union in church affairs could reflect unfavorably on Father O'Connell.[43]

O'Connell, too, believes that Catholic laymen and conservative clergymen in the Archdiocese of New Orleans wanted him removed since they objected to his labor views. He believes that antiunion forces pressured a bishop whose church operated a heavily mortgaged parochial school. At their request, the bishop asked the provincial of O'Connell's order to reassign him.[44]

Certainly, though, as a member of a religious order, for about twelve years O'Connell enjoyed far more independence than regular diocesan priests assigned to particular parishes and subject to direct pressure from the parishioners. Once he had been assigned chairman of the Social Action Committee, pastors brought problems related to race and labor to him. Priests deferred to him, knowing that he had the knowledge

42 Hasiwar to Churchill, April 22, 1952, 67:1299, Mitchell to Galarza, April 21, 1952, 67:1298, [Galarza] to Hasiwar, June 3, 1952, 67:1304, all in STFU.
43 Hasiwar to George Higgins, August 1, 1952, 67:1308, STFU; Mitchell, interview, June 23, 1970.
44 O'Connell, interview, September 11, 1970, and VPO interview.

and training to handle such matters and the trust and support of the archbishop. Also, as a teacher at Notre Dame Seminary, O'Connell could use his classroom as a forum and sounding board for discussing sensitive matters.[45]

Fortunately for Mitchell's union, Archbishop Rummel found a capable replacement for Father O'Connell. The Archbishop, too, had trusted and relied on O'Connell's judgment and ability: he could be forceful when necessary, yet tactful and diplomatic when the situation called for magnanimity. His replacement as chairman of the Social Action Committee, the Jesuit Louis J. Twomey, in time won the same respect from Archbishop Rummel, whom he personally represented in many social action matters. Ordained in 1939, Twomey had come to New Orleans in 1947 and opened the Institute of Industrial Relations at Loyola University. He had observed cigar-union activity during his youth in his native city of Tampa, Florida, and had written about sharecroppers and about the National Industrial Recovery Administration while in training for the priesthood. The chain-smoking Jesuit once encouraged janitors working at Loyola to form a union. In New Orleans he collaborated with O'Connell, who introduced him to many labor leaders, industrialists, and priests active in the archdiocesan area.[46]

Prior to the annual wage hearings in July, Hasiwar gathered data from workers in Louisiana while Mitchell in Washington studied the legal ramifications of the Sugar Act. The NAWU president wondered what personal interest Senator Ellender had in the sugar industry. Then, in August, 1952, Hasiwar reported to Mitchell that he had signed up 100 new members in Raceland along Bayou Lafourche, and told AFL officials that he had picked up 350 members on several plantations without any trouble. He predicted that within a year the NAWU would be set to "move in" on the sugar industry.[47]

The National Sharecroppers' Fund, for many years a major financial

45 Ibid.; Joseph Vath, VPO interview.
46 Mitchell, "The People at the Bottom of Our Agricultural Ladder," October 7, 1952, 67:1311, STFU; Plauché, interview, March 22, 1972, and VPO interview; John R. Payne, "A Jesuit Search for Social Justice: The Public Career of Louis J. Twomey, S.J., 1947–1969" (Ph.D. dissertation, University of Texas, 1976), 22, 35, 44, 46, 62, 84; O'Connell, VPO interview.
47 Mitchell to Hasiwar, July 3, 1952, 67:1306, Hasiwar to Mitchell, August 19, 1952, Hasiwar to Lew Rhoades [Rhodes], August 20, 1952, both in 67:1309, all in STFU.

contributor to the NAWU, based its fund-raising appeal in 1952 on the Louisiana sugarcane workers. American Sugar Cane League officials discussed a promotional pamphlet circulated by the group at several sessions of their executive committee meetings, and in May T. M. Barker recommended asking for some kind of government investigation of the pamphlet. By August the League had gathered evidence with which it hoped to prove that the Sharecroppers' Fund, by distributing fallacious information, had employed fraudulent means to solicit money. Senator Ellender asked the chairman of the House un-American Activities Committee to provide information on H. L. Mitchell and other NAWU leaders and on the National Sharecroppers' Fund, which the Cane League's Josiah Ferris had requested. From the committee Ellender received routine background information on Mitchell, and on Norman Thomas, Fay Bennett, Sidney Hertzberg, Frank Graham, and Charles S. Johnson, all members of the Sharecroppers Fund. Presumably, he passed the information on to Ferris.[48]

As the National Agricultural Workers Union moved closer to a confrontation with leaders in the sugar industry in Louisiana, Mitchell shared with his union colleagues the knowledge he had gained from years of dealing with the agricultural establishment. He cautioned them that USDA people were mainly Farm Bureau appointees. He also advised Hasiwar to act while farm workers were fired up with enthusiasm. But he warned Hasiwar not to become too involved in their affairs and become too much one of them. Mindful of Hasiwar's personal sympathy for the poor, Mitchell told him not to become unduly concerned about plantation workers who lost their jobs for joining the union. "If they are driven out," he wrote, "they will be a damn sight better off personally than they are now." Mitchell hoped the NAWU research director could soon relieve the president of the tedious and technical task of studying the Sugar Act, a job Mitchell did not enjoy.[49]

Meanwhile, in Assumption Parish along Bayou Lafourche the NAWU organizing campaign moved on a confrontation course with Clarence

---

48 National Sharecroppers' Fund, "Minutes of Board of Directors Meeting," June 18, 1952, 67:1305, STFU; Cane League, Minutes of Executive Committee Meeting, May 28, 1952, p. 4, August 27, 1952, pp. 5–6; Harold Velde to Ellender, September 25, 1953, in "Agriculture, Sugar, 1953" folder, Box 83, Josiah Ferris to Wurzlow, November 25, 1953, both in "Misc. 'F' 1953" folder, Box 113, November 24, 1953, all in AEP.

49 Mitchell to Hasiwar, August 9, 1952, 67:1308, and August [2]0, 1952, Mitchell to Galarza, August 28, 1952, both in 67:1309, all in STFU.

Savoie, a wealthy and influential planter who was also a member of the House of Representatives of the state legislature. With help from the Catholic church the union won a Pyrrhic victory in this first encounter with Savoie, who resented the influence of local priests assisting the NAWU. In Bertrandville, near Napoleonville, the Josephite priest, Harry J. Maloney of St. Benedict the Moor Church, a black Catholic parish, encouraged his parishioners to join the union. Angry Catholic growers asked Archbishop Rummel to remove Maloney. Local priests had given Savoie conflicting reports on the likelihood of his successfully pressuring the archbishop to oust the Josephite. Instead of removing the priest, Rummel called him in for a conference. Although the church won that round, Savoie reacted by using his influence thereafter to oppose the unions and the priests. Encouraged by Archbishop Rummel's refusal to remove Father Maloney, Hasiwar told E. H. Williams to ask Clarence Savoie if he was ready to sit down and negotiate with the NAWU. "We got his people organized," Hasiwar said with obvious delight. To facilitate organizational work in the cane country Hasiwar and his followers had formed the Sugar Cane Workers Organizing Committee earlier in 1952. In August, 1952, Hasiwar reported that thirty-five laborers signed union application cards for membership following a meeting near Plattenville. They became members of Local 312.[50]

As Mitchell often implied, the agricultural establishment in Louisiana stymied union efforts in a number of ways. Local offices of the Department of Agriculture, such as the Production and Marketing Administration, presented any obstacles they could to the NAWU. "These parish PMA's are really terrible," Hasiwar wrote. "Hell, they're violating the Act themselves." In February, 1952, the Secretary of Agriculture appointed T. M. Barker to serve on the state PMA committee. Hasiwar informed the Sugar Division of the USDA that Moise Hymel, chairman of the St. James Parish Production and Marketing Committee, had violated the Sugar Act on his Gramercy, Louisiana, plantation by not giving workers a specific lunch hour, by collecting for a group insurance

50 Plauché, interview, March 22, 1972; Hasiwar to Mitchell, October 31, 1952, 67:1311, STFU; Notes of report by Harry J. Maloney to Rummel, October 31, 1952, in "Farmers Union" folder, JFR Papers; T. Harry Williams, *Huey Long: A Biography* (New York: Alfred A. Knopf, 1969), 261; Twomey to Rummel, May 22, 1953, in "Rummel, Archbishop" folder, Louis Twomey Collection, Documents Center, Loyola University, New Orleans; Hasiwar to E. H. Williams, November 19, 1952, in "Farmers Union" folder, JFR Papers; Mitchell to National Executive Board, NAWU, October 3, 1952, 67:1311, Hasiwar, "Weekly Report," August 31, 1952, 67:1309, both in STFU.

policy that did not cover workers, and by failing to specify other deductions made from the workers' wages. In Thibodaux and in Napoleonville, Production and Marketing Administration officials refused to give unpaid-wage claim forms to the NAWU. Only individuals could secure these forms, the Lafourche and Assumption parish offices told Henry Pelet, a CIO sugar factory worker who was helping to organize field workers. The union, Hasiwar said, would use its own forms containing the same information.[51]

After the death of AFL President William Green in November, 1952, Mitchell planned ways to persuade George Meany, the new AFL leader, to continue subsidizing the NAWU. He intended to emphasize Catholic church support for the NAWU to Meany, a Catholic. Meanwhile the strain of financial and agricultural problems began to catch up with Hasiwar. Commenting on Hasiwar's possible ulcers, Mitchell cautioned him to follow his doctor's orders and get some rest. "One damn case [of ulcers] in this outfit is enough." Responding to Mitchell's letter saying that Hasiwar had fainted, Ernesto Galarza said if Hasiwar had not passed out from martinis, he was worried. "If it was [the martinis], I'm still worried," he added. Hasiwar did not have ulcers, after all, and he felt better after cutting down on his smoking and taking Sundays off.[52]

In 1952 two CIO sugar refinery workers, interested in the cause of field workers, began helping Hasiwar to get to the field and meet plantation workers. Henry Pelet, whose father came from Switzerland to Bayou Teche where Henry was born, later moved to the sugar country of Bayou Lafourche. The elder Pelet's liberal views influenced his son, a member of Local 1422 at Supreme Sugars in Labadieville. Henry Pelet worked from six o'clock in the morning until two o'clock in the afternoon at the sugar refinery and then spent much of his free time contacting workers whom he invited to union meetings at church halls, including the one at Saint Benedict the Moor in Bertrandville, where Father Maloney encouraged workers to join the NAWU. In one year

51 Hasiwar to Mitchell, November 25, 1953, 67:1309, STFU; Cane League, Minutes of Executive Committee Meeting, January 27, 1954, p. 5; Ellender to M. W. Scanlan, telegram, February 20, 1952, in "Agriculture, Production & Marketing, 1952" folder, Box 118, AEP; Hasiwar to Thomas Allen, November 3, 1952, in "Farmers Union" folder, JFR Papers.
52 Mitchell to Hasiwar, November 24, 28, 1952, both in 67:1312, Galarza to Mitchell, December 1, 1952, Hasiwar to Mitchell, December 2, 1952, both in 67:1313, all in STFU.

Pelet traveled sixty thousand miles by automobile, organizing mostly black workers, never receiving expense money. Similarly, in the Reserve area along the Mississippi River, Frank Lapeyrolerie, a black who worked at the Godchaux refinery, called workers to meetings at Our Lady of Grace Church, a black parish in Reserve, where Josephite Father Joseph G. Turner explained to workers the significance of a labor union.[53]

Like Henry Pelet, Frank Lapeyrolerie often contacted plantation workers at night, traveling from house to house. This method offered several advantages, including easy access to workers and a measure of anonymity for organizers who appeared to be visiting friends in their homes at night. Workers and organizers were less afraid of physical abuse from growers than of economic pressure against those who joined the union. Sugar factory workers received higher wages than plantation workers, but a planter could prevent a field worker from taking a higher-paying factory job by complaining to the factory manager. Thus, a grower's labor needs, or even his vindictive attitude, could thwart a worker's chance for financial advancement.[54]

In 1952 Mitchell considered asking AFL President William Green to hire Henry Pelet to help Hank Hasiwar in Louisiana, and in November he endorsed Hasiwar's appointment of Lapeyrolerie as secretary of the rapidly developing sugar local. The next month Hasiwar asked for expense money for Pelet and Lapeyrolerie, whose assistance he said was invaluable. "Both these boys haven't asked for a dime in expense," he wrote, "and they are using gas as well as plenty of time." In 1952 the NAWU also discussed plans for using George Stith, a veteran black organizer, in the sugar industry.[55]

If Mitchell and his colleagues envisioned a world they hoped to create for agricultural workers, they failed to articulate these dreams and aspirations either among themselves or to their union members. They never elaborated on how a living wage took priority over industry profits, how workers could come to own their own homes, or how meaningful minimum standards fitted into the larger scheme of union plans. In short, they did not formulate long-range objectives for themselves. Even so, they undoubtedly felt a strong sense of mission, a determina-

53 Henry Pelet, interview, February 29, 1972; Mitchell, interview, June 23, 1970.
54 Frank Lapeyrolerie, interview, October 5, 1975.
55 Mitchell to Hasiwar, August [2]0, 1952, 67:1309, November 21, 1952, 67:1312, Hasiwar to Mitchell, December 25, 1952, 67:1313, all in STFU.

tion to make a better life for agricultural workers. Mitchell often spoke of "continuing the fight" and of some day "winning the struggle" against the lords of agribusiness. Hasiwar once scolded a West Coast colleague for his lack of idealism and for his disappointment at being underpaid. "We are doing this [job]," Hasiwar wrote, "to make the society we live in more tolerant, democratic and abundant."[56]

Perhaps the NAWU leaders, like Mitchell, Galarza, and Hasiwar, discouraged idle dreams of changing the world of the rural poor until they had developed a self-supporting union. Like starving men more concerned about subsistence than cholesterol levels, union leaders thought mainly in terms of survival. Preoccupied with financial matters, they philosophized more about subsidies from the AFL, grants from the National Sharecroppers' Fund, and collecting sufficient dues to meet the payroll than about future goals of farm workers. Union leaders hoped to win recognition as legitimate representatives of farm laborers in the sugar industry and to receive the benefits enjoyed by organized labor. Then, perhaps, they could think about creating a new world for agrarian outcasts.

The National Agricultural Workers Union reached a crossroads in Louisiana during the summer of 1952. Acute financial problems plagued the union which had not yet recovered from the collapse of the dairy farm locals. In addition, the union faced legal bills, fines, and possible jail sentences for leaders of the strawberry local charged by the Justice Department with violating antitrust laws. These developments left the NAWU with only one remaining major group of agricultural laborers to organize: sugarcane workers. If the union hoped to remain in Louisiana, it would have to contend with the legal, economic, and political might of the agricultural establishment. Perhaps deciding to persevere was easy for leaders who realized that any other course would have meant the end of the union. Where else could Mitchell's agrarians, the perennial voice of distressed agricultural laborers, operate if they withdrew from the fray in Louisiana?

56 Hasiwar to Becker, February 25, 1952, 66:1293, STFU.

Chapter 6

The Archbishop and the Cane Growers

The Sugar Workers Organizing Committee of the NAWU did its job well, and in January of 1953 the NAWU chartered Local 317, a sugar workers' local. Once again the Catholic Church participated directly in the union effort. In discussing the role of priests, Mitchell wrote to a union colleague: "They do everything except sign up the members and collect the dues. There is no fear of loss of jobs by union members, the cane planters don't dare fire them because of the possibility of encurring [sic] the wrath of the church." From three to a dozen priests attended various union meetings at which 562 workers joined Local 317, Mitchell said.[1]

Mitchell personally presented Local 317 its charter at its installation ceremony at Our Lady of Grace church hall in Reserve on January 30, 1953. Father Louis Twomey delivered the principal address to union members representing sixteen sugar-producing parishes with district offices in Napoleonville, Raceland, and Reserve. Father Harry J. Maloney of Bertrandville provided school buses to transport members from the Napoleonville area to the meeting hall provided by Father Joseph Turner. The local elected Paul Chaisson, a white, and Frank Lapeyrolerie, a black, president and vice-president respectively.[2]

After the sugar local became a reality, the NAWU decided to make Louisiana the center of its operations. H. L. Mitchell wanted continued aid from the AFL and hoped that its new leader, George Meany, who

1 H. L. Mitchell to Arthur Churchill, February 3, 1953, Box 68, Folder 1321 of Southern Tenant Farmers Union Papers, housed in the Southern Collection (and photoduplicated by the Microfilm Corporation of America in 60 rolls), University of North Carolina, Chapel Hill, hereinafter cited as STFU, with box and folder or roll number.

2 The *Union Farmer*, February, March, 1953, Roll 58, STFU.

was a Catholic, would be swayed by the support the NAWU was receiving from the church. He felt that a diplomatic letter to Meany from "someone high in the New Orleans Diocese," suggesting that the AFL continue its subsidy to the NAWU would help. He also specified that if Meany sent someone to investigate conditions in Louisiana, that investigator should meet priests like Louis Twomey, Alexander Sigur, and the archbishop, if possible, for "he would be more impressed with the church angle than with the workers themselves." The NAWU must "make it plain that the first job is to be done in Louisiana and afterwards California," Mitchell stressed.[3]

Hasiwar asked the Chancellor of the Archdiocese of New Orleans and E. H. Williams of the State Federation of Labor to write to Meany along the lines suggested by Mitchell. Mitchell requested aid for a campaign about twice the size of anything the NAWU had mustered over the previous years and told Meany: "The support given by the Catholic Church to the Union's campaign in rural Louisiana is not to be discounted." When someone mentioned other religious groups contributing significantly to the NAWU, Mitchell replied: "However, we have never had any sort of local support of the type the Catholic Church is in the position to give in rural Louisiana."[4]

The NAWU nearly lost Hasiwar, its key man in Louisiana, in April, 1953. Depressed by news that his father in New York was suffering a fatal illness and discouraged by setbacks and sacrifices demanded of him and his family, Hasiwar planned to retire from the union to manage his father's oil distributorship. The NAWU was an anachronism, he told Galarza. Maybe, he said, it was in "the wrong historical slot." Galarza learned from Mitchell the following month that Meany was planning to stop paying NAWU organizers. Mitchell, who had spoken to the CIO sugar workers about joining the NAWU, observed: "If it ever works out we can tell AFL to go to hell." In the meantime Mitchell wanted Galarza to conduct an educational campaign among the agricultural workers in Louisiana, who were inexperienced in labor matters. They reminded Mitchell of sharecroppers he had organized in Arkansas in 1934 and Mexican-Americans in California after World War II. Hasiwar had decided by early summer to remain with the union, and so he moved to Reserve, even though Mitchell had suggested that he settle in New

3 Mitchell to Churchill, February 9, 1953, 68:1321, STFU.

4 Henry Hasiwar to Mitchell, February 11, 1953, 68:1321, Mitchell to George Meany, [January 6, 1953], 68:1318, Mitchell to Nelson Cruikshank, February 16, 1953, 68:1322, all in STFU.

Orleans. "You know Hank has to be in the center of a three ring circus to be happy," Mitchell said.[5]

In June, Meany quit paying the salaries of three NAWU organizers and instead pledged a grant of $1,200 per month to the union for one year. Upon hearing this Galarza told Mitchell to do everything possible to keep Hasiwar from resigning. "The rest of us will walk the plank," he said, adding, "I'll go to Louisiana just as soon as I am satisfied that we have burned out [our] last match out here and it won't be long now." Mitchell regretted having to abandon six years of work in California but commented on union finances in his usual Micawberesque manner. He jokingly worried about Hasiwar, who wanted a union organizer to postpone his wedding in order to plan strategy for organizing sweet potato farmers. "Hank must not have any sense of humor," Mitchell said. "Don't see how he keeps going without a little."[6]

After Galarza left California in midsummer 1953, the NAWU had no other organizer on the west coast. For a time the union considered sending Hasiwar back to California and letting Joe Guidry, the Acadian organizer, supervise the entire Louisiana operation. Later at an executive board meeting in September the NAWU apparently decided to abandon California in favor of Louisiana. It gave Local 317 jurisdiction over workers west of the Mississippi River and Local 312 authority over those east of the river. Dorothy Dowe, Mitchell's wife, resigned her position as NAWU secretary-treasurer but stayed on as office secretary in the Washington, D. C., office that the union decided to maintain because legislation, publicity, and contacts with other labor organizations were essential.[7]

In December, 1952, the National Agricultural Workers Union took its first step toward negotiation with the big sugar interests. Hasiwar wrote to Godchaux Sugars and requested a session to discuss the wage claims of plantation workers. Noting good relations between the company and CIO factory workers, Hasiwar hoped the same would be true for the NAWU–Godchaux Sugars association. The NAWU charged that the cane

5 Ernesto Galarza to Mitchell, April 29, 1953, 68:1325, Mitchell to Galarza, [May, 1953], 68:1333b, both in STFU.

6 Meany to Mitchell, June 18, 1953, Galarza to Mitchell, June 17, 1953, Mitchell to Galarza, June 22, 1953, all in 68:1328, STFU.

7 Mitchell to F. R. Betton, July 31, 1953, 68:1330b, Mitchell to C. Paul Barker, August 31, 1953, 68:1333b, Minutes of Executive Board meeting of the NAWU in New Orleans, Louisiana, September 12–13, 1953, 68:1334a, all in STFU.

growers were violating the Sugar Act by paying workers for nine hours and making them put in nine and a half. The union expected the Department of Agriculture to curtail benefit payments to growers until the wage dispute had been resolved and filed for back pay totaling $32,000. That February Mitchell felt confident that the tactic would succeed, but in April the USDA dismissed the wage claims against the big planters.[8]

In a detailed letter to Archbishop Rummel the next month, Hasiwar reported on the progress of Local 317 and outlined tentative plans as the fall cane-grinding season approached. He acknowledged the importance of Father Harry Maloney to the success of the movement which now claimed a membership of over a thousand, each paying one dollar each month in dues. Local 317, he said, maintained executive boards and field stewards in Reserve, Raceland, Thibodaux, Houma, Labadieville, Klotzville, and Central. This permitted union members, eighty percent of whom were black, to attend meetings near their homes. The local maintained good race relations, and blacks held important positions. But growers fired workers for joining the union. Anticipating proposed meetings with industry spokesmen in June, union leaders studied legal aspects of the Sugar Act.[9]

In July, 1953, Local 317 sent the biggest sugar producers in Louisiana registered letters asking them to enter into collective bargaining with the union over wages and working conditions. Although Hasiwar quoted popes from Leo XIII to Pius XII on the right of workers to be "organized and recognized as an organization by their employers," planters continued to oppose collective bargaining. They denied that Local 317 represented plantation workers, and they refused to meet with its leaders.[10]

At the July wage-price hearings conducted by the Department of Agriculture in Thibodaux, the NAWU and other groups asked for higher pay and better working conditions for plantation workers. The Ameri-

8 Hasiwar to Walter Godchaux, Jr., December 3, 1952, Mitchell, news release, December 17, 1953, 67:1313, The *Union Farmer*, January, 1953, Roll 58, Mitchell to Churchill, February 3, 1953, 68:1321, Mitchell, news release, April 23, 1953, 68:1325, all in STFU.

9 Hasiwar to Joseph Francis Rummel, May 20, 1953, in "Farmers Union" folder, Joseph Francis Rummel Papers, Archives of Archdiocese of New Orleans, hereinafter cited as JFR Papers.

10 Frank Lapeyrolerie, identical letters, July 29, 1953, to Charles A. Farwell, Walter Godchaux, Jr., William McCollam, J. J. Munson, Francis Robicheaux [sic], L. J. Rodrigue, Clarence Savoie, Moise Hymel, and Felix Savoie, 68:1330b, all in STFU; *Godchaux Sugars, Inc.* v. *Chaisson et al.,* So. 2d 673 (1955), 678.

can Sugar Cane League and the Louisiana Farm Bureau proposed a five percent increase over the previous year's wages to "insure a better labor supply," while the Catholic Daughters of America and union representatives presented facts in support of the workers' viewpoint. A Napoleonville paper objected to union demands of one dollar per hour for skilled workers and seventy-five cents per hour for unskilled workers. In an editorial it complained about unions that held a "public be damned attitude." Mitchell disliked the idea of minimum rates, for "minimums become the maximum rates paid." For the first time labor spokesmen questioned the validity of Louisiana State University cost studies. They had perennially served as the sole authority in the Louisiana sugar industry and the basis for Sugar Cane League contentions that growers could ill afford wage increases. Loyola Professor Rudolf Coper raised doubts about evidence from so-called impartial witnesses after an LSU professor became flustered by Coper's questions about his accounting procedures.[11]

The Cane League considered the LSU cost studies reliable research projects conducted by disinterested scholars. T. M. Barker of the League insisted, "these are completely disinterested agencies."[12] It is true that Cane League records do not reveal collusion between the League and the LSU economists who prepared the cost studies. Nevertheless, the relationship between the two groups was far from impersonal and disinterested. In fact, the authors of the cost studies sometimes served on League committees. In 1945 Arthur Keller resigned from the League's executive committee upon returning to his teaching duties at Louisiana State University. The following year the League unanimously approved a motion by Frank L. Barker to donate $250 to Dr. J. N. Efferson of LSU for assembling and preparing cost studies of sugar operations. That same year the League gave $300 to Dr. Keller to use in his study of cane-cleaning equipment in Hawaii. In 1948 the League authorized an expenditure of $2,000 by Efferson to study the reduced recovery of sugar per ton of sugarcane. When the National Agricultural Workers Union and several labor priests began actively

11 *Lafourche Comet* (Thibodaux), July 23, 1953; *Assumption Pioneer* (Napoleonville), July 24, 1953; Mitchell, news release, August 14, 1953, 68:1332, STFU; Raymond Witte to Rummel, July 24, 1953, in "Farmers Union" folder, JFR Papers.

12 American Sugar Cane League, Minutes of Executive Committee Meeting, Nicholls State University Library, Thibodaux, Louisiana, July 30, 1952.

organizing plantation workers in 1952, Efferson may even have been serving as a member of the League's labor committee. He joined the members of the labor committee at a meeting to draft a reply to Father O'Connell's promise to organize the cane industry. In the mid-1950s the League sponsored scholarships to LSU instead of making cash grants or donations for research, and even as recently as 1973 an LSU professor made cost studies free of charge for the Cane League.[13]

Experienced Cane League veterans attempted to put spokesmen for plantation workers on the defensive. After Loyola Professor Raymond Witte admitted at a hearing that he could not distinguish between a stalk of cane and a stalk of corn, T. M. Barker of the Sugar Cane League told the hearing that it was ludicrous for the professor to discuss economic phases of the sugar industry. Hasiwar, speaking for the NAWU, recommended a four-point program including, in addition to the wage increases, features to assist small farmers, provisions for greater supervision of the sugar industry by the USDA, and efforts to stabilize the labor force in sugarcane and improve the education of the workers. He sent a copy of his proposal to Archbishop Rummel.[14]

In mid-August the conciliator for the Louisiana Department of Labor, to whom the union had appealed when growers refused to bargain, told Local 317 he would meet with its leaders on August 19, 1953, to obtain detailed information regarding the controversy with sugar growers. Local 317, then, in order to imply it was already bargaining with the growers and had reached a stalemate, sent another batch of letters to the growers, which stated: "We appreciate a point of contention raised in your letter regarding the recognition of our union." The letters, further, suggested conciliation talks with officials of the Louisiana Department of Labor to settle the dispute. The Department of Labor, in turn, informed the growers of what union records the NAWU agreed to make available and scheduled a meeting with the sugar planters for August 26, 1953, at the Civil Courts Building in New Orleans.[15]

13 Ibid., May 30, 1945, p. 2, January 30, 1946, p. 8, May 29, 1946, p. 3, January 28, 1952, p. 10, April 30, 1952, p. 4, January 25, 1956, p. 3; Lafourche Comet (Thibodaux), June 6, 1973.

14 T. M. Barker, interview, May 10, 1972; Hasiwar, "Statement," July 16, 1953, 68:1329, STFU; Hasiwar to Rummel, July 17, 1953, in "Farmers Union" folder, JFR Papers.

15 A. P. Harvey to Lapeyrolerie. August 13, 1953, 68:1332, Lapeyrolerie to nine sugar growers, August 18, 1953, Harvey to nine sugar growers, August 19,

Because agricultural workers were not specifically mentioned in Louisiana laws under the definition *employee,* the NAWU was unable to require the Department of Labor to compel sugar growers to attend the conciliation meetings. "We do not believe that it would be to our agricultural employees' best interest to be represented by such a union," a Godchaux Sugars representative wrote. Holding a union election, another company official stated, would serve no useful purpose, because "our workers" do not want union representation and no contention between management and labor exists. Claiming an obligation to protect workers who did not wish to belong to a union, the Godchaux official turned down conciliation attempts by citing Louisiana law which "prohibits anyone from taking any action whatever which would have the result of coercing an employee to become a member of union organization." The other growers refused to attend for various reasons.[16]

Local 317, next, consulted Dr. Paul Hebert, dean of the Louisiana State University Law School and chairman of the State Labor Mediation Board, for assistance in bringing about conciliation. Just one day after the appeal to Dean Hebert, Hasiwar explained to Archbishop Rummel how Local 317 had written letters to nine sugar producers who had refused to bargain with the NAWU. The union then turned to the Louisiana Department of Labor for conciliation but again failed to get planters in for talks. "The Service has no compulsory or mandatory powers," Hasiwar complained, and growers had simply refused to negotiate. The growers who had been contacted by the union had, however, raised their wages at least one dollar per day, in spite of T. M. Barker's contention that growers could not even afford a five percent increase. Hasiwar felt that the raise indicated the falsity of the growers' position. He also told Rummel that, since voluntary pay increases had failed to diminish union fervor, planters, such as Clarence Savoie, had fired some workers and had threatened to evict others for their union activity.[17]

1953, L. H. Simmons to nine sugar growers, August 20, 1953, 68:1333a, all in STFU.

16 *Godchaux Sugars, Inc.* v. *Chaisson et al.,* So. 2d 673 (1955), 678; Lapeyrolerie to Simmons, August 10, 1953, 68:1332, Richard McCarthy, Jr. to Louisiana Department of Labor, August 25, 1953, 68:1333b, William McCollam to Lapeyrolerie, August 21, 1953, McCollam to Simmons, August 23, 1953, 68:1333a, all in STFU.

17 Lapeyrolerie to Paul Hebert, August 27, 1953, 68:1333b, STFU; Hasiwar to Rummel, August 28, 1953, in "Farmers Union" folder, JFR Papers.

Meanwhile Mitchell's union was laying the groundwork for its offensive against the sugar industry. The harvest season was to begin in October. In September, 1953, after sugar planters refused collective bargaining, Hasiwar met with Archbishop Rummel. The archbishop apparently promised to try to change the minds of recalcitrant growers, who had demurred even after the state Department of Labor offered conciliation service. Several days after the scheduled meeting with Rummel, Hasiwar sent the archbishop a list of nine growers who had refused to meet with the union and included photostatic copies of their letters to Local 317. A week later the archbishop invited the nine sugar men in for an informal discussion of "certain problems" in the sugar industry. He assured the men that no representatives of organized labor would be present, "but only three or four nonpartisan priests and laymen, whose counsel in matters of this kind I regard with confidence."[18]

One layman whose counsel the archbishop considered invaluable was Charles Logan, former regional director of the National Labor Relations Board. He had also been, for many years, the consultant to whom church leaders turned whenever the archdiocese became involved in labor disputes. A few days after Rummel wrote to the nine sugar growers, Logan gave him a step-by-step outline of how to conduct the meeting. First of all, Logan said, having anyone present besides Monsignor Charles Plauché, the Chancellor, and Monsignor Lucien Caillouet, the Vicar General, could ruin the chances for success because the growers might resent outside participants. The archbishop should not begin by asking for a labor contract, Logan felt; instead, he should simply pledge to work toward settling a specific problem, such as housing or worker efficiency. In confidence Logan told the archbishop that Godchaux Sugars liked the idea of this informal approach. If the participants requested an impartial referee, Logan volunteered to serve, without pay, upon the archbishop's request. To make certain that Rummel understood the subtleties of choosing an impartial referee, Logan wrote him a second letter the day after his first. The archbishop, he explained, should allow the growers to choose the impartial referee; only if they could not find one, he said, should the archbishop recommend him. The

18 Rummel to Hasiwar, September 1, 1953, Hasiwar to Rummel, September 8, 1953, Rummel to Charles Farwell, Clarence Savoie, W. C. Kemper, Roland L. Toups, Sabin Savoie, Walter Godchaux, Jr., Moise Hymel, and F. A. Robichaux, September 17, 1953, all in "Farmers Union" folder, JFR Papers.

idea was to avoid the appearance of implementing a preconceived plan.[19]

Archbishop Rummel found sugar growers reluctant to discuss the sugar industry, even with him. One planter, who said he was unaware of any unusual or novel problems confronting the industry, refused to meet for fear of stirring up new issues. A Terrebonne Parish refinery manager would not discuss any controls on the cane industry and called Father Drolet's comments to the press about labor a "provocation for violence." Southdown Sugars sent its attorney to confer with the archbishop several days before the scheduled meeting, and one planter gave no reason at all for declining the invitation. Another planter, who was afraid that the archbishop would force him to accept unionization that would bankrupt him, went to his parish priest and inquired whether a large church donation would free him of labor problems. Archbishop Rummel informed the priest, who had relayed his parishioner's concern, that he would not use coercion and that rumors of unusual church-labor collusion were untrue. The growers who did attend the conference remained unconvinced that they should negotiate with the NAWU.[20]

While Catholic church leaders were trying to reason with sugar growers, the NAWU went into the Bayou Teche area of Louisiana in the western portion of the cane country. Hank Hasiwar, Henry Pelet, Joe Guidry, and Irving Upton, a black organizer from Houma, scheduled a meeting at the Odd Fellows Hall in Franklin on September 25, 1953, but were disappointed by the attendance. When they made a hasty departure after menacing looks from some well-dressed men, their car was followed for some distance. Nevertheless, despite intimidation of would-be union members by growers in Franklin, Joe Guidry reported several days later that St. Mary Parish was "fully or partly" organized. Planters accused Guidry of making exaggerated statements to entice workers into joining the union.[21]

19 Mitchell, interview, June 23, 1970; Charles Logan to Rummel, September 17, 18, 1953, both in "Farmers Union" folder, JFR Papers.

20 Charles Farwell to Rummel, September 23, 1953, Roland Toups to Rummel, September 22, 1953, Joseph M. Jones to Rummel, September 23, 1953, Robichaux to Rummel, telegram, September 23, 1953, George Meiluta to Rummel, September 23, 1953, all in "Farmers Union" folder, JFR Papers; Joseph Vath, interview, April 4, 1972, with Monsignor Charles Plauché and Reverend Vincent O'Connell, hereinafter cited as VPO interview.

21 Lafourche Comet (Thibodaux), October 1, 1953; Henry Pelet, interview, February 29, 1972; New Orleans Times-Picayune, September 26, 1953.

Because the NAWU seemed determined to organize plantation workers, Cane League officials intensified their quest for foreign labor. Since the end of World War II, sugar industry leaders had complained about problems associated with using foreign laborers from Cuba and the British West Indies. The Immigration and Naturalization Service refused to permit the use of foreign workers as strikebreakers and, therefore would authorize their importation only if the Department of Labor stated that local workers could not be found. In 1951 Senator Ellender learned from Cane League contacts that Department of Labor officials had removed Mexican nationals from California's Imperial Valley while H. L. Mitchell's union conducted strike activity there. Louisiana sugar growers also noted the efforts of the Florida Fruit and Vegetable Growers Association to obtain labor from the British West Indies despite complaints from local laborers.[22]

Mitchell, whenever he could, used the importation restrictions to thwart the Cane League. He informed the Bureau of Employment Security that five hundred workers from his union's Mid-South division would be available for the January, 1953, harvest season in Florida and told Hasiwar that the offer to supply workers had the bureau on the run. But he admitted, "They may have us on one if they agree to accept 500 men for the Florida job." The NAWU did not have that many laborers. A few days later, though, he instructed the director of the Mid-South office to prepare a list of workers in case the bureau asked for particulars. Mitchell later declared that a bureau recruiter sent to the Memphis area had actually discouraged hiring American citizens in favor of British West Indians.[23]

After growers had asked the Louisiana Employment Service to permit several hundred Jamaicans to enter Louisiana for the sugarcane harvest, Mitchell instructed a colleague in Memphis to write to Frank Lapeyrolerie, secretary-treasurer of Local 317, to tell him that he had five hundred laborers available who were willing to do cane-field work at the rates paid members of Local 317. Mitchell did not think the NAWU

22 "W. A. Rolston" to C. J. Bourg, April 24, 1947, in "Justice Department, General, 1947" folder, Box 371, Maurice Tobin to Ellender, July 16, 1951, Howard Bond to Frank Wurzlow, telegram, November 5, 1951, Wurzlow to Bond, telegram, November 5, 1951, all in "Labor, General, 1951" folder, Box 637, all in Allen J. Ellender Papers, Division of Archives, Nicholls State University, Thibodaux, Louisiana, hereinafter cited as AEP.

23 Mitchell to Robert Goodwin, January 2, 1953, Mitchell to Hasiwar, January 5, 1953, Mitchell to Churchill, January 7, 1953, all in 68:1321, STFU.

would have to supply the five hundred men, but he felt the step would keep the foreign workers out. Galarza, who had agreed to come to Louisiana about September 1, 1953, had seen Mexican laborers used as strikebreakers in California, and was not surprised by this recent threat to the NAWU.[24]

Large sugar growers had begun recruiting workers of Mexican descent in Texas specifically to break up the sugar local in the fall, Hasiwar told Mitchell in late August, 1953. They may even have offered these workers wages higher than the current rate, Hasiwar said, adding that he was afraid that this tactic could force Local 317 to strike before the union was ready. Meanwhile, Local 317 conducted a strike vote and assessed its members two dollars for a strike fund, and Mitchell told a union colleague, "there is sure to be a strike in the cane fields." Because chances for success looked good, Hasiwar told Galarza that he and Mitchell should come to Louisiana to help out. Avoiding a premature strike, Mitchell felt, was Hasiwar's responsibility. Nevertheless, he asked labor leaders in Cuba to apply pressure in behalf of the NAWU by threatening to withhold Cuban raw sugar from Louisiana refineries if the NAWU went on strike.[25]

Joe Guidry, NAWU leader in the Lafayette area, scheduled a meeting for September 27 at Bertrandville in Assumption Parish where the union would promulgate the results of the secret strike balloting conducted after September 7 "under the auspices of the clergymen." If a majority of Local 317 members votes to walk out, Guidry said, the union would choose a strike committee to set a date for the work stoppage. On September 27 Local 317 announced a vote of 1,808 to 8 in favor of a strike, the date of which, Hasiwar said, would be set if the big growers did not negotiate with the union. For the first time in Louisiana history workers had threatened to strike a major crop, reported one local journalist, evidently unaware of the militant strikes in sugarcane fields in the 1880s. American Sugar Cane League officials, for the time being, had no comments on the union proposals.[26]

Not surprisingly, the NAWU and the Cane League had different versions of what was happening in Louisiana. H. L. Mitchell asked the

24 Mitchell to Churchill, July 27, 1953, 68:1330a, Galarza to Mitchell, August 24, 1953, 68:1333a, both in STFU.

25 Mitchell to Galarza, August 20, 26, 1953, Mitchell to Churchill, August 21, 1953, both in 68:1333a, Mitchell to Eusebio Mujal, August 31, 1953, in 68:1333b, all in STFU.

26 Baton Rouge *Morning Advocate,* September 25, 28, 1953.

Secretary of Labor to curtail the importation of foreign labor in the cane fields and submitted an affidavit from Hasiwar attesting to the dispute between the NAWU and the sugar growers. Officials in the Labor Department forwarded the NAWU affidavit to the Attorney General along with a statement in which Governor Robert Kennon said he knew of no dispute between the NAWU and the sugar planters. Senator Ellender became involved in the dispute, no doubt at the behest of the Cane League. He conferred with Labor Department officials about requests for 167 British West Indian laborers for Godchaux plants in Raceland and Reserve and the South Coast plant in Houma. The Labor Department sent him a copy of its letter to the Attorney General which referred to the conflicting views of the union and Governor Kennon concerning the situation in Louisiana. When the Department of Labor authorized the use of Jamaicans for cane field work, Paul Chaisson, president of Local 317, said this ruling had "opened the flood gates to foreign labor in an attempt to submarine our union." Citing the 1,808-to-8 vote in favor of a strike as evidence of a dispute, Chaisson said the union had no choice but to strike and hinted that bringing in foreign laborers could lead to trouble, possibly violence.[27]

The NAWU had conducted a hasty strike vote partly because of the controversy over the use of foreign labor in sugarcane fields at the time growers were refusing to negotiate with the union. To counter the growers' approach, which was to ignore the union and ask for clearance from the Bureau of Employment Security to import labor from the British West Indies, the NAWU needed to convince the bureau that there was a labor dispute. If there were a bona fide dispute, the bureau could halt the importation of foreign laborers. The union also attempted to refute the growers' argument that the domestic labor market was incapable of handling the seasonal demand for workers.

In late September the NAWU sent fifteen other sugar plantations letters similar to those sent earlier to the nine big concerns. The letters requested collective bargaining sessions on wages and working conditions, and asked growers to reply before October 9, 1953. In early October a follow-up letter to both groups of sugar growers asked them to reconsider their original positions. The strike vote mentioned in the press, Hasiwar asserted, was not a threat. The NAWU had a genuine desire to

27 Mitchell to Martin P. Durkin, September 10, 1953, 69:1334a, Acting Secretary of Labor to Herbert Brownell, Jr., October 6, 1953, 69:1335, both in STFU; Rocco Siciliano to Ellender, October 14, 1953, in "Labor, General, 1953" folder, Box 62, AEP; Baton Rouge Morning Advocate, October 9, 1953.

prevent a work stoppage and intended, if recognized, to work for harmony in the sugar industry.[28]

Once again, though, the sugar interests refused to meet with the
NAWU. One grower mentioned what the NAWU had already painfully
observed: "We disagree with your statement that agricultural workers
are guaranteed the right to form a union. Indeed the policy of the Federal Government as well as the State of Louisiana has been to exclude
agricultural workers from any legislation granting the right of workers
generally to organize and to act in concert." Responsibility for any work
stoppage, which could bring economic ruin to the area, according to an
advertisement, "will be entirely upon your union and its leaders."[29]

In late September, Charles Logan conferred with Archbishop Rummel again and explained to him that Joe Guidry's news release which
referred to conducting a strike vote "under the auspices of clergymen"
had caused some resentment among parishioners. No strike date had
been set, Logan said, but the union was considering October 12–15.
Hasiwar was committed to the strike program, and, according to Logan,
"unless some unforeseen situation or influence is brought to bear, the
strike is certain."[30]

This news prompted the archbishop to schedule another meeting with
a large number of sugar growers for October 3, 1953. He had cancelled
his meeting with cane farmers scheduled for the previous week after
learning that sugar growers were to meet the same day in Thibodaux.
Once again the growers begged off. A Southdown representative said
he would not meet with the prelate because doing so violated the public
policy of the state. Several growers sent telegrams saying they could
not attend.[31]

When growers mentioned violating public policy of the state of Louisiana and of the United States, they meant simply that agricultural
workers had been excluded by definition from the provisions of most
labor laws. By negotiating with the NAWU or agreeing to State Depart-

28 Lapeyrolerie to various growers, September 29, 1953, 69:1334, October 2,
1953, 69:1335, both in STFU.

29 McCollam to Hasiwar, October 8, 1953, Munson to Hasiwar, October 10,
1953, both in 69:1335, STFU.

30 Logan to Rummel, September 28, 1953, in "Farmers Union" folder, JFR
Papers.

31 Logan to Rummel, September 28, 1953, W. C. Kemper to Rummel, September 29, 1953, T. M. Barker, Arthur Lemann, Jr., Roland Toups, Charles Farwell, F. A. Robichaux, and Richard McCarthy, telegrams to Rummel, September
30–October 3, 1953, all in "Farmers Union" folder, JFR Papers.

ment of Labor conciliation service, growers would be granting *de facto* recognition to the NAWU. Any negotiation would be an admission that farm laborers had organizing rights, when in fact, most laws specifically excluded them. Leaders of the NAWU disagreed with this position and opposed it strenuously. They contended that, despite being left out of most labor legislation, farm workers had a fundamental right to organize for their own protection—a right protected by the Constitution of the United States, and reinforced by Catholic doctrine.

Prevented from meeting the growers face to face, Archbishop Rummel wrote letters to those the NAWU had contacted, saying that he had read Hasiwar's letter in behalf of the union and had found his proposal for avoiding a strike reasonable. "It is my conscientious opinion," the prelate wrote, "that the proposal should be seriously considered and accepted." He ended: "The issue of a strike is too grave to be faced with indifference, while a conference is possible."[32]

Soon, letters of explanation from growers poured into the archbishop's office. Meeting with an agricultural union would violate public policy, Southdown reiterated. If his workers struck, Charles Farwell said, his company could not feed, clothe, and house them during the winter. Furthermore, if labor problems persisted, his company might discontinue sugar operations and enter the cattle business, which required only a small labor force. Another grower thought that meeting with Hasiwar would not end the possibility of a strike at all, but would be a dangerous precedent violative of public policy. More bluntly, one sugar farmer wrote: "Please tell me what business is it of yours that you should side with the union leaders and non-Catholic people." The grower, a contributor to the Catholic church and to Catholic education, believed "bad preaching" in church had contributed to labor problems in the sugar industry.[33]

Not all of the growers were recalcitrant, however. The Levet brothers, part owners and managers of San Francisco Planting and Manufacturing Company in St. John Parish near Reserve, were more liberal than most growers. The brothers and a neighbor went to the union office in Reserve and offered to sign a contract with Local 317 if other

32 Rummel to twenty-nine growers, October 7, 1953, in "Farmers Union" folder, JFR Papers.
33 Kemper to Rummel, October 9, 1953, Charles Farwell to Rummel, October 8, 1953, Munson to Rummel, October 10, 1953, C. J. Arcement to Rummel, October 10, 1953, all in "Farmers Union" folder, JFR Papers.

cane producers did likewise. Following Archbishop Rummel's admonition closely, they even offered to open their account ledgers to union officers to demonstrate their sincere desire to establish an equitable rate of pay for plantation workers. The Levets were the only growers to make such gestures, however, and Local 317 signed no contracts with them or with any other growers.[34]

Perhaps sugar growers who had met with Archbishop Rummel on labor matters knew of his toughness and so preferred not to confront him directly. When irate Catholics visited him to protest about union activity, the archbishop would greet them cordially at the door of his study, lead them to comfortable chairs, and introduce Father O'Connell, whom he seated at his side. He would attempt to keep the discussion within the broad perspective of the church's economic and social doctrines, but would allow Father O'Connell to field technical and detailed questions concerning labor problems. At the conclusion of the discussion the archbishop would always accompany his callers to the door and thank them for coming, no matter how fiery the exchanges had become. Then, privately, he would suggest to Father O'Connell alternative proposals or how certain points might have been made more diplomatically.[35]

Sugar growers from Bayou Lafourche visited Archbishop Rummel to ask for the removal of Father Jerome Drolet, Pastor of Saint Charles parish. Drolet's statements on the rights of labor and his testimony before Tennessee Senator Estes Kefauver's crime-investigation committee had stirred controversy. As executive secretary of the Lafourche Social Action Committee, an antivice citizens' group, he had shocked local sensibilities with a campaign against an infamous Thibodaux brothel known as "Jeanette's." When planters came to confer with Archbishop Rummel, he seated Father Drolet at his side thereby forcing the complainers to make their charges in the presence of the outspoken priest. The archbishop frequently interrupted loud criticisms of Father Drolet to ask if the charges about prostitution were not true. Even though influential parishioners complained, the archbishop did not remove Drolet.[36]

34 Mitchell, interview, June 23, 1970.

35 O'Connell, vpo interview.

36 Jim Russell, *Labor's Daily*, June 12, 1953, Jerome Drolet Scrapbook, lent to author; Vath, vpo interview.

In September, 1953, the Thibodaux *Lafourche Comet* published what became known as Drolet's "two-arm bandit" comment on page one:

> Fortunately Louisiana is at long last free of the one-arm bandits called slot machines; it will be a happy day when our state will enact and enforce laws strong enough to repress and restrain the small but dangerous minority of business leaders who are white-collar, two-arm bandits in their inhuman treatment of their laborers.
>
> Labor unions are good and necessary. This is recognized by God's word. This is recognized by the public policy of the United States government. This is recognized by the public policy of Louisiana. The minority of business men today who refuse to recognize this right of their workers are guilty of a criminal immoral act. They are responsible for strikes. It is the duty of governments, State and Federal, to restrain such employers effectively for the sake of the public good.
>
> It is the duty of government to remove the causes which force labor to strike in an attempt at self-preservation against unjust aggression by antiunion management. It is shameful abuse to force police to take management's side in such strikes, and such unnatural collaboration to smash unions and break just strikes itself constitutes the worst kind of violence, which causes and is responsible for other kinds of violence, which flow from the original violence—the refusal to recognize God's law and accord genuine union recognition.[37]

The controversial Drolet boldly accused the Federal Bureau of Investigation of helping gamblers and antilabor forces in Louisiana. He charged the FBI with arresting Warren "Puggy" Moity, who had been beaten up after testifying before the Kefauver committee, on evidence submitted by gamblers and prostitutes. The arrest was a means of intimidating Moity. "Recent developments show that even our wonderful FBI may have been reached by our State Dixiecrats to do the dirty work against those who dare to follow the Kefauver recommendations," he wrote, and he asserted that the FBI had done little to check prostitution in Thibodaux, New Iberia, and Lafayette where white slavers "are very strongly entrenched throughout So. La."[38]

Labor consultant Charles Logan had contact with all three of the parties in the unfolding confrontation among the National Agricultural Workers Union, the Catholic Church, and the Agricultural establishment. A labor mediator in the New Orleans area, Logan had often dis-

---

37 *Lafourche Comet* (Thibodaux), September 10, 1953.
38 Drolet to Francis Case, October 15, 1951, in "Federal Bureau of Investigation" folder, Box 459, AEP.

cussed labor matters with Archbishop Rummel and, on one occasion, had reviewed collective bargaining possibilities with the Archbishop and eight or ten growers, including representatives from the prominent Barker, Savoie, and Godchaux sugar interests. Logan had a low opinion of Hank Hasiwar. He considered him a phony, using his Catholicism to get help from the chancery office and stirring false hopes among poor agricultural workers, whom he could not really help. Logan thought Father Drolet naive and incompetent, noting that when he had told Drolet about the payoff a labor leader had offered him, Drolet had not grasped the significance of the attempted bribe.[39]

Catholic sugar growers apparently resolved their church-union dilemma by choosing economic self-interest over the spiritual. Generally, Catholic priests did not influence public opinion as Archbishop Rummel might have wished. The public in the cane country basically did not understand the labor movement, according to Mitchell, but the American Sugar Cane League, nevertheless, tended to influence the public with its talk of Communists and outsiders in union activity.

The union failed to capitalize on the vulnerable economic position of the Louisiana sugar industry and its dependence on government subsidies. If ever an industry offered an opportunity for the imposition of meaningful government minimum standards, Galarza believed, it was the sugar industry in which adequate compensation to workers could be tied to the system of tariffs, quotas, acreage allotments, and benefit payments. The subsidized industry had criticized government-set wage rates and acreage allotments as mere restrictive procedures, using praise for the free enterprise system to distract attention from the fact that the growers were receiving government-set benefit payments. The sugar lobby had made the status quo seem the only way to maintain a valuable industry. The union, spokesman for ignorant, impoverished workers, mostly members of a racial minority, simply could not compete effectively against the League's paid lobbyists and spokesmen.

Without support from Catholic church leaders, Mitchell's union probably never would have come to Louisiana. With active church encouragement and aid, the NAWU was able to make Louisiana the center of its operations from 1951 to 1958. At every step of the Louisiana movement, church leaders provided not only institutional backing but also financial aid, advice, leadership, and contacts with workers. Some parish priests followed Archbishop Rummel's labor policies despite personal

39 Logan, interview, September 26, 1974.

misgivings. Two older clergymen in the cane country, Monsignor Dominic Perino and Monsignor Jean Eyraud, experienced difficulty not only in reconciling their views with those of the prelate, but also with those of young assistant pastors assigned to their parishes. Father Roy Patterson probably left his position at Holy Savior in Lockport because of differences with Monsignor Perino.

Archbishop Rummel's closest advisers considered him a great leader. With Joseph Vath and Charles Plauché in the Chancery office, Vincent O'Connell and later Louis Twomey of the Social Action Committee, and the layman Charles Logan advising him on matters of social justice, the late archbishop became a liberal reformer of the first magnitude. Josephite pastors, including Harry J. Maloney in Bertrandville, Joseph Turner in Reserve, and R. A. Auclair of St. Rose of Lima Mission in Cecilia, provided solid support for his policies, as did parish priests such as Jerome Drolet, Roy Patterson, Roland Boudreaux, Alexander Sigur, and others in the Lafayette area. Even though their efforts in behalf of the NAWU failed, Charles Plauché and Joseph Vath did not consider the attempt to have been in vain. Nor did they consider the work of such controversial priests as Joseph Coulombe or Drolet wasted. These pioneers provided a catalyst to a popular movement to ameliorate oppressive conditions.

Because it did not qualify for the normal collective bargaining guarantees afforded to industrial unions, the NAWU had resorted to unorthodox methods after normal trade union tactics failed. Nonetheless, it threatened to use the ultimate weapon of the trade union—the strike—when atypical bargaining methods attempted by Catholic church leaders failed to achieve results. This seemed to be a longshot gamble, especially after the NAWU had failed to get typical union machinery into motion. But Mitchell's agrarians usually faced overwhelming odds against success. If the union carried through on it threats to strike, the agricultural establishment in Louisiana would be no different from the formidable opposition the NAWU usually faced—that is, unless the Catholic church could work some miracle and persuade sugar growers to make concessions to agricultural workers.

Chapter 7

The Cane Mutiny

Sugarcane planters worried about the National Agricultural Workers Union's threat to call a strike, but they did not respond publicly at first. Gilbert Durbin, general manager of the American Sugar Cane League, spoke to the Thibodaux Rotarians about problems of the sugar industry in September, 1953, apparently without mentioning the union. Later in the month L. A. Borne of Raceland, outgoing president of the Cane League, said his organization did not plan to recognize the union, but before surrendering leadership to J. P. Duhe of New Iberia, the new president, he acknowledged that a strike seemed imminent.[1]

The American Sugar Cane League prepared for the strike by circulating mimeographed instructions among its members. The instructions consisted of twenty-three questions and answers in four sections: general status of labor, the NAWU's organizational drive, ways to combat the strike, and specific steps to take if a strike occurred. A typical question and answer illustrate the League approach: "Am I actually 'unfair' or 'anti-labor' if I refuse to deal with such a Union? No. Both the Wagner Act and the State Mediation Law expressly exclude agricultural laborers from coverage." In responding to union overtures, the guide advised, "Either ignore the demand or reply that you do not recognize the Union." It said that workers "can be discharged at any time for any reason or without reason." If a strike came, "Call your lawyer. Also immediately call upon your Sheriff, inform him of the situation, and request your sheriff to assign a deputy to your farm to afford protection to your laborers." The guide said, also, that violence was entirely possible: "Yes . . . 'goons' are imported by a Union from other areas to do

---

1 *Lafourche Comet* (Thibodaux), September 10, 1953; Baton Rouge *Morning Advocate,* September 25, 1953.

violence to nonstriking employees and to sabotage equipment." The
Cane League recommended that growers destroy all correspondence
from the NAWU and distributed leaflets encouraging field laborers to
return to work and listing ways in which the NAWU supposedly de-
ceived plantation workers. Another leaflet proclaimed: "Don't give up
your liberty. Be a free man. Don't join the union."[2]

During the first week of October, 1953, the Sugar Cane League prepared an extensive news release on the pending strike in the sugarcane
fields where harvesting was to begin the next week. Referring to the
"fallacious and misleading" views of the NAWU, the Cane League said
that a strike in a perishable agricultural crop would be an "unprecedented calamity." It encouraged the public to oppose a strike by plantation workers. The story repeated arguments made earlier to Archbishop Rummel and to the NAWU and added a few new wrinkles about
hurting small farmers, interfering with interstate commerce, and cutting
off necessary foodstuffs. The League complained of governmental restrictions imposed on sugarcane operations but, as usual, said nothing
about governmental benefits enjoyed by the industry.[3]

Prior to the start of the cane-field strike, Father Drolet offered to
lead the picketing when the walkout began. Fearful that Drolet's zeal
and strong statements would provoke violent antiunion responses or
make union members overly rambunctious, Hasiwar and his colleagues
persuaded Drolet to serve, instead, as a fund raiser. Mitchell and the
chief NAWU benefactor, the National Sharecroppers' Fund, carefully
planned his itinerary, listing various union leaders he should see and
suggesting that Drolet sign all telegrams with his "Father title." While
in Washington he should see Father George Higgins of the National
Catholic Welfare Conference, who had "the best contacts with Catholics
who have money." Later Mitchell's wife reported that Drolet had arrived in Washington after successful stops in Chicago, Detroit, and
Pittsburgh, and that he was to go to New York next. "Wouldn't it be
wonderful if we could really win a victory," she mused optimistically,
"in the South of all places?" From the Meat Cutters, Packinghouse
Workers, United Auto Workers, and the Machinists, Drolet received
pledges for contributions of $1,000 to $5,000, but George Meany, the

2 American Sugar Cane League, mimeographed "Questions and Answers,"
"Attention All Sugar Cane Workers," and "Stop, Look, Read," October 5, 1953,
in possession of E. J. Clement; E. J. Clement, interview, February 23, 1972;
Warren Harang, interview, May 9, 1972.
3 New Orleans Times-Picayune, October 5, 1953.

new head of the AFL, did not make a contribution in the name of his organization.[4]

The strike started on Monday, October 12, 1953, when laborers did not show up for work on the plantations of the four biggest sugar corporations. Sugar Workers Union Local 317 of the NAWU struck Godchaux Sugars with holdings in Reserve, Raceland, and Napoleonville; Southdown Sugars, with operations in Houma, Thibodaux, and Vacherie; South Coast with properties in Houma and Mathews; and Milliken-Farwell with operators in Napoleonville, Donaldsonville, and West Baton Rouge Parish. Officials of the big companies said the strike did not affect factory operations, but they acknowledged that most harvesting work forces were skeletal. George Stith and Hasiwar termed the walkout by twelve hundred men almost complete.[5]

By the second or third day both labor and management had made so many charges, denials, and counter charges that the strike became a major propaganda war. Conflicting versions circulated concerning the extent of the strike, the propriety and frequency of evicting strikers from plantation homes, the likelihood of violence, the effect of the strike on small sugar farmers, the use of nonunion labor, and the picketing of mills and refineries.

As the strike continued the NAWU expressed a willingness to negotiate with growers. "It is not our intention to paralyze the harvest," Hasiwar said. The day the strike started, Local 317 sent letters to growers seeking collective bargaining agreements. Meanwhile, in Washington, Mitchell solicited support from union members in Puerto Rico, who he hoped would help end the strike in Louisiana by curtailing the shipment of raw sugar to Louisiana. Not surprisingly Catholic priests in the Archdiocese of New Orleans assisted the sugar workers union. "You have begun a movement of tremendous importance not only to Louisiana," Father Twomey told union members, "but to fellow men in the Texas and Florida cane fields." Father Drolet, having completed his fund-raising tour for the sugar workers, lent his automobile to union

4 H. L. Mitchell, interview, June 23, 1970; Fay Bennett to Mitchell, October 7, 1953, 69:1335, Dorothy Dowe to Arthur Churchill, October 16, 1953, 69:1337a, both in the Southern Tenant Farmers Union Papers, housed in Southern Collection (and photoduplicated by the Microfilm Corporation of America in 60 rolls), University of North Carolina, Chapel Hill, hereinafter cited as STFU, with box and folder or roll number.

5 Baton Rouge *Morning Advocate*, October 13, 1953.

organizers during the strike and aided strikers with personal problems.[6]

During the strike, the NAWU called members out to several central locations in the cane country early each morning and kept them variously occupied all day to prevent planters from coaxing or intimidating them into returning to work. A Cane League news release referred to the all-day meetings as "indoctrination" and "brain-washing." The daylong demands taxed the organizers' stamina. Galarza was managing the union office during the strike, and Hasiwar was supervising matters in the field. "Both are almost at the breaking point and more help would be a Godsend to them," Mitchell told Arthur Churchill of the NAWU's Memphis office. He asked Churchill to go to Louisiana with his movie projector and as many films as he could locate to help at the long sessions that started at five o'clock in the morning and were "a combination of union meeting, preaching, singing, etc." Henry Pelet got little sleep during the strike, and in Washington, daily press releases and appeals for money occupied Mitchell's days, and telephone calls at night made matters hectic as well. "He has not had a chance to take his usual after lunch siesta," his wife wrote later.[7]

Mitchell's telegram to the secretary of labor announcing the start of the sugar strike emphasized two areas of NAWU concern: the right of agricultural workers to organize and bargain collectively and fear that cane growers would bring in foreign strikebreakers. To the attorney general, Mitchell complained of pressure against union members, especially in Assumption Parish. Generally, NAWU publicity and propaganda suggested that the union had attempted to prevent a strike, the growers were undemocratic, the major objective of the strike was recognition, the strike was successful and spreading, outside help was pouring in, the union wanted to assist small farmers and raw sugar mills in harvesting their crops, growers were encouraging scabs and pressure tactics, and local merchants who suffered financial loss were circulating a petition demanding that the big corporations meet with the union to settle the strike.[8]

6 Henry Hasiwar, mimeographed news release, October 12, 1953, Frank Lapeyrolerie to various growers, October 12, 1953, Mitchell to E. G. Moreno, October 12, 1953, all in 69:1336, STFU; Williard S. Townsend, "Priest Fights for Workers," unidentified clipping, n.d., in Jerome Drolet Scrapbook, lent to author.

7 Henry Pelet, interview, February 29, 1972; New Orleans *Times-Picayune,* October 22, 1953; Mitchell to Churchill, October 28, 1953, 69:1337b, Dowe to Churchill, November 2, 1953, 69:1339 and November 18, 1953, 69:1340, all in STFU.

8 Mitchell to James P. Mitchell, telegram, October 12, 1953, Mitchell to Herbert Brownell, telegram, October 14, 1953, 69:1336, both in STFU.

Only in an academic and rather negative sense did the NAWU ever win the point that agricultural workers, like other American workers, had the right to organize and bargain collectively. "The central issue in this dispute is not wages," Hasiwar stated on the strike's first day. "The issue is the right, guaranteed under our constitution, of agricultural workers to have an organization that will represent their interests." After Mitchell had telegraphed the secretary of labor, he asked the secretary to specify that agricultural workers had the right to organize as do other workers and to ask the United States Employment Service not to refer foreign strikebreakers to jobs on sugar plantations. Mitchell also asked AFL President Meany to help the NAWU counter the idea that certain state and federal laws exempting agricultural workers also forbade them to join a union or to engage in strikes.[9]

The United States Employment Service agreed to send no foreigners to replace strikers, and Meany acceded to Mitchell's request for help. The Director of the Federal Mediation and Conciliation Service suggested, perhaps facetiously, that the NAWU turn to the National Labor Relations Board to settle its dispute with cane growers. Mitchell replied sharply: "We would gladly follow your suggestion of taking the matter of representation up with the National Labor Relations Board, however, you no doubt know that the NLRB is not permitted to handle matters involving agricultural workers." He asked the Mediation and Conciliation Service to look into the matter as the Assistant Secretary of Labor had suggested. Cane growers, meanwhile, did not budge from their position regarding the NAWU. "Recognizing the union," one said, "would be like putting our heads on the chopping block." Discussing the pros and cons of sugar wages and work conditions was as close as Cane League officials would come to negotiating with the NAWU. The union felt that their refusal to recognize the rights of agricultural workers to organize peacefully was subversion of the Constitution, and Department of Agriculture officials finally agreed with that assessment, declaring that no federal statute could prevent their organizing "for the purpose of dealing with their employers."[10]

9 Hasiwar, mimeographed news release, October 12, 1953, Mitchell to James P. Mitchell, telegram, October 12, 1953, Mitchell to George Meany, October 13, 1953, 69:1336, all in STFU.

10 Rocco Siciliano to Mitchell, October 14, 1953, Meany to Mitchell, October 15, 1953, both in 69:1336, Whitley McCoy to Mitchell, October 19, 1953, Mitchell to McCoy, October 20, 1953, both in 69:1337a, Local 317, news release, October 22, 1953, 69:1337b, Lawrence Myers to Frank Graham, November 2, 1953, 69:1338, all in STFU; New Orleans *Times Picayune,* October 20, 1953.

Even though Senator Ellender officially assumed a hands-off posture during the strike, his office quietly aided cane growers. To individual growers who complained about the strike he expressed disappointment that the dispute had delayed the harvest, but he did not offer any suggestions for solving the problem. Frank Wurzlow, Jr., and George Arceneaux, Jr., of the senator's staff helped the South Coast Corporation receive certification from the United States Employment Service for importing British West Indian laborers. "They used their positions in your office to secure information and to urge approval of the application," a company spokesman wrote Senator Ellender in a thank-you letter at the end of the strike. The South Coast executive sent copies of his letter to other prominent Cane League members to remind the senator that the sugar industry had not overlooked his behind-the-scenes help. During the strike Ellender communicated with Walter Godchaux, Jr. about proposed modifications of the Taft-Hartley Act.[11]

Senator Ellender also heard from those unhappy with developments in the sugar industry. The Reverend R. A. Auclair complained to Ellender about wages for plantation workers, set in 1951 by the Department of Agriculture at $3.10 for a nine-hour workday. "Such a wage is not decent and you know it, Senator," Auclair wrote. "Such a damnably low wage is a crime that cries to heaven for vengeance. Please do something to give the sugar cane workers a fair deal." Margaret Smith, an outspoken critic of the agricultural establishment, wrote to Ellender several years later about a sugar program that enriched big producers at the expense of laborers and the DPs, who had fled depressed conditions on sugar plantations. A farmers' market, she thought, would help plantation workers become self-sufficient.[12]

Senator Ellender's attitude toward small cane growers and laborers had changed substantially through the years. His response to critics of the sugar industry in the postwar era lacked the concern for small growers and tenants he had expressed earlier as a lieutenant of Huey Long,

11 Frank Wurzlow, Jr., to Henry Landeche, October 20, 1953, Allen J. Ellender to Landeche, October 30, 1953, both in "Agriculture, General, 1953" folder, Box 83, Howard Bond to Ellender, November 9, 1953, in "Agriculture Dept." folder, Box 46, Ellender to Walter Godchaux, Jr., October 26, 1953, in "Legislation" folder, Box 46, all in Allen J. Ellender Papers, Division of Archives, Nicholls State University, Thibodaux, Louisiana, hereinafter cited as AEP.

12 R. A. Auclair to Ellender, January 12, 1951, in "Agriculture, Sugar, 1951" folder, Box 109, Margaret Smith to Ellender, January 18, 1954, in "Agriculture, Sugar, 1955" folder, Box 478, all in AEP.

champion of the little man in Louisiana. He seemed no longer to weigh the effects of various programs on big and little growers, respectively, as in the past. Instead he echoed spokesmen for the American Sugar Cane League, which represented big planter interests. He cited the financial problems of growers and fluctuating sugar prices and said that consumers paid a reasonable price for sugar and that the Department of Agriculture set wages for plantation workers after conducting public hearings. He also remarked that domestic sugar production was advantageous to the local economy during war and peace.[13]

The executive committee of the American Sugar Cane League called a special meeting at the Agricultural Building in Thibodaux for October 13, the second day of the strike. Many Cane League members not on the executive committee attended. T. M. Barker, chairman of the League's labor committee, asked the support of all members to defeat the strike. The executive committee approved proposals to form a publicity committee directed by Gilbert Durbin, to publicize the union oath, to seek the assistance of clergymen sympathetic with Cane League views, to evict from plantation houses union leaders only (and not laborers *en masse*), and to form a committee to assist growers in need of workers. Barker read an appeal from Archbishop Rummel for settlement of the strike, but the committee postponed acting on the appeal.[14]

Once the strike had begun, Roman Catholic planters reacted even more vehemently to Archbishop Rummel's pleas to consider the appeals of the NAWU. "Tend to your own knitting," one grower told the prelate. Claiming that union recognition would lead to the destruction of the sugar industry and great suffering by innocent people, he added: "I do not want that blot on my conscience." Another grower termed union methods organized gangsterism and supplied the archbishop with facts, which he said the union had ignored. "The Church as I understand, is to bring to the people the teachings of Christ and not be envolved [*sic*] in a labor dispute," an anonymous Catholic Napoleonville farmer wrote. "I also know that the morals of these negro Laborers are

13 Ellender to Smith, March 13, 1954, in "Agriculture, Sugar, 1955" folder, Box 478, Ellender to Auclair, January 26, 1951, in "Agriculture, Sugar, 1951" folder, Box 109, both in AEP.

14 American Sugar Cane League, Minutes of Executive Committee Meeting, Nicholls State University Library, Thibodaux, Louisiana, October 13, 1953, pp. 2–3.

rock bottom and again not worthy of being represented by our Church."[15]

Archbishop Rummel reproved Hasiwar for the timing of the strike because it brought considerable financial hardship to workers, who usually earned more money during grinding season that any other time of the year. The archbishop nonetheless provided the NAWU vice-president money to wage a maximum effort. Surreptitiously Hasiwar visited a priest in the archdiocese who handed over money to him. The archbishop's personal secretary recalled that a union official came by for money periodically.[16]

Archbishop Rummel also provided a more orthodox form of aid to people in the strike area. To each dean of the five deaneries in the sugar-growing regions of the Archdiocese of New Orleans, he sent a check for $2,000 for food for needy families with the directive: "Catholic families will naturally receive first consideration but charity prompts us to aid deserving non-Catholics—and there should be no color line." The Baton Rouge deanery returned the grant since no parishioners applied for aid. Monsignor Joseph Wester of the Houma deanery reported on conditions in such areas as Saint Lucy, a black parish in the city that needed assistance. He said that back pay, credit at company stores, and aid from the big unions tended to minimize the suffering. The monsignor, after conferring with Senator Ellender, concluded only that the matter was complicated and that great hardship would result if the strike continued. The Thibodaux deanery reported the cutting of credit at plantation stores and some evictions from plantation houses. Monsignor Jean Eyraud in Reserve gave $500 to nearby Our Lady of Grace Parish.[17]

The Catholic Committee of the South, a social action group of clergy and laymen, also supported the NAWU strike which they called a strug-

15 B. Thibaut to Joseph Francis Rummel, October 13, 1953, Warren Harang to Rummel, October 17, 1953, "Cane Farmer" to Rummel, undated, all in "Farmers Union" folder, Joseph Francis Rummel Papers, Archives of Archdiocese of New Orleans, hereinafter cited as JFR Papers.

16 Vincent O'Connell, interview, April 4, 1972, with Bishop Joseph Vath and Monsignor Charles Plauché, hereinafter cited as VPO interview.

17 Rummel, identical letters to deans Jean Eyraud in Reserve, Edwin J. Gubler in Donaldsonville, Raphael Labit in Thibodaux, H. P. Lohmann in Baton Rouge, and Joseph A. Wester in Houma, October 23, 1953, Lohmann to Rummel, October 27, 1953, Wester to Rummel, October 27, 1953, Labit to Rummel, October 27, 1953, Eyraud to Rummel, October 27, 1953, all in "Farmers Union" folder, JFR Papers.

gle over "the basic, moral right of any workers, industrial or agricultural, to organize." The social action group labeled the sugar industry noneconomic and said "without tariffs and price support subsidies, it could not meet competition of a foreign market." By refusing to bargain collectively, the Committee said, growers denied workers a basic human right.[18]

A few days after the canefield strike had begun, sugar plantations cut off the utilities of striking workers and issued eviction notices to union leaders, including Paul Chaisson, president of Local 317. On October 25 Mitchell sent a telegram to Attorney General Brownell protesting that planters were evicting strikers in an attempt to drive them back to the fields. Mitchell asked the social activist Jesuit Louis Twomey to provide him with the names of priests who knew of violations of the constitutional rights of cane-field workers. The next day the American Sugar Cane League said "ring-leaders" of the strike who did not return to work would have to vacate plantation houses. The NAWU publicized a large number of evictions, but Gilbert Durbin of the League denied that growers had resorted to mass evictions, and Sheriff A. P. Prejean said no eviction notices had been issued in Terrebonne Parish prior to October 20. Later, however, Durbin admitted that cane growers were evicting strikers *en masse*. "We have no choice in the matter," he said. "If the workers living in the houses don't want to work then we have to get someone who will, and they need a place to live." Sheriff Fernand Richard of Assumption Parish said that eviction proceedings would be heard in the Napoleonville Courthouse on October 23, 1953.[19]

C. Paul Barker and Fred Cassibry, attorneys for the NAWU and the CIO, respectively, assisted strikers in combatting the threatened evictions. Chaisson and other strikers, claiming to be "temporarily withholding their labor from the defendants to persuade them to recognize, meet and bargain collectively," sought an injunction in the 17th Judicial District Court of Louisiana forbidding evictions. However, Judge P. Davis Martinez found in favor of Godchaux Sugars and Southdown and against fifteen strikers, who claimed growers had evicted them in violations of the Sugar Act. The plaintiffs appealed to the federal district court, but at the hearing on October 28, 1953, Federal District Judge Herbert Christenberry denied the petition, ruling that: "The Court is

18 Baton Rouge *Morning Advocate*. October 17, 1953.

19 *Ibid.,* October 15, 18, 20, 21, 1953; Mitchell to Louis Twomey, October 28, 1953, in "La. Sugar Cane" folder, Louis Twomey Collection, Loyola University, New Orleans, Louisiana, hereinafter cited as LTC.

of the view that a federal question has not been sufficiently alleged to warrant this court's taking jurisdiction." He said "the complaint does not state a claim on which the court can grant relief." One cane country newspaper ran this headline: "Planters Can Evict Strikers Says Judge." Sheriffs in Lafourche and Assumption parishes believed the decision prompted a back-to-work feeling in the cane fields. Mitchell felt that the court action was worthwhile, however, because it at least delayed the evictions.[20]

In the propaganda contest between labor and management, both versions of events were, undoubtedly, slanted, for the accounts are not compatible. The NAWU pictured the strike as a tightly organized movement, picking up momentum and new adherents daily; eventually, they said, planters would be forced to recognize the influence of Local 317 among sugar workers. American Sugar Cane League releases played down the extent of the strike with reports of uninterrupted operation and a growing back-to-work sentiment among plantation laborers. During the first week of the strike, growers said that the strike had slowed cane harvesting but that grinding in the mills was continuing uninterrupted because of returning strikers, hired replacements, and assistance from farmers unaffected by the strike. Durbin said strikers were returning "in droves" and added, "Even if all the union's members went on strike they still couldn't stop us from harvesting this crop."[21]

Propaganda increased in tempo after the appearance of an article in *Time* called "Cane Mutiny." The national news weekly not only quoted growers protestations of the necessity of subsidies for their existence, but also their advertisement predicting victory over the union. *Time* said that four-fifths of the strikers were black, two-thirds were illiterate, many spoke no English, and most lived in company houses ("some of them hovels, some adequate") and traded at the company store. They had gathered at Masonic lodges and burial society halls to await recognition and an end to the strike. The article continued: "After generations of precarious existence on the big plantations, the cane workers were out on an organized strike." Indicating widespread support for the union from the Catholic Church and organized labor, the article quoted Father Twomey: "The workers are apparently willing to take

20 Mitchell, interview, June 23, 1970; Pelet, interview, February 29, 1972; *Lafourche Comet* (Thibodaux), October 29, 1953; New Orleans *Times-Picayune*, October 21, 29, 1953.

21 New Orleans *Times-Picayune,* October 13, 14, 21, 24, 1953.

whatever risks are involved to free, if not themselves, at least their children from this environment."[22]

Not surprisingly, Father Twomey heard from those who thought he should stay out of plantation labor disputes. One correspondent wondered why Twomey consented to the *Time* interview and interfered with blacks who did not need "elaborate food" or much money to be happy. "Why disturb their peaceful adaption [*sic*] to life?" he wrote. "Why encourage them to gain monies to become suckers for manufactured products which cannot increase their human values."[23]

The Cane League executive committee, which voted unanimously not to respond to the *Time* article, instead pushed its own vituperative attack on the NAWU. Entitled "The Issue," this attack first appeared in the press on October 22. Treated in the smaller papers as a paid advertisement, the strongly worded release listed the usual arguments of the Cane League but with considerably more invective. The author used such expressions as "manufactured in Moscow," "Alias Hank Hasiwar," "so-called labor union," "union dictatorship," and "convicted bank robber and ex-convict" to describe Hasiwar, Felix Dugas, and the ideology of the NAWU.[24]

Besides having to contend with Cane League publicity, which Mitchell readily admitted was effective, the union received editorial reprimands in the local press. For three consecutive weeks the *Assumption Pioneer* at Napoleonville criticized the union for, among other things, a lack of success. "The sugarcane crop here will be harvested—strike or not!" the editor said. "So far things here are not even bad enough to declare an emergency and call for volunteers to aid the farmers." On the question of union recognition, he declared: "THAT WILL NEVER BE. With the continued help of the Lord, the crop will be harvested on schedule." And, adding a parting word about the workers, he proclaimed: "They . . . have missed . . . getting some of the highest harvesting wages ever paid." The following week the editor said that "no outside or inside goons will ever make us stop working when we so desire or scare us with threats or reprisals."[25]

22 "Cane Mutiny," *Time*, November 2, 1953, p. 26.

23 J. Wiltz Emmer to Twomey, October 30, 1953, in "La. Sugar Cane" folder, LTC.

24 Cane League, Minutes of Executive Committee Meeting, November 6, 1953, p. 3; *Assumption Pioneer* (Napoleonville), November 6, 1953.

25 Mitchell, interview, June 23, 1970; *Assumption Pioneer* (Napoleonville), October 16, 23, 30, 1953.

The local press sometimes expressed generalized antiunion hostility. The *Assumption Pioneer* complained that the union leaders "hold the money bags of members" and that in matters of double-dealing "these birds are past masters." The editor closed with a reminder that peace and harmony in the cane country had been the order for so long that the current problem was a strange one. A *Lafourche Comet* editorial entitled "Which Way Do We Head?" warned Local 317 that, although, unions had been helpful in the past, sugarcane growers faced big problems and had constitutional guarantees, too. "Our Parish," he said, "can not and will not stand for cane burnings or similar malicious action." Sheriff Frank Ducos announced that despite rumors of violence against those who did not join the union, his office would protect the rights of all who wanted to work.[26]

Mitchell, who had come to appreciate the value of publicity, especially in obtaining funds to operate the NAWU, decided to battle the sugar growers in the press. "We believe that the only way the agricultural workers can win a decent life," Mitchell said, "is by putting their case before the bar of public opinion." A common Mitchell tactic was to send somewhat exaggerated telegrams to public officials complaining of certain conditions affecting union members, and then to use the telegrams as the basis for widely distributed news releases. The mimeographed articles he prepared and marked "for release" usually listed the background causes for a strike, explained the role and position of the NAWU, and quoted the forcefully worded telegram by the union as evidence of determination by outraged union leaders to correct the abuse whatever the odds. The NAWU also prepared handbills, one of which contained four pictures of dilapidated housing on a sugar plantation and a promise by the NAWU to correct such conditions. Norman Thomas, Mitchell's friend and political mentor, suggested that the NAWU use the radio networks and newspapers to publicize their plight to a larger audience.[27]

Mitchell's propaganda barrage would have succeeded better in areas where critical journalism and investigative reporting flourished. Most people in the bayou country received limited news about the strike.

26 *Assumption Pioneer* (Napoleonville), October 2, 1953; *Lafourche Comet* (Thibodaux), October 8, 1953.

27 Baton Rouge *Morning Advocate*, October 25, 1953; Mitchell to James P. Mitchell, telegram, October 12, 1953, Mitchell to Herbert Brownell, telegram, October 14, 1953, Mitchell, mimeographed NAWU news release, October 15, 1953, all in 69:1336, Mitchell, mimeographed "Why the Strike," [October, 1953], 69:1337b, Norman Thomas to Mitchell, October 16, 1953, 69:1337a, all in STFU.

Editors of small weeklies did not have the time, the staff, or the financial resources to learn the facts, and so most of them printed sketchy details of the strike after New Orleans and Baton Rouge dailies had first run the news.

Critics of the agricultural establishment knew that the American Sugar Cane League was dodging offers to discuss labor conditions and the strike and pretending that plantation workers had no real problems. Like nineteenth century slave owners, who concocted theories about slavery's benefit to society in order to justify its existence and assuage their own guilt feelings, moderns in the cane country blamed problems on outside agitators, Communists, and extremists. One grower, unaware of earlier cane-field strikes, complained to Senator Ellender: "We cane planters are faceing [*sic*] a problem we have never faced before, we are informed the labor unions plan to make us pay our plantation labor $1.00 per hour?" Margaret Smith later accused the Cane League of political intrigue and of having suppressed news of the strike. After the CIO had become active in Lafourche Parish, she wrote, "an Army of Lafourche Parish Deputy Sheriffs guarded the labor for 90 days.... Not one word got published about it. It got exciting for a while, but the lid was kept on." She blamed Ellender for allowing the sugar program to grow through the years. "You are not a sugar planter," she declared, "this situation has developed before your eyes. It is time to end this farce. Let the Federal Government get out of the Louisiana sugar business." According to another of her letters, everyone knew "about the Political Chicancery [*sic*] of the so-called Louisiana Sugar Cane League."[28]

Covert attempts by union leaders to infiltrate Cane League strategy sessions reflected frustration and naïveté on on the part of union leaders. During the strike, for example, Galarza bought one share of stock in a large sugar corporation, thinking that as a stockholder he would be privy to strategy used by the company to combat the union. Mitchell, who realized the folly of such action, refused to use union funds to reimburse the Mexican-American vice president of the NAWU for his capitalistic venture.[29]

Keeping track of the cane-field strike in the press after the end of the second week became increasingly difficult because of the large num-

28 Landeche to Ellender, October 12, 1953, in "Agriculture, Dept." folder, Box 46, Smith to Ellender, January 18, 1954, March 7, 1955, both in "Agriculture, Sugar, 1955" folder, Box 478, AEP.

29 Dowe to Churchill, November 18, 1953, 69:1340, STFU.

ber of contradictory reports. Cane League releases during the last week
of October contained much that must have been discouraging to labor
leaders. Durbin reported that returning strikers, laborers from outside
the strike area, and strikebreakers were maintaining the harvest and
keeping the mills running at almost capacity. At the end of the month
the union claimed that 2,000 men were still on strike; the Cane League
said only 1,000 remained away from work. After saying that the entire
labor force in the sugar industry totaled 45,000, Durbin said that, even
if all 3,000 union members went out on strike, the harvesting would
not stop because the entire labor force totaled 45,000 workers. Union
figures showed an increase in the number of strikers from 1,200 the
first day to 1,600 by the middle of the first week; the figure was 2,000
after 400 workers from the Labadieville area joined on October 20,
1953. NAWU President Mitchell flew to Louisiana from Washington for
a two-day tour of the strike area at about this time and reported that
ninety percent of the regular employees at the big-four plantations remained on strike. Only a few strikebreakers from Mississippi and Alabama remained in the fields, and they were cutting little cane. Hasiwar
claimed that newly arrived laborers refused to work after they learned
of the strike.[30]

The NAWU attempted to deny the damning charges of the Cane
League's "The Issue" with its own "A Reply from the Cane Field
Workers." The union countered the League's charges point by point. It
traced the futile attempts to negotiate with the cane growers, who had
assumed that agricultural workers had been denied the right to organize
and bargain collectively. Hasiwar's indictment for alleged antitrust violations with the strawberry local, the union claimed, did not indicate
guilt. It also noted that calling NAWU member Felix Dugas a convicted
bank robber and a hardened criminal created an incorrect impression.
Dugas had been convicted as "an immature youth" for implication in
a robbery, but his parents had restored all the money. A family outcast,
Dugas had served two years in prison for a bank robbery in 1947 after
his military service. He had later had problems finding and holding a
job, and in July, 1953, at a union meeting in Labadieville, had asked
for membership. Local 317 officials were suspicious of him because he
was Clarence Savoie's nephew, and they hesitated until Father Maloney
suggested he be allowed to join. Finally, the NAWU denied that it had

30 New Orleans *Times-Picayune,* October 21, 22, 28, 30, 1953.

"brainwashed" union members; its all-day union meetings had kept members from becoming involved in violence.[31]

To charges that the strike had hurt small farmers, the NAWU replied that it was directing the strike primarily against the four largest sugar producers in the state. "The Union is encouraging workers who are employed in the grinding mills to remain on the job, so that small farmers' crops may be saved." The union claimed that the big-four had enlarged the scope of the strike when they borrowed union workers from plantations not affected by the strike. This was not true. Mitchell's wife wrote to a NAWU colleague at that time, "In case you give out any of this information—do not indicate the part about all these plantations. For publicity purpose, we are sticking to the fact that workers are striking on the 4 big plantations." Meanwhile, Hasiwar in Louisiana had promised that Local 317 would assist any small farmer adversely affected by the strike. The strike did hurt small farmers, according to Sheriff Richard of Assumption Parish, and Durbin supplied the names of several in the Napoleonville area. Still, Hasiwar insisted that the NAWU was calling out only members working for small farmers who had gone to the aid of the big-four.[32]

Associating one's opponent with communism was a potent attack during the McCarthy Era of the 1950s, and the League used that tactic during the strike, charging that Local 317 was receiving aid from a Communist-front organization. The National Sharecroppers' Fund, long a supporter of the union, had been cited as a Communist front by the California state senate's fact-finding committee on un-American activities, Durbin said. Although Mitchell made an effective reply to most of Durbin's charges, he could do little about their initial impact. "Some unmitigated liar may have made the statement to the California legislative committee that this charitable fund was operated by the Communists," Mitchell said. "But Mr. Durbin has no right to repeat . . . these statements." Pointing out that the chairman of the fund, Frank Graham, was a former United States senator from North Carolina, Mitchell added that Durbin "shall be called to account in a court of

---

31 *Ibid.*, October 29, 1953; unidentified clipping, Drolet Scrapbook.

32 NAWU mimeographed news release, October 15, 1953, 69:1336, Dowe to Churchill, October 16, 1953, 69:1337a, both in STFU; Baton Rouge *Morning Advocate*, October 20, 21, 1953.

law as soon as it is physically possible for attorneys to prepare and file the necessary papers."[33]

Graham, who demanded an apology from the Cane League, disavowed any association with Communists and said the attorney general's office had never listed the National Sharecroppers' Fund as a subversive group. At first refusing to comment on the issue, Durbin later replied to Graham's telegram but, because of the California committee's findings, he did not apologize. Later, repeating his charges against the fund, Durbin speculated: "Frankly we do not know the real objective behind the strike." A strike wrecking the sugar economy would "undoubtedly cause much delight behind the iron curtain."[34]

Although there was little violence during the strike, several physical clashes made it more than a contest of words and ideas. Mitchell exaggerated somewhat in his telegram to the attorney general two days after the strike began, when he said that armed strikebreakers, deputized plantation foremen, and sheriff's deputies in Assumption Parish had invaded workers' homes and used force and violence to drive laborers to the fields. Mitchell had asked the Justice Department to inquire whether the state police had assisted local authorities in serving eviction notices, but State Police Superintendent Francis Grevemberg reported that his men were merely enforcing the law and patrolling "in case of violence." Sugar grower Charles Farwell labeled the union charges "false and libelous." One Labadieville laborer, who had been fired and evicted for union activity, found a job on a small farm owned by Angelo Russo. The NAWU helped him to move his belongings to his new home, and, according to their account, Clarence Savoie and a deputy sheriff followed their truck. Several days later Russo fired the man at the insistence of John Thibaut, son of the Glenwood Mill manager, who said he would not grind Russo's cane otherwise.[35]

Savoie, surprised at the extent of union influence early in the strike, admitted restricting credit of strikers at the plantation store, but he denied cutting off water, gas, and electricity. "They don't want to strike," Savoie said, "but they are scared of what might happen to them.

33 New Orleans *Times-Picayune,* October 24, 1953; Mitchell, news release, October 25, 1953, 69:1337b, STFU.

34 New Orleans *Times-Picayune,* October 26, 27, 28, 1953.

35 Mitchell to Brownell, October 14, 1953, 69:1336, STFU; Oliver Pilat, New York *Post,* November 10, 1953.

I'm against all unions." Referring to Felix Dugas of the NAWU, his nephew by marriage, he said: "A boy caused all this trouble. Felix Dugas is the cause of it all, born on the plantation, played ball with the others. He led the poor people wrong. I couldn't recognize him. If his union should win, I'd go out of business."[36]

The only shooting incident during the strike occurred in Houma on October 22 when men lying in ambush fired two shotgun blasts at a truck transporting workers to the Southdown refinery. A. P. Prejean, sheriff of Terrebonne Parish, reported that three of the workers, Mechanicville residents, had suffered minor flesh wounds. Southdown offered a $500 reward for information leading to the arrest and conviction of those responsible, and Prejean added: "Up to this time we have had no trouble. But if that's the way they want it, that's the way they'll get it." Governor Robert Kennon promised protection of life and property to all, regardless of which side of the controversy they were on. Later Prejean arrested four black strikers and charged them with attempted murder. One of them was actually charged with firing birdshot at the truck from a car parked beside the road. One newspaper said eyewitnesses saw him fire the shots, and a Houma paper reported that the arrested men had admitted participating in the incident. A New York concern posted the bail for the four men, which Judge Robert Lottinger had set at $5,000 each.[37]

Toward the end of the first week of the strike the Reverend J. E. Poindexter, a black Baptist minister of New Orleans, made periodic broadcasts over radio station WBOK, calling on NAWU members to return to work since the union had made false promises. The fifty-year-old minister of Greater Pleasant Green Baptist Church replied to threats of ridicule by union men if he did not stop his broadcasts, by saying: "I'm not a union buster. . . . I'm simply trying to help my people." The NAWU reported the outcome: a union delegation had given the preacher "his baptism in Christian ethics and social problems." Later, however, when Mitchell was seeking assistance from Norman Thomas in getting American Civil Liberties Union funds to fight legal battles, Mitchell said: "Our fellows had nothing to do with the proceedings.

36 Baton Rouge *Morning Advocate,* October 17, 1953; unidentified clipping, n.d., Drolet Scrapbook.
37 New Orleans *Times-Picayune,* October 24, 1953; Houma *Courier,* October 27, 30, 1953.

. . . Negro leaders of the ILA and Teamsters Union were responsible."[38]

Father Drolet, back in Louisiana after a fund-raising tour, became embroiled in a heated incident late in the strike. When Welton Lestrick, a union worker, sought his aid, Drolet decided to speak up in his usual blunt style. According to Drolet, Lestrick had come to Thibodaux to pay a judgment against his brother who had been jailed after an automobile accident. Chief Deputy Eddie J. Ste. Marie recognized the union man in the courthouse and approached him saying, "I'm tired of you and the union." Drawing his pistol, Ste. Marie allegedly struck Lestrick on the head several times, causing severe cuts and bleeding. He then ordered the black man to clean up in the washroom and to leave Lafourche Parish. The next day, November 8, a Sunday, Father Drolet described the beating of Lestrick from his pulpit. He quoted Ste. Marie as saying that he would show who was "king of the niggers around here." Drolet concluded his sermon with an ironic and forceful comment on American life: "You are thankful that God has placed you in the land of the free, where the poor enjoy equal justice under the law. It's so different here from the communist countries behind the Iron Curtain, where human dignity is outraged, and human freedoms are ruthlessly trampled upon by godless dictators." The priest secured medical attention for Lestrick's cut eye and head and found a safe place for him to hide until he could move his family. Later, Drolet corrected the impression that it was a plantation deputy who had beaten the union man. The man responsible, he said, was "the high sheriff of the county. His name, and I am sorry to say it, is Eddie Ste. Marie, a big and important man."[39]

Archbishop Rummel in late October wrote to clergymen requesting that Sunday, November 1, 1953, be a day of special prayer for settlement of the strike. In a letter read in all Catholic churches of the archdiocese on that Sunday, the archbishop told parishioners: "Divine guidance and aid will bring about the material recognition of the principles of justice and charity, which alone can guarantee enduring peace in the social order." In an attempt to lessen tension over conflicting views of the strike, he urged the clergy in another letter to refrain "from discussing

38 Baton Rouge *Morning Advocate,* October 2, 1953; Ernesto Galarza, telephone report to NAWU, October 17, 1953, Mitchell to Norman Thomas, November 12, 1953, both in 69:1339, STFU.

39 Oliver Pilat, New York *Post,* November 10, 1953, various clippings, dateline New York, October 11, 1954, Drolet Scrapbook.

social problems in the pulpit." He suggested forming study groups instead. "Under all circumstances," he ordered, "personal references and complications should be avoided."[40]

Meanwhile the Catholic Committee of the South, Holy Name societies, and the Christian Family Movement all provided food packages or services for the families of strikers. The Reverend Robert Guste, assistant pastor of Saint Cecilia Parish in New Orleans, organized a motorcade to deliver food and clothing to needy families on strike. The New York *Post* in November ran a feature article, based on material supplied by Local 317, detailing hardships endured by union members, but cash grants, such as the $5,000 check from the United Auto Workers, combined with local aid, made life more tolerable for those on strike.[41]

After the strike was about a week old, the NAWU had placed ten pickets at the Godchaux refinery at Raceland in Lafourche Parish to inform factory workers of field worker demands.[42] The pickets handed out leaflets encouraging the factory workers to join the NAWU in order to strengthen their own position: "If any unionized sugar factory workers take their stand with us, we will stand with them until they get recognition, too." Hasiwar estimated that three hundred mill workers left their jobs in support of Local 317.

Four days after the picketing began, however, Judge J. Louis Watkins of the 17th Judicial District Court of Louisiana signed a temporary order restraining members of the United Packing House Workers of America (CIO) from walking off their jobs at the Southdown Sugars plant in Terrebonne in sympathy with the field workers strike. The next day he restrained Local 317 from picketing the Southdown plant which, the company said, had suffered "irreparable damage." The latter order named such important union leaders as Hasiwar, Frank Lapeyrolerie, Joe Guidry, Felix Dugas, Paul Chaisson, and Irving Picou. On October 30 Judge Watkins heard evidence to decide whether the injunction against picketing should be made permanent. Southdown brought in witnesses to show intimidation of non–union members, while Local 317

40 Houma *Courier,* November 10, 1953; Rummel to all clergymen in Archdiocese of New Orleans, October 28, 1953, in "Farmers Union" folder, JFR Papers.

41 Oliver Pilat, "Brother, Can You Spare a Drink of Water?" New York *Post,* November [11], 1953, Drolet Scrapbook; Walter Reuther to Galarza, October 23, 1953, 69:1337b, STFU.

42 Galarza, telephone report to NAWU, October 17, 1953, 69:1337b, STFU.

claimed that the right to picket was as basic as the right to strike. Watkins granted an indefinite restraining order against Local 317. Mitchell complained that the injunction was based on the idea that picketing was an illegal conspiracy since agricultural workers were not under National Labor Relations Board jurisdiction.[43]

Judge Watkins, who communicated with Senator Ellender on a first-name basis, had lived on sugar plantations for twenty-five years (most of them on the Southdown plantation) "as the son of an employee and as an actual employee for brief periods." He acknowledged difficulty in being objective: "We are placed in the awkward, unhappy and extremely difficult position of attempting to draw a line of demarcation between the testimony in the record and our own personal knowledge. . . . harvesting without processing is as unthinkable as liberty without law."[44]

Two days later in St. John Parish the state district court ruled similarly against picketing by Local 317 at the Godchaux Sugars refinery, and on November 5, a ruling in Lafourche Parish halted picketing at Godchaux's Raceland refinery. In the Lafourche proceedings, Judge P. Davis Martinez heard testimony from Hasiwar and from Roland Toups, who testified that South Coast had lost from $7,500 to $8,000 since the strike had started and that his company had lost business to plants unaffected by the strike. The union tried to bring the matter before the Louisiana Supreme Court, but, on November 6, the court announced that it would not "exercise its supervisory jurisdiction to disturb the orderly procedure in trial below except in cases of irreparable injury." Union attorneys argued that the Louisiana high court should have heard the case because the injunction violated the constitutional rights of union members, appellate procedures were inadequate, and appeals would have taken months to reach a higher court.[45]

43 Houma *Courier*, October 20, 23, 1953; Mitchell to Patrick E. Gorman, October 28, 1953, 69:1337b, STFU.

44 J. Louis Watkins to Ellender, April 17, 1952, Ellender to Watkins, April 25, 1952, both in "State Dept., General, 1952" folder, Box 481, AEP; *Southdown Sugars, Inc.* Vs. *No. 15,432, Irving Picou et al.*, 17th Judicial District Court, State of Louisiana, Parish of Terrebonne, November 2, 1953, mimeographed transcript in 69:1338, STFU.

45 *Godchaux Sugars, Inc.* Vs. *No. 304, Frank Lapeyrolerie et al.*, 29th Judicial District Court, State of Louisiana, Parish of St. John the Baptist, November 4, 1953, *Godchaux Sugars, Inc.* Vs. *No. 10,672, Paul Chaisson et al.*, 17th Judicial

Injunctions determined the outcome of the strike. Mitchell had no funds to use fighting legal battles and, in desperation he asked E. H. Williams of the State Federation of Labor to urge George Meany to help finance the legal struggle to clear away the injunctions and make continued organizational activity possible in the sugar industry. Mitchell also asked the American Civil Liberties Union for legal aid. An NAWU attorney who discussed the possibility of success in overturning lower court rulings in the United States Supreme Court submitted a bill for $3,200 that he knew the union could not pay in full. "If you were well heeled we would charge more," he said in a letter asking the NAWU to pay what it could afford.[46]

Because it was enjoined by court order from picketing or otherwise performing its function as a labor union, the NAWU had no choice but to halt the strike. It ended on November 10. Later, the union issued a forcefully worded news release composed mainly by attorney C. Paul Barker, urging its members to return to work and declaring: "Although we feel we have been betrayed by our courts, the strike has succeeded in unifying our people. . . . The Union will continue this fight. The organization of the plantation workers will go forward. The suffering and sacrifice of our people will not be in vain. We will organize and we will be recognized." Mitchell informed Norman Thomas of the strike's end and of the Justice Department's willingness to settle the antitrust case against strawberry Local 312 if Hasiwar and others pleaded guilty. Galarza would return to the West Coast, the sugar local would survive, and Hasiwar would remain in Louisiana unless sent to jail because of the strawberry suit.[47] The National Agricultural Workers Union cane-field strike had come to an ignominious end.

When Louisiana courts had enjoined the NAWU to prevent it from interfering with sugar factory workers, Mitchell knew that the strike was

District Court, State of Louisiana, Parish of Lafourche, November 5, 1953, mimeographed transcripts, C. Paul Barker to Fred Piper [Pieper], November 8, 1953, all in 69:1338, STFU; Houma *Courier*, November 6, 1953.

46 E. H. Williams to George Meany, November 6, 1953, Mitchell to Irving Ferman, November 6, 1953, Barker to Piper [Pieper], November 8, 1953, Barker, "Legal Proceedings to Date, Sugar Workers Strike," November 8, 1953, Barker to Mitchell, November 8, 1953, all in 68:1338, STFU.

47 Local 317 mimeographed news release, November 19, 1953, Mitchell to Norman Thomas, November 10, 1953, Mitchell to William Becker, November 12, 1953, all in 69:1339, STFU.

lost. The plantation workers strike could not halt sugar production, and financial problems and antitrust suits had just about wrecked the NAWU. Only if factory workers had supported the plantation workers and stopped sugar production completely, could Mitchell possibly have won recognition and a union contract with growers. Given the racial composition of the NAWU, the weakness of all sugar worker unions, the strength of the sugar lobby, the attitude of the public toward unions during the McCarthy Era, and the organizational problems of the NAWU, the 1953 strike had been a longshot gamble that had not paid off.

The 1953 cane-field strike was useful because it exposed conditions in Louisiana, but the strike itself was a failure and a setback for unionism in agriculture. The sugar workers failed, as had the sharecroppers in the 1930s, to win collective bargaining concessions from the big agricultural corporations. The older type of strike, which the NAWU was forced to conduct without the advantages of collective bargaining and the closed or union shop, could have succeeded only if the union had been able to exert overwhelming economic pressure. The injunctions that ended the strike resembled those described by Irving Bernstein, which were used against unions during the lean years for organized labor before 1933.

The 1953 strike also resembled the cane-field strikes of the 1880s more than modern industrial strikes. In both eras growers either openly or subtly stirred racial prejudices against the predominantly black unions and called union leaders Communists or Communist-supported. Planters, in both cases, combatted union influence by evicting the blacklisted workers, requesting additional police protection, and charging the unions with violating property rights.

The NAWU attempt to align small cane farmers with union workers against outside-owned giants of the industry was a throwback to the 1890s. Perhaps *neo-Populist* best describes the effort to join the two groups against the big sugar corporations. Galarza claimed that the small growers were paying the American Sugar Cane League dues that were "all but compulsory." They were subject to arbitrary trash penalties, complicated purity tests, and unsupervised sucrose analyses. Agricultural co-ops, which were originally designed to help small farmers, benefitted wealthy processors in the sugar industry. The NAWU claimed that small cane growers paid higher wages than the big corporations, as part of its attempt to direct its sharpest barbs at the corporations. The union also advocated a processing tax on sugarcane to finance programs beneficial to laborers and to small farmers. The union appeal failed, however, since small growers could see few direct benefits to themselves from unionization and since they were afraid that unionization would bring demands for higher wages. Union promises to help small farmers harvest their crops during the 1953 cane-field strike had not impressed small growers, who knew that the strike was not directed solely against the big-four corporations as the NAWU claimed.

Chapter 8

Caught Between the AFL and the CIO

For the National Agricultural Workers Union the days following the 1953 cane-field strike afforded time for reevaluation, readjustment, and introspection to determine its prospects. What went wrong? Why had the strike failed? The answers provided by union and church leaders emphasized plots and conspiracies of various kinds but overlooked salient economic and political points.

NAWU President Mitchell felt that the sugar local had developed so quickly that there was insufficient time to mobilize public support for its plantation workers, but Father O'Connell marveled at the support demonstrated by longshoremen and other international unions. Both men felt that, when Eddie Sutton, a leader of the CIO-affiliated United Packinghouse Workers of America (UPWA), had crossed a NAWU picket line at the Godchaux plant in Raceland, all chance for success in the strike had vanished. According to this version, Godchaux Sugars officials in New York had instructed their Louisiana plant managers to sign a contract with the NAWU, but word of CIO men crossing the picket line changed the company's plans about signing a contract.[1]

This simplistic explanation ignores both the injunction and the union's failure to halt the harvesting of cane and to stop sugar operations. Despite the injunctions the strike would have succeeded, O'Connell feels, if various union elements had worked together. Years later he admitted what he had always been reluctant to say: that he would have been able to prevent the CIO from crossing NAWU picket lines. With Teamsters Union cooperation, he said, "not a truck would have

---

1 H. L. Mitchell, interview, June 23, 1970; Vincent O'Connell, interview, September 11, 1970.

moved," and eventually the NAWU would have gained recognition.[2] How such action—had it been forthcoming—would have bypassed court injunctions or Taft-Hartley restrictions against secondary boycotts O'Connell did not explain.

Union leaders, blacklisted and evicted as a result of the strike, required immediate attention. By mid-November sugar growers had begun to fire workers, but the Catholic church quickly tried to meet the challenge, and the NAWU planned to use some members, whom the church had been unable to place in jobs, as part-time organizers.[3]

Father Twomey, head of the Industrial Relations Department of Loyola University, brought together leaders of the Christian Family Movement, the Saint Vincent de Paul Society, the Commission on Human Rights of the Catholic Committee of the South, the Urban League, the AFL, and the CIO. Ninety-seven men, responsible for six hundred dependents, had been fired because of the strike, Ernesto Galarza told the gathering. Those who had not been blacklisted had found jobs, but sixty or sixty-five heads of families required temporary refuge at union headquarters in Reserve. Union men received $15 cash and groceries each week. Some commuted to jobs in New Orleans but needed help in finding new homes there. Frank Lapeyrolerie worked part-time for more than a year conducting a survey for the NAWU before he found a job in Reserve as a motion picture projectionist, and Paul Chaisson, with the assistance of Father Twomey, found an organizer's job with a large industrial union. Joe Guidry remained with the NAWU organizing rice mills, but when that effort failed, he had trouble returning to his teaching position in the Lafayette area. In December, Mitchell was still trying to find common laborer jobs with construction companies for blacklisted NAWU members.[4]

Hopeful that federal courts would overturn state court rulings, Mitchell

2 Vincent O'Connell, interview, April 4, 1972, with Bishop Joseph Vath and Monsignor Charles Plauché, hereinafter cited as VPO interview.

3 Mitchell, "The Strike of the Sugar Cane Plantation Workers in Louisiana," [November, 1953], 69:1340, C. Paul Barker to Mitchell, November 13, 1953, 69:1339, both in the Southern Tenant Farmers Union Papers, housed in the Southern Collection (and photoduplicated by the Microfilm Corporation of America in 60 rolls), North Carolina, Chapel Hill, hereinafter cited as STFU with box and folder or roll number.

4 New Orleans *Catholic Action of the South*, November 19, 1953; Frank Lapeyrolerie, interview, October 5, 1975; Mitchell, interview, June 23, 1970; Mitchell to E. J. Bourg, December 29, 1953, 69:1342, STFU.

tried to obtain funds from the industrial unions of the state. Injunctions, which had prevented the union from picketing sugar mills, threatened the well-being of all unions, Mitchell said, but the big unions were unimpressed with that argument. Although union attorneys contributed considerable free legal time to the case, the NAWU could not finance much of a legal struggle. Therefore, attempts to overturn the injunctions failed and wealthy Louisiana unions refused to help.

NAWU attorney C. Paul Barker complained to a CIO official that a Louisiana court had ruled "that a labor dispute and picket line is permissible if not effective, but regardless of the nature of the dispute, if effective, it is unlawful." Mitchell sent Barker's law firm $500 in mid-November "as a token payment" and promised to send more for an appeal, the total cost of which Barker said would be between $3,500 and $5,000. Later in the month Mitchell sent $400 more so that Barker could proceed with the appeal of *Godchaux Sugars, Inc.* v. *Paul Chaisson*. The NAWU owed Barker $500 for a portion of a legal action against Hasiwar, which the attorney himself paid.[5]

Not until January, 1955, more than a year after the cane-field strike, did the Louisiana Supreme Court rule on the permanent injunction against Local 317. Chief Justice John Fournet delivered the opinion which said that picketing of sugar refineries violated no-strike agreements of the factory workers' union and was "not secured to union under right of freedom of speech." He stated further that "injunctions . . . did not deprive . . . [unions of the] right to organize and peacefully picket." Local 317 had complained of being denied rights guaranteed by the First, Fifth, Thirteenth, and Fourteenth amendments to the Constitution. Godchaux had charged the union with forming "a conspiracy or combination in restraint of trade" in picketing some plants and not others and with using "artifice, force, [and] intimidation, as well as threats of force, intimidation and body injury, [to induce] the agricultural workers on the plantations to cease work through the guise of a so-called 'strike'." Fournet agreed with Watkins—harvesting a perishable crop "transcends the right of the defendants to picket."[6]

The NAWU failed to convince Judge Louis Watkins of the state's 17th Judicial District Court to set aside the temporary injunctions, and

5 C. Paul Barker to Fred C. Piper [Pieper], November 8, 1953, 69:1338, Mitchell to Barker, November 13, 1953, 69:1339, Barker to Mitchell, November 17, 1953, Mitchell to Barker, November 23, 1953, 69:1340, Dorothy Dowe to Arthur Churchill, May 10, 1954, 70:1361, all in STFU.

6 *Godchaux Sugars* vs. *Chaisson*, 78 So. 2d 673–75 (1955).

in upholding Watkins' injunction against delaying the harvest, Justice A. L. Ponder of the state high court ruled: "writs refused, not sufficient showing to warrant the exercise of our supervisary [sic] jurisdiction." Watkins stated: "So vital does the element of time appear to us to be in the joint harvesting and processing operations, that we are disposed to regard any affirmative act intended to disrupt, deter, or prevent such operations as wrongful." CIO attorney Arthur Goldberg promised to defray legal fees if the United States Supreme Court agreed to hear the case of *Godchaux Sugars, Inc.* v. *Paul Chaisson et al*, while the American Sugar Cane League pledged to pay up to one-fourth the legal costs incurred by Godchaux Sugars if the high court agreed to hear the case. Attorney Daniel Pollitt stressed to C. Paul Barker that the Supreme Court would agree to hear the case only if the union could demonstrate that the state court had ignored a federal question that had been properly raised in the lower court. That same year the United States Supreme Court denied a writ of certiorari, declaring the case moot. Chief Justice Earl Warren and Justice Black dissented, but the highest court in the land had ruled against the troubled NAWU.[7]

Meanwhile, American Sugar Cane League officials planned to capitalize on their organization's victory over the National Agricultural Workers Union. In November the League forwarded statistical data regarding the strike to the Bureau of Labor Statistics, whose requests for information the League sometimes met with reluctance. T. M. Barker, chairman of the League's labor committee, reminded members that before signing contracts with CIO unions, refiners should include tight no-strike clauses. The League thanked Governor Robert Kennon for maintaining law and order during the strike and, presumably, for helping earlier with statements about labor disputes.[8]

Just when the union's position in the cane-field strike became untenable, the NAWU faced an indictment against its strawberry local. In order to clear up the antitrust suit against Local 312, NAWU attorneys proposed a consent agreement, tantamount to a plea of guilty. They felt that the

7 Houma *Courier*, November 24, 1953; Mitchell to C. Paul Barker, January 17, 1955, 71:1379, Daniel Pollitt to C. Paul Barker, February 9, 1955, 71:1381, all in STFU; American Sugar Cane League, Minutes of Executive Committee Meeting, Nicholls State University Library, Thibodaux, Louisiana, May 25, 1955, pp. 3–4; *Paul Chaisson et al.* v. *South Coast Corporation,* 350 U.S. 899 (1955).

8 Cane League, Minutes of Executive Committee Meeting, November 6, 1953, p. 3.

Justice Department wanted to consummate a consent agreement but hated to set a precedent by allowing a cooperative union marketing arrangement to remain intact. Assistant Attorney General Stanley N. Barnes informed union attorneys that the Capper-Volstead Act did not permit a labor union to form a farmers' co-op. Mitchell told Norman Thomas that the NAWU would accept the consent agreement if it provided for fines only and not prison terms for union leaders.[9]

Mitchell came to Louisiana to confer with those of his people involved in the strawberry case. He spoke with Archbishop Rummel and thought that the church leader would put in a good word with the judge for the strawberry local. But in mid-April, Judge Herbert Christenberry told union attorney C. Paul Barker that the local would have to make its plea and take its chances. Mitchell felt that, because of the cane-field strike, those eager to put Hasiwar out of action were demanding stiffer penalties. "If we los[e] our most effective organizer," he asked Galarza, "what can we do?"[10]

On April 28, 1954, Judge Christenberry heard the case. He fined the local $4,000 and Hasiwar, Louis Edwards, and Casel Jones $1,000 each. He also sentenced the three to nine-month jail terms but suspended their sentences and imposed one-year probation.[11]

Besides losing the strike and having to pay antitrust fines, the NAWU lost its AFL subsidy in 1954 and saw its membership drop to a mere five hundred dues payers. That year Mitchell's wife, who handled office affairs, prepared gloomy financial reports. "I haven't even told him [Mitchell] yet that we will not be able to meet the payroll the first of the month unless a miracle happens," she wrote later. Discouraged over the antitrust case and the critical illness of his father, Hasiwar planned to leave the union. "I feel like quitting too," Mitchell told Galarza, "but you and I have the bear by the tail so we can't let go." The next week he wrote: "As you know I try so many schemes to get us money to operate on that by the law of averages . . . one of them clicks occa-

9 Pollitt to C. Paul Barker, October 30, 1953, 69:1337b, Stanley Barnes to C. Paul Barker, October 14, 1953, 69:1336, Mitchell to Norman Thomas, November 10, 1953, 69:1339, all in STFU.

10 Mitchell to Ernesto Galarza, January 26, 1954, 69:1354, C. Paul Barker to Joseph Rauh, April 19, 1954, 69:1360, both in STFU.

11 *United States of America* v. *Louisiana Fruit and Vegetable Producers Union, Local 312, Et Al.*, U. S. District Court, Eastern La. Division, New Orleans, Louisiana, Criminal Action Number 24,906, April 28, 1954, certified copy in 69:1360, STFU.

sionally. I'll keep at it as long as you, Hank and others hang on." Hoping that wealthy union brethren would lend a hand, Mitchell proposed a budget of $87,000 for 1954 to organize the entire Louisiana sugar industry.[12]

The NAWU cut corners in an attempt to stay alive. Union dues fell to about $1,000 a month, and the union sent Galarza to Louisiana to build up membership among rice, strawberry, and sugarcane workers. In September, 1954, Mitchell called the union's financial status the worst it had been in fifteen years. In October the union reduced the president's salary (Mitchell earned $4,600 a year plus travel and other reimbursements at a time when the Cane League was paying Gilbert Durbin $12,000). Union headquarters was moved to a cheaper office ($75 a month) in the same building in Washington, D. C.[13]

Hank Hasiwar's father died in February, 1954, the day before the eighteenth convention of the National Agricultural Workers Union convened in New Orleans. Mitchell felt that the strike had contributed more to Hasiwar's depressed state of mind than even his father's death. Hasiwar took a one-year leave from the NAWU to work for Ohiolene Company in New York, his father's business.[14] He never returned to union activity.

In June, 1954, Mitchell planned to close the Washington office and open a new one in New Orleans. He wanted Galarza to work in Louisiana with Joe Guidry, who needed help. Mitchell wondered about the effect of a right-to-work law the Louisiana legislature had passed that summer. Union attorney Aubrey Hirsch told him that an agricultural campaign would do well despite right-to-work because industrial unions, unhappy with planters for helping contractors pass right-to-work legislation, would assist the NAWU. Hirsch thought that growers, who were miffed at the defeat of their measure to outlaw agricultural strikes,

12 Mitchell to several union members, September 22, 1954, 70:1369, Dowe to Churchill, February 23, 1954, Mitchell to Galarza, March 10, 1954, both in 69:1356, Mitchell to Galarza, March 17, 1954, 69:1358, Mitchell, duplicate appeal letters to large industrial unions, December 4, 1953, 69:1341, all in STFU.

13 Mitchell to Fay Bennett, May 28, 1954, 70:1362, September 20, 1954, 70:1369, Audit Report, A. G. Hall and Co., Blytheville, Ark., December 31, 1953, 69:1342, Dowe to Churchill, October 5, 1954, 70:1370, all in STFU; Cane League, Minutes of Executive Committee Meeting, March 26, 1954, p. 4.

14 "Proceedings—18th National Convention of the NAWU, February 6, 7, 1954," 69:1355, Mitchell to Bennett, March 7, 1954, 69:1357, Mitchell to Galarza, May 5, 1954, Dowe to Churchill, May 10, 1954, both in 70:1361, all in STFU.

would be eager to settle with the industrialists, who were responsible. His interest aroused, Mitchell wrote to learn if C. Paul Barker agreed with the optimistic report he had received from Hirsch.[15]

When Mitchell blamed the failure of the cane-field strike on inability of AFL and CIO unions to coordinate efforts, he seemed more interested in promoting future cooperation than in reviewing past failures. One CIO-sponsored organization, the Southern Sugar Cane League, gave the NAWU hope during the strike. Its leader, Antoine Songy, who had co-operated closely with Local 317 during the strike, said, "What is now happening to the A. F. of L. in the cane industry may later happen to the C. I. O." The following month Ralph Helstein, an official of the United Packinghouse Workers of America (CIO), which had jurisdiction in a number of sugar refineries, suggested that his union and the NAWU combine forces to organize the Louisiana sugar industry. Mitchell liked the idea, but the AFL saw many possible obstacles to organizing fifty-four sugar mills and the many plantation workers as well. The NAWU readily agreed to the AFL-CIO no-raiding agreement which served as a preliminary to the 1956 merger; but Mitchell admitted to Galarza that he sometimes complained to Meany about CIO raids on NAWU jurisdiction, hoping that the competition would provoke AFL and CIO leaders to form one joint committee to organize agricultural workers. When his subtle scheme failed, Mitchell sent Meany a proposal for a joint AFL-CIO organizing campaign for agricultural and packinghouse workers. Periodically, thereafter, he mentioned the proposed joint effort, on which he based his future hopes.[16]

While waiting for top leaders of the AFL and the CIO to negotiate the details of the hoped-for joint effort, Local 317 worked out tenuous agreements with CIO locals in the cane country. Frank Lapeyrolerie of Local 317 and CIO Packinghouse Workers pledged to consolidate their locals' efforts in the sugar mills and the cane fields. Mitchell would have preferred teaming up with the Amalgamated Meat Cutters and Butcher Workmen of North America (AFL), whose leaders had worked

15 Mitchell to Galarza, June 4, 1954, 70:1363, Mitchell to Aubrey Hirsch, July 6, 1954, Hirsch to Mitchell, July 9, 1954, Mitchell to C. Paul Barker, July 14, 1954, all in 70:1365, all in STFU.

16 Mitchell to Meany, November 10, 1953, 69:1339, Ralph Helstein to Mitchell, December 1, 1953, Mitchell to Helstein, December 3, 1953, both in 69:1341, Peter McGavin to Mitchell, December 29, 1953, Mitchell to Meany, January 4, 1954, both in 69:1353, Mitchell to Galarza, June 2, 1954, 70:1363, Mitchell to members of NAWU Executive Board, August 4, 1954, 70:1368, all in STFU.

well with the NAWU for several years. Nonetheless, the NAWU had, for a time, considered joining the CIO, despite Mitchell's dislike for the Communist influence with Packinghouse. Mitchell hoped the NAWU could win some sugar mills over from Packinghouse, and he knew that E. H. Williams of the State Federation of Labor would not try to block such attempts.[17]

In early November, 1954, Henry Pelet telephoned Ernesto Galarza in California to tell him that the men of Local 1420 at the South Coast refinery in Mathews had gone on strike. Pelet was president of Sugar Workers Local 1422 at Supreme Sugars at Labadieville. These two CIO locals had become semi-independent local industrial unions although they were nominally under the jurisdiction of United Packinghouse Workers of America (UPWA). Both Pelet, who had helped the NAWU organize field workers, and George Parr, the diminutive but pugnacious leader of Local 1420, saw a need for organizing both mill and field workers. The CIO had given Packinghouse jurisdiction over agricultural workers, but because that group had not organized field workers, Galarza assumed that it had conceded plantation workers to the NAWU. Once this *modus vivendi* had been worked out, Galarza reminded Mitchell that Victor Reuther of the CIO had promised to take the initiative in an organizing campaign if the AFL did not. Meanwhile, Pelet and Parr were allowing Galarza to sit in on their strike strategy sessions. Local 1420 had decided to call a strike because the South Coast Corporation refused to follow the usual company policy of granting contract terms similar to those negotiated by 1422 in Labadieville. Pelet had hoped to capitalize on Galarza's wide knowledge and experience in labor disputes and on his expertise in publicity campaigns.[18]

Father Drolet, to no one's surprise, pitched into the Mathews fray with his usual abandon. His old feud with Chief Deputy Eddie Ste. Marie flared up again when Drolet accused the Lafourche Parish sheriff's office of aiding South Coast against the workers and of harassing strikers instead of closing down notorious houses of prostitution in the parish. Ste. Marie complained that Father Drolet had criticized him from the pulpit for convoying scabs from neighboring Terrebonne Parish to work at Mathews. Earlier he had explained that he was "escorting

17 Mitchell to Galarza, October 4, 1954, Mitchell to C. Paul Barker, October 13, 1954, both in 70:1370, Mitchell to Galarza, undated, 70:1371, all in STFU.
18 Galarza to Mitchell, November 3, 6, 1954, 70:1372, STFU; Henry Pelet, interview, February 29, 1972.

millworkers in a bus and a 6 or 7 car convoy because someone fired on a busload of workers during the 1953 sugar strike. I don't want anything like that to happen in this parish." T. M. Barker's firm was transporting cane from Mathews and grinding it at Valentine Sugars to prevent the loss of the crop. Barker did not believe, however, that convoying was a major factor in the strike's failure, nor did Henry Pelet. Nevertheless, when Ste. Marie crossed picket lines, Drolet spoke over Thibodaux radio station KTIB to say that he had taken sides against the working men and women of Lafourche Parish.[19]

Ste. Marie replied simply "no comment" to Drolet's questions about his refusal to testify before a Senate crime-investigating committee and his failure to enforce laws against "so-called night clubs" in Thibodaux. These must have been embarrassing questions for law enforcement personnel and other public officials in Lafourche Parish, for every high school boy in the area knew about the infamous Jeanette's. Asked by the chancellor of the archdiocese if he could substantiate his charges, Drolet spelled out the names of people who managed Jeanette's and several other "disreputable places" and whose names were usually deleted from local press accounts. Drolet also mentioned the pistol-whipping of Welton Lestrick during the cane-field strike the year before.[20]

When Galarza reminded Mitchell that Deputy Sheriff Ste. Marie had pistol-whipped Lestrick, he had hopes of waging a publicity campaign against antilabor forces in Lafourche. Ste. Marie had recently arrested Fred Wansley, a union worker at a local paper mill, partly owned by T. M. Barker's firm, and had held him for seventeen days before releasing him. The union undoubtedly hoped to link Barker and the Cane League with Ste. Marie's actions, but its case was apparently weak.[21]

When Ste. Marie arrested George Parr on November 24, 1954, for disturbing the peace and released him half an hour later, Local 1420 called the incident a police campaign against the union. The Chief Dep-

19 *Lafourche Comet* (Thibodaux), November 18, 25, 1954; T. M. Barker, interview, May 10, 1972; Pelet, interview, February 29, 1972.
20 Unidentified clipping, December 28, 1954, Jerome Drolet Scrapbook, lent to the author; Drolet to Charles Plauché, Thanksgiving 1954, in "1954 Cane Strike —Mathews" folder, Joseph Francis Rummel Papers, Archives of Archdiocese of New Orleans, hereinafter cited as JFR Papers.
21 Galarza to Mitchell, November 27, 1954, 70:1372, STFU; Local 1420 Strike Bulletin No. 8, November 29, 1954, in "1954 Cane Strike—Mathews" folder, JFR Papers.

uty, however, claimed that Parr had cursed deputies George Rebstock and Albert Duet, and said that he would not tolerate "uncalled for cursing by a union official of my men when they are simply doing their duty."[22]

Members of Local 1420 welcomed Father Drolet's support for their strike, but they were outraged by the actions of Monsignor Dominic Perino, patsor of the Holy Savior Church in Lockport, whose parish included the Mathews community. T. M. Barker and Roland Toups, a South Coast vice-president, were feeding him [Perino] "a line of bull," the union claimed. Union leaders suggested that Archbishop Rummel remove Monsignor Perino because he was antilabor and unsympathetic to the working man. A representative of Local 1420, asserting that Perino's statements criticizing the strike contradicted Catholic labor policy, asked to meet with Archbishop Rummel or Chancellor Charles Plauché to discuss the effect of the pastor's stand on Catholic strikers, who considered him a spokesman for Barker and Toups. The correspondent said that workers wondered why their spiritual leader often visited the South Coast office but never the union hall, and why he implied to strikers' wives that praying would do no good. Father Drolet told the archbishop that Monsignor Perino's statements hurt the union cause at Mathews, and that the Lockport pastor's chief adviser on social matters, Barker, had used a Protestant document to support his right-to-work views the previous summer.[23] Nevertheless, Rummel issued no censure of Perino.

By mid-January Local 1420 was bargaining from a weakened position, unable even to insist that South Coast dismiss the twenty-five scabs it had hired during the Mathews strike. In February, 1955, Local 1420 and South Coast Corporation finally signed a new two-year contract, which Galarza thought provided few real benefits to the union. Later, CIO leaders, thinking perhaps that Galarza had profited unduly, sent auditors to check the Mathews strike fund. The Mexican-American labor leader reacted: "So help me, Mitch, do I have to take this kind of bull at my stage of life. . . . I'm remembering the week I turned over

22 Local 1420 Strike Bulletin No. 5, November 25 and No. 6, November 25, 1954, in "1954 Cane Strike—Mathews" folder, JFR Papers; *Lafourche Comet* (Thibodaux), December 2, 1954.

23 Local 1420 Strike Bulletin No. 8, November 29, 1954, Felix J. Dugas to Plauché, November 28, 1954, Drolet to Rummel, November 30, 1954, all in "1954 Cane Strike—Mathews" folder, JFR Papers; Local 1420 mimeographed information sheet, n.d. [1954], Drolet Scrapbook.

my salary check to the strike fund—the week I went six days with 27 cents in my pocket because I was able to get meals here and there and in [a] striker's home and on the picket line and because I was likewise able to get free flops." Mitchell advised him to ignore the accusations, saying, "I have been accused of everything from stealing money to selling sharecroppers clothes off their backs."[24]

Because the CIO gave the small union inadequate support, Local 1420 made a weak showing in the Mathews strike. Galarza felt that Packinghouse, hoping to force the local independent union back under UPWA jurisdiction, had encouraged Local 1420 to strike and expend its resources. "CIO and PH have done an efficient job of breaking Parr and Pelet," he wrote. "I am almost sick over what has happened to those half dozen boys in Mathews and it's the same godam [sic] complacency of those at the top," he said. Mitchell thought that the CIO was supporting the Packinghouse leaders because Victor Reuther was afraid that Packinghouse would merge with the Butchers before Meany and Reuther could consumate their "unity deal." He claimed that Reuther was ashamed of the CIO double cross of Galarza at Mathews and, therefore, refused to talk about it.[25]

Even after failing to elicit support from prominent national labor leaders, NAWU and CIO local leaders Parr and Pelet played up the AFL-CIO unity theme whenever possible. Since locals 1420 and 1422 had come to the assistance of Local 317 in the cane-field strike the year before, Galarza said, the NAWU was returning the favor in an attempt to thwart the Sugar Cane League's strategy of trying to destroy one union at a time. Galarza asked Mitchell to drum up more AFL support for the Mathews strike and probably wrote the flyer circulated by Local 317 entitled "Don't Cut Scab Cane." The dodger stressed helping Local 1420 but did not actually call cane-field workers to strike. Mitchell reminded Galarza to request E. H. Williams' support for the strike, but admitted, "None of these top guys in either AFL or C.I.O. [is] concerned about what happens to agricultural workers."[26]

24 May and George Parr to Galarza, January 11, 1955, 71:1381, Galarza to Mitchell, February 21, 1955, Mitchell to Galarza, February 25, 1955, both in 71:1382, all in STFU.

25 Galarza to Mitchell, February 2, 1955, Mitchell to Galarza, February 4, 1955, both in 71:1381, Mitchell to Fay Bennett, January 7, 1955, 71:1378, all in STFU.

26 "Don't Cut Scab Cane," Local 317 flyer, n.d. [1954], in "1954 Cane Strike —Mathews" folder, JFR Papers; Galarza to Mitchell, telegram, November 7, 1954, Mitchell to Galarza, November 8, 1954, both in 70:1372, STFU.

Galarza carefully appealed to Victor Reuther and George Meany, hoping somehow to get them to sponsor a joint campaign in the sugar industry. He explained to Reuther that Mitchell had sent him to assist the CIO local on strike at Mathews specifically to check the tendency of small farmers to side with the American Sugar Cane League, which allegedly refused to grind their cane and imposed higher-than-usual penalties for trash content in their cane if they did not abide by Cane League labor policies. He asked Reuther to send an expert on labor-farm relations to various high-level union meetings and to protest to the Department of Agriculture about trash content deductions, volunteering, himself, to help draft a statement on the subject. Galarza told Meany how the NAWU and Packinghouse had come to an agreement about field workers and how he was assisting the CIO local on strike by pressuring South Coast Corporation through NAWU influence with plantation workers. Hinting that the NAWU might join the CIO, Galarza pointedly inquired if the AFL was interesed in a united effort in the sugar industry. A week later the NAWU had received no word from either Meany or Reuther. Galarza and Joe Guidry were also disgusted with Louisiana Federation of Labor president E. H. Williams' reluctance to act.[27]

Then, George Meany made a statement to the AFL's Miami Beach convention in 1955, and his words fell like an executioner's axe on the NAWU. The individual farm hand, said Meany, "is the type of worker who will not benefit from unionizing." Mitchell became so angry, after reading Meany's remarks, that he could not eat his breakfast.[28] The NAWU had indeed been caught in the AFL-CIO unity move—and neither side of the proposed merger had indicated any interest in agricultural workers. Unless the AFL or the CIO acted soon, time would run out for the NAWU, whose leader indeed held a bear by the tail.

Disgusted by the inaction of labor leaders in general, Mitchell lashed out at important union officials and at the racial policies of unions in the South. AFL and CIO leaders, he believed, were overlooking the propaganda value an organizational drive among the agricultural poor could generate. "Of course," Mitchell said, "that means nothing to George Meany, he is too stupid. But Walter Reuther knows its danger to him,

27 Galarza to Victor Reuther, November 16, 1954, Galarza to Meany, November 18, 1954, Mitchell to Galarza, November 22, 1954, Galarza to Mitchell, November 28, 1954, all in 70:1372, STFU.

28 Mitchell, mimeographed news release, February 12, 1955, 71:1381, [Dowe] to Galarza, February 24, [1955], 71:1382, both in STFU.

therefore he is ready to help keep us quiet. The result—we get $5,000 from the Industrial Union Department." In July, 1956, Mitchell decided to use the threat of adverse publicity against Walter Reuther. Mixing his metaphors, he said that the NAWU was undertaking a last-ditch stand in Louisiana on a shoestring, and if the AFL and CIO had no interest in the welfare of two million human beings, "then the public should be told about it."[29] His not-so-subtle threat produced no response.

In late November Mitchell expressed concern about the possibility of a Catholic independent union in the sugar country. Rumors that such a union was being formed grew, he told Galarza, because Father Louis Twomey did not get along well with Packinghouse. "I don't know what the hell to say about all this," Mitchell observed, "however it is now obvious to all of us that neither AFL or C. I. O. have any intention of spending money on an agricultural worker organization." Mitchell went to Louisiana to discourage talk of the Catholic independent union. In view of the coming AFL-CIO merger, he said, using Local 1420 as the basis for an independent union, backed by the Catholic church, would be misunderstood not only by bigots but by devout Catholics like Meany. Mitchell wanted attorney C. Paul Barker to ask Charles Logan to talk Archbishop Rummel into putting a damper on the independent union notion. Logan's partner then forwarded word of Mitchell's concern about the proposed new union to Chancellor Plauché. The archbishop apparently received the information and agreed with Mitchell, for by the end of the year the NAWU leader had been able to stop the movement.[30]

Mitchell wanted, instead, a huge organizing campaign in the Louisiana sugar and rice industries supported by aid from the AFL and the international unions. To succeed, he said, the NAWU would need $5,000 per month for twenty-four months. Mitchell's organizing prospectus referred to Catholic church support for the cane-field strike and to Archbishop Rummel's role in the right-to-work controversy. Either the archbishop or his advisers thought the specific references to the church's role should be omitted, and when Logan asked Mitchell to delete the

29 Mitchell to Walter Reuther, July 19, 1956, Mitchell to Bennett, April 24, 1967, both in 71:1382, STFU.

30 Mitchell to Bennett, November 30, 1954, Mitchell to Barker, November 30, 1954, both in 70:1372, Mitchell to Bennett, December 29, 1954, 70:1373, all in STFU; J. Michael Early to Plauché, December 6, 1954, in "1953 Sugar Cane Strike" folder, JFR Papers.

references, he did so. Mitchell planned to move NAWU headquarters to New Orleans if Logan and Williams found ways to raise the $5,000 per month needed for an agricultural campaign. In the union's Mid-South region, where black and white Protestant preachers exerted considerable influence, some members feared that moving to New Orleans would give the Catholic church too much influence in union affairs. "I don't want to think our office will be DOMINATED BY THE CATHOLICS, but I do have this feeling," a black NAWU vice-president wrote to the Mid-South director, a Protestant minister.[31]

As the proposed merger of the two giant union conglomerates neared, Galarza, already angry at the CIO for reneging on its promise to finance an agricultural organizing campaign and for implying that he had profited personally from the 1954 Mathews strike, wondered if being broke and in debt were not too great a price to pay for being affiliated with the AFL. Galarza and Mitchell wondered about the NAWU's future in the new AFL-CIO in light of Meany's statement that farm laborers would not benefit from unionization. Although Mitchell had not presented an optimistic view of its prospects to the union's executive board, he emphasized that the union should continue to be the spokesman for defenseless and unorganized workers. "If we fail," he said, "we must go down fighting in the same manner in which we rose 21 years ago."[32]

Mitchell did not realize that "Lige" Williams had blamed the NAWU for passage of the 1954 right-to-work law, but he recognized indications of union scabbing by Williams and reacted quickly to them. The director of the state Federation planned to enroll agricultural workers in a new AFL federal labor union, Mitchell cautioned his organizers. Because forming a federal labor union where a national union already operated was a violation of AFL policy, Mitchell complained to the secretary-treasurer of the AFL about Williams. He told Williams, though, that he could hire organizers as long as they remained under the NAWU banner. Mitchell warned Galarza that Williams was telling people that Hank Hasiwar had made $30,000 in Hammond on the strawberry deal-

31 Charles Logan to Plauché, December 27, 1954, Logan to Mitchell, December 27, 1954, Mitchell to Logan, December 29, 1954, all in "1953 Sugar Cane Strike" folder, JFR Papers; Mitchell to Barker, December 16, 1954, Mitchell to Bennett, December 29, 1954, both in 70:1373, F. R. Betton to Churchill, February 1, 1955, 70:1381, all in STFU.

32 Galarza to Mitchell, March 2, 10, 1955, Mitchell to Churchill, March 3, 1953, Mitchell, report to NAWU Executive Board, April 3, 1955, all on Roll 38, STFU.

ings. Williams also told Father Twomey that the NAWU had failed with dairy, strawberry, and cane and was a dying outfit destined to be displaced by another international union unless conditions changed quickly. The federal union scheme fell through, though, because of Mitchell's letters and disclosures. According to Williams, Joe Guidry had lied about the whole matter.[33]

NAWU relations with Williams deteriorated rapidly after this. Mitchell searched for documented evidence of Williams' alleged insurance business connections in Lafourche Parish with Harvey Peltier, hoping that the journalist Murray Kempton could use it for an exposé of Williams. Mitchell also suspected Williams of having encouraged the Seafarers' International Union (SIU) to advance Joe Guidry $800 and hire him as an organizer. "I am convinced," Mitchell said, "it was to keep us from moving fast into the sugarcane areas where he [Williams] personally has business and political connections." Later, Williams attempted to entice Local 1420 president George Parr, whose brother worked for the Seafarers, into joining the SIU. Mitchell told Galarza he thought Williams was involved with various welfare funds and "insurance rackets."[34]

As merger talk increased in intensity, Mitchell and his lieutenants were afraid that a rival union would spring up and deny the NAWU a chance finally to prove itself in a well-financed AFL-CIO organizational drive. Rumors that Packinghouse vice-president A. T. "Tony" Stephens would launch a drive to organize field workers as soon as his union and the Butchers merged also alarmed the NAWU. Mitchell explained to his old friend Patrick Gorman, secretary-treasurer of the Butchers, his understanding that the NAWU would have jurisdiction over agricultural workers in the AFL-CIO. The NAWU's seven top-flight organizers had years of experience with agricultural workers, Mitchell said.[35]

To inform the Butchers of the latest charges against Packinghouse, Mitchell sent Gorman notes detailing the Communist influence in the CIO union. He did not think that Packinghouse leader Ralph Helstein

33 Mitchell, identical letters to Joseph Guidry, Felix Dugas, Frank Lapeyrolerie, Mitchell to William Schnitzler, all on May 23, 1955, Mitchell to E. H. Williams, telegram, May 23, 1955, Mitchell to Galarza, May 25, 1955, all on Roll 38, STFU.

34 Mitchell to Galarza, April 30, July 2, 1956, Mitchell to Bennett, April 24, 1957, all on Roll 38, STFU.

35 Mitchell to Patrick Gorman, January 6, 1956, Roll 38, STFU.

was a Communist, but Communists in the organization found him tractable and kept him in office. Vice-president Stephens admitted he was once a Communist, Mitchell added, and in 1953 Packinghouse had rejected an amendment that would have barred Communists from membership. Helstein wanted the NAWU and his UPWA to match funds and organizers for a cane industry drive, but the NAWU did not have the matching funds, and the AFL refused to underwrite the campaign. If Gorman, who had promised never to raid NAWU territory, and leaders of other big unions supported the NAWU, Mitchell felt, the AFL-CIO would make concessions.[36]

In June, 1955, sugar locals 1420 and 1422, which, by that time, included field workers in their membership, disaffiliated from Packinghouse, which had begun to organize field workers again. Unless the NAWU started its own drive soon, George Parr and Henry Pelet warned, Packinghouse would displace the weakened agricultural union. Both threatened to rejoin Packinghouse before that happened. Mitchell reminded the Butcher Workmen that the Catholic church disliked the Communist influence in Packinghouse. Galarza had little hope that the NAWU could benefit in the meantime from a Packinghouse strike at the Godchaux plant in Reserve. If UPWA lost the strike, sugarcane workers would think the situation hopeless; if UPWA won, it would not need the NAWU.[37]

In September, 1955, Mitchell asked Pelet of Local 1422 to postpone his proposed return to Packinghouse because of the confusion regarding the proposed AFL-CIO merger. The NAWU leader, who exchanged information with Father Twomey about the Communist links to Packinghouse, also asked the priest to dissuade Pelet from leading his local back into the UPWA. Apparently the tactic worked; soon both Pelet and Parr expressed interest in joining the NAWU, and in February, 1956, Local 1422 voted sixty-two to ten to join the National Agricultural Workers Union. Walter Reuther approved, and Mitchell promptly asked him for money for a campaign to organize sugar workers. In March, though, after Parr's local applied for a charter, Mitchell had to go to Louisiana

36 F. S. O'Brien, "The 'Communist-Dominated' Unions in the United States Since 1950," *Labor History*, IX (Spring, 1968), 184–209, did not list the UPWA among unions having strong Communist connections; Gorman to Mitchell, January 12, 1956, Mitchell to Gorman, January 19, 1956, Mitchell, notes on NAWU-UPWA negotiations, n.d. [1957], all on Roll 39, STFU.

37 George Parr and Pelet to Mitchell, June 16, 1955, Mitchell to Harry Poole, June 3, 1955, Galarza to Mitchell, August 29, 1955, all on Roll 39, STFU.

to persuade Pelet's group to remain with the NAWU. Personality clashes caused leadership problems in the union's new Thibodaux office between Pelet and Parr over the influence of the secretary.[38]

After Joe Guidry took a job with the Seafarers International Union at a salary of $750 a month in 1956, the NAWU campaign in rice and sugarcane suffered; and Mitchell's ulcers acted up again. Guidry had been organizing rice mills in southwest Louisiana since the end of the 1953 cane-field strike. His usual procedure was to petition for National Labor Relations Board elections when he felt he had a chance of winning NAWU jurisdiction at a mill. Late in 1954 Mitchell urged a concentrated effort to win elections in several mills and to secure a base of operations from which to stage a comeback in sugarcane and strawberries.[39]

The NAWU campaign to organize rice mills had faced so many problems that, in retrospect, failure seemed inevitable. There was little progress in negotiating contracts, even after the union had won elections, and so Mitchell, who had been with Guidry for his first election, considered sending Galarza to help in southwest Louisiana. There was also the perennial money shortage. Mitchell, in May, 1955, asked Guidry to remain silent about an NAWU appeal to John L. Lewis for funds to finance a campaign in rice mills because competing CIO unions, such as the Brewery Workers, claimed jurisdiction of the mills. An argument among organizers Guidry, George Stith, and Felix Dugas over supervision of the drive so complicated matters that Mitchell had to intervene to soothe tempers. Furthermore, the Catholic church in the Diocese of Lafayette did not provide the forceful backing that the union had received from Archbishop Rummel in New Orleans. After the union had lost three consecutive rice mill elections, Mitchell canceled future scheduled elections. Thus, Guidry's defection to the Seafarers Union was an effect of the setback in the union's rice campaign, not a cause of it. Earlier, when a rice mill shut down after the union had won an election,

38 Mitchell to Pelet, September 7, 1955, Mitchell to Louis Twomey, September 6, 1955, Galarza to Mitchell, November 23, 1955, February 22, March 21, 1956, Parr to Victor Reuther, August 26, 1955, Mitchell to Walter Reuther, February 24, 1956, Parr and others, Charter Application to NAWU, March 12, 1956, Mitchell to Bennett, March 19, 1956, Mitchell to Galarza, March 19, 1956, all on Roll 39, STFU.

39 Mitchell to Bennett, March 29, 1956, Galarza to Mitchell, May 9, 1956, Mitchell to Galarza, May 28, 1956, all on Roll 39, November 8, 1954, 70:1372, all in STFU.

Guidry pleaded with Mitchell: "Please, Mitch, don't let me down—blast man, blast!"[40] By that time, though, Mitchell could do nothing.

Mitchell attended the AFL-CIO merger convention in New York in December, 1955, and returned somewhat buoyed in spirit. Henry Pelet, George Parr, and the NAWU high command had met in Washington before the convention to develop a plan for organizing sugar workers, which they intended to present to Walter Reuther. Tony Songy, CIO leader in Reserve, had attended the meeting also. Mitchell told him that Packinghouse would either merge with Amalgamated Meatcutters and Butcher Workmen of North America or be thrown out of the AFL-CIO because of its Communist connections. At the convention Mitchell received some reason to hope that, eventually, the AFL-CIO would give him some financial help. "We at least have the feeling," his wife said, "that we will not be left out in the cold completely."[41]

Ernesto Galarza was skeptical, however. He was unimpressed by Mitchell's perennial optimism and impatient with AFL-CIO inaction. "I want to get shed of that feeling that we are hanging around waiting for Lefty and he isn't coming," he wrote to Mitchell. In January, 1956, when the merger occurred, Galarza knew that the NAWU had no place in AFL-CIO plans. "I believe," he told Mitchell, "you ought to abandon Washington to the squirrels and set up in Louisiana to do what can be done with the sugar country."[42]

40 Mitchell to Peter McGavin, February 25, 1955, 71:1382, Galarza to Mitchell, November 6, 1954, 70:1372, Galarza to Mitchell, March 15, 1955, Mitchell to Joseph Guidry, May 19, July 5, 20, 1955, all on Roll 38, Guidry to Mitchell, September 18, November 16, 1955, both on Roll 39, all in STFU.

41 Mitchell to Tony Songy, November 21, 1955, Dowe to Churchill, December 13, 1955, both on Roll 39, STFU.

42 Galarza to Mitchell, November 23, 1955, Roll 38, STFU.

Chapter 9

The Right-to-Work Controversy in Louisiana

Right-to-work laws prevent an employer from requiring an employee to become a union member as a condition for obtaining or retaining employment. Such laws came under intense scrutiny during the 1940s, but the idea of prohibiting a requirement that employment be contingent upon union membership dates back to the early twentieth century. In 1901 antiunion forces in San Francisco staged a big open shop campaign designed to prevent any union from gaining exclusive bargaining privileges in a plant, and in 1903 David M. Parry, president of the National Association of Manufacturers, launched his "crusade against unionism." Meanwhile, the National Civic Federation, under the leadership of Ralph M. Easley, attempted to maintain a large nonunion labor force, and Eugene Grace of Bethlehem Steel pressured unions by refusing to sell steel to union builders or contractors in New York and Philadelphia. After World War I industrialists emphasized the American Plan—another version of the open shop. When these frontal approaches failed antiunion forces encouraged company, or independent, unions and helped them to become bargaining agents.[1]

Rerum Novarum, the 1891 papal encyclical which asserted the basic rights of workers to join together for their mutual protection, provided church leaders a justification for defending the closed or union shop. Monsignor George G. Higgins, influential secretary of the United States Catholic Conference, went one step further and denounced right-to-work as an outright antiunion technique. Right-to-work guaranteed no specific job security to workers, he and other church leaders stressed. They showed that it was employers' organizations, not employees, who

1 "Position Papers on 'Right-to-Work'," *Blueprint*, XXIX (September, 1976), 9–10.

were demanding a freedom workers had not requested. Commutative justice, they insisted, demanded that all workers contribute to the well-being of the labor force; allowing nonunion members a "free ride" at the expense of dues-paying workers is a worse evil than demanding that a man join a union in order to work in a plant.[2]

Proponents of right-to-work laws usually stressed the right of a man to take a job without having to join a union. Opponents of such laws called them misnomers that made strikebreaking easy, encouraged company unions, and allowed nonunion workers to enjoy the fruits of a union without contributing to the organization that made the benefits possible. Eventually the union representing workers would decline in strength and workers would lose bargaining power.

The Taft-Hartley Act of 1947 restricted the activities of labor unions and made possible widespread passage of right-to-work laws. Anti-labor forces thought that it balanced the Wagner Act of 1935, which protected unions from unfair labor practices. Influenced by troublesome strikes and concern about Communist-dominated labor unions during the postwar era, Congress wrote legislation that held union leaders accountable for their actions by requiring them to file detailed financial reports and to sign anti-Communist affidavits. Taft-Hartley outlawed secondary boycotts and provided for a cooling off period before strikes. Section 14 (b), which authorized states to legislate open shop policies, removed doubts about the legality of right-to-work laws and encouraged energetic efforts by supporters of such legislation. By granting the states jurisdiction in writing labor-control laws more stringent than existing federal laws, it reversed a trend toward greater control of interstate commerce by the federal government.[3]

In the early 1940s a Houston, Texas, reactionary named Vance Muse found success campaigning for "Anti-Violence-in-Strikes" and "God-Given Right-to-Work" laws. Since 1936 his Christian American Association had played on racial and religious bigotry without attracting many converts. But when he turned to antiunion causes, he received unexpected support. The American Farm Bureau Federation and the Southern States Industrial Council joined Christian American in criticizing union practices during World War II in Arkansas, Alabama, Florida, Texas, and Louisiana.[4]

2 *Ibid.*, 2–8.
3 *Ibid.*, 1; F. S. O'Brien, "The 'Communist-Dominated' Unions in the United States Since 1950," *Labor History*, IX (Spring, 1968), 184–209.
4 See Chapter 1 for further discussion of Christian American Association activities.

Right-to-work proponents scored their most impressive victories in the South. Arkansas and Florida amended their constitutions in 1944 with provisions outlawing compulsory unionism. Vance Muse collected $67,000 from right-to-work supporters in Arkansas alone for lobbying expenses. In 1947 Georgia, North Carolina, Tennessee, Texas, and Virginia passed laws outlawing the closed shop. By 1953 Arizona, Nebraska, and South Dakota had passed similar legislation. Among southern states only Alabama, South Carolina, Kentucky, Mississippi, and Louisiana had resisted right-to-work legislation.[5]

Pressure from antiunion forces on Louisiana legislators to pass right-to-work legislation increased after World War II. Because Louisiana had not joined other Deep South states in passing "antiviolence in strikes" laws, Christian American labeled the Pelican State "The Red Spot on the Gulf Coast". J. Tom Watson, Florida's attorney general, who explained significant points of his state's right-to-work law to Senator Ellender, thought Florida had been opportunistic in outlawing the closed shop. Another correspondent told Ellender in 1946 that in the state legislature "sentiment against [John L.] *Lewis* and the *Wagner Labor Bill* is very strong. Louisiana will undoubtedly vote out the closed shop, just as Florida did." A friend of the senator encouraged him to support right-to-work legislation and to encourage a national movement against the closed shop.[6]

On May 15, 1946, State Representative W. B. Cleveland, an automobile dealer from Crowley, introduced House Bill 105 that would prohibit compulsory unionism. Cleveland felt that organized labor's economic influence was far more dangerous than its political influence. He claimed that Florida had prospered after passing right-to-work legisla-

5 George Brown Tindall, *Emergence of the New South, 1913–1945* (Baton Rouge: Louisiana State University Press, 1967), 711; William Havard (ed.), *The Changing Politics of the South* (Baton Rouge: Louisiana State University Press, 1972), 152.

6 F. Ray Marshall, *Labor in the South* (Cambridge: Harvard University Press, 1967), 242; J. Tom Watson to Ellender, L. M. Haynie to Ellender, both July 17, 1945, in "Ed. & Labor, Labor Problems—General 1943, '44, '45" folder, George T. Goodman to Ellender, May 23, 1946, in "Education and Labor Committee, *Case Bill*" folder, all in Box 211, Allen J. Ellender Papers, Division of Archives, Nicholls State University, Thibodaux, Louisiana, hereinafter cited as AEP.

tion. On June 10 the House approved H.B. 105 by a 55 to 43 margin and sent the bill to the Senate. Several representatives from the sugar country, including Robert Angelle (St. Martin), James Beeson (Jefferson), Horace Dugas (St. Charles), and J. R. Fernandez (St. John), voted against H.B. 105. However, R. Norman Bauer (St. Mary), P. Davis Martinez and Marc J. Picciola (Lafourche), and Clarence Savoie (Assumption) voted for the right-to-work bill. After receiving the Senate version of the bill and concurring on minor amendments, legislative leaders sent it to Governor Davis on June 27. On July 8, Davis returned H.B. 105 to the House with his veto message.[7]

Considerable behind-the-scenes activity had prompted the veto by the usually conservative governor. During the summer of 1946, E. H. "Lige" Williams, Father O'Connell, and others had welded warring unions and labor leaders into a strong labor movement. In the Heidelberg Hotel in Baton Rouge union leaders had met again and again until they had decided on a common course of action against right-to-work. Father O'Connell of the Social Action Committee spoke for Archbishop Rummel against the antilabor legislation. A group of Catholic laymen had denounced his Social Action Committee's stand, asserting that it did not express the feelings of all Catholics, but still another group, called Informed Catholic Laymen, countered with an endorsement of the Committee's position.[8] After Davis received H.B. 105 from the legislature on June 27, E. H. Williams asked him to meet with labor leaders and other opponents of right-to-work. Representatives of many labor factions, along with social activist priests from the New Orleans archdiocese, greeted the governor on the appointed meeting date. They promised an all-out campaign against those responsible for right-to-work, including the governor, if he signed H.B. 105. The governor called in his legal advisor, George Wallace, and asked him to prepare a justification for rejecting H.B. 105. Davis vetoed the bill on the grounds that it "impedes collective bargaining and impose[s] criminal sanctions on labor, forbids activities which in themselves are functions of collective bargaining," contradicts acts of Congress and decisions of the Supreme Court, and is unnecessary and more drastic than the Florida measure approved by voters in a referendum there. On July 9, 1946,

7 *Louisiana House Journal*, 1946, p. 480; Baton Rouge *State Times,* June 8, August 5, 1946; New Orleans *Times-Picayune*, May 31, 1946.

8 Vincent O'Connell, interview, April 4, 1972, with Bishop Joseph Vath and Monsignor Charles Plauché, hereinafter cited as VPO interview.

supporters of the bill could not produce enough votes to override the veto.[9]

Proponents of right-to-work legislation in Louisiana capitalized on more favorable conditions in 1954 and achieved their long-sought objective. With the help of the agricultural establishment, they pushed through a measure that Governor Robert Kennon signed into law. Since 1946, when Governor Davis had killed right-to-work with a veto, conditions had changed not only in Louisiana but in the entire South. For one thing, the Taft-Hartley Act of 1947 made things easier for those bent on ending the closed shop. By the 1950s ten southern states had right-to-work laws.[10] In addition, Louisiana had experienced a violent paper mill strike in Elizabeth in 1952, a strike of plantation workers in 1953, and strikes in sugar refineries as well. Farm Bureau, American Sugar Cane League, and U.S. Chamber of Commerce elements joined forces in 1954 to promote right-to-work, while Archbishop Rummel, through his spokesman, the Reverend Twomey, opposed right-to-work even more vigorously than he had supported Mitchell's National Agricultural Workers Union during the cane-field strike of 1953. Father Drolet added sparks to an explosive political climate with his usual fiery oratory. When the agricultural establishment helped defeat an amendment that would have made right-to-work apply to agricultural operations only, industrial union leaders became convinced that the farmer had become a stalking horse for opponents of industrial unions. If farmers wanted right-to-work primarily to prevent interference with harvesting, why did they help kill an agricultural right-to-work bill and then support another that applied to all workingmen?

During the 1954 regular session of the legislature, Senator W. M. Rainach of Summerfield introduced Senate Bill 127, a right-to-work measure. It moved steadily through legislative channels, despite determined efforts to stop it, and sailed through the Senate after receiving a favorable report from the Committee on Industrial Relations. Senators Guy W. Sockrider, Jr. of Lake Charles and B. B. Rayburn of Bogalusa tried unsuccessfully to amend S.B. 127 by making it apply only to agricultural matters. Then, on June 9, the Senate passed S.B. 127 by a vote

9 O'Connell, VPO interview; *Louisiana House Journal*, 1946, pp. 1813–14, 1835.

10 Charles Roland, *The Improbable Era: The South Since World War II* (Lexington: University Press of Kentucky, 1975), 17–18.

of 22 to 14 and sent the measure to the House. On June 13 floor leaders in the House received the bill and sent it to the Committee on Labor and Capital, which later returned it to the floor of the House with an unfavorable report. Unwilling to admit defeat, proponents by a 56-to-42 vote of the entire House refused to let the bill die. Then, several representatives tried the same tactic used by Sockrider and Rayburn in the Senate, but they too failed to make the measure apply only to agriculture. After long, intense debate the House passed S.B. 127 by a 58-to-41 vote. On July 2 legislative leaders sent it to Governor Kennon, who signed the bill—it became Act 252 the same day—saying "it secures to every man and woman in Louisiana a freedom of choice."[11]

Both agrarian and industrial interests realized the significance of making right-to-work apply only to agriculture. The agricultural establishment had cooperated with industrial interests to pass a right-to-work law applicable to all workingmen in the state—and labor leaders knew it. E. H. "Lige" Williams of the State Federation of Labor criticized the actions of the Right-to-Work Council and explained what had transpired:

> The Farm Bureau and the Sugar Cane League permitted themselves to be used as a front for this powerful special interest group. They did so in order to use the influence of Louisiana's small farmers for the passage of this anti-labor law. . . . This was proved when labor's friends in the Legislature offered a challenge to the sincerity of the right-to-work group by presenting an amendment that would have made the measure applicable to agricultural workers only.

Earlier a union man had complained to Archbishop Rummel that proponents of right-to-work talked about helping farmers, "but they are far-removed from agricultural pursuits." Fred Cassibry, a union attorney, blamed farm lobby groups and the American Sugar Cane League's T. M. Barker in particular for pitting farmers against workingmen. Louisiana Farm Bureau president Malcolm Dougherty said he supported S.B. 127 because of recent strikes in the sugar industry. William Dodd, a prolabor politician in the Earl Long camp, viewed passage of right-to-work with obvious disgust: "I can't understand how the Louisiana Farm Bureau, which represents a lot of fine, rich people, who work for

11 *Louisiana Senate Calendar*, 1954, pp. 44–45; *Louisiana Senate Journal*, 1954, pp. 452–591; *Louisiana House Journal*, 1954, pp. 1964–65; *Louisiana Acts of the Legislature*, 1954, pp. 541–44; New Orleans *Times-Picayune*, June 24, July 31, 1954.

$15 to $20 a week, can liberate pipefitters and carpenters making $35 to $40 a week. . . . I haven't found anyone who wants to be liberated in that fashion." New Orleans legislators Joseph Carey, Edward LeBreton, and J. Marshall Brown opposed S.B. 127, saying, "we have been a little amazed at the combination of agriculture, manufacturing and contractors." The legislators felt that some type of agricultural right-to-work measure would have passed with little opposition. Addressing himself more specifically to the unlikely alliance of farmers and industrialists, Representative D. Elmore Becnel from St. John Parish wondered how farmers could have been duped by industrialists into supporting a general right-to-work law. Becnel, who supported an agricultural right-to-work measure, did not favor restricting industrial unions.[12]

Involvement of the agricultural establishment in efforts to pass right-to-work legislation surprised lawmakers and political analysts alike. The American Sugar Cane League and the Farm Bureau actively supported a general right-to-work law—not a measure limited to agriculture alone. On Saturday, May 8, 1954, prior to the opening of the legislative session in Baton Rouge, the Lafourche Parish Farm Bureau hosted a combination barbecue–political rally in Raceland for about 350 people. Gilbert Durbin, a full-time director of the Cane League, attended, along with Irving Legendre, a sugar grower and a member of the Lafourche Parish Police Jury, and state legislators Richard Guidry and R. J. Soignet. F. A. Graugnard, Jr., a Cane League official and legislator from St. James Parish, discussed right-to-work and other pending antiunion legislation at the get-together. Malcolm Dougherty, chairman of the Louisiana Right-to-Work Council, bought advertising in newspapers throughout the state. On three different occasions during the summer of 1954 the New Orleans *Times-Picayune* editorially supported right-to-work. Rural weeklies in the cane country carried multicolumn advertisements, and editorials echoed the ads. The police juries of several sugar parishes endorsed S.B. 127. In Lafourche, T. M. Barker's resolution of support won unanimous jury support. Iberia Parish had endorsed S.B. 127 but reneged and opened public hearings on the matter when the Reverend A. O. Sigur complained and applied pressure. The Board of Directors of the New Orleans Chamber of Commerce joined

12 Printed letter from Typographical Union to Joseph Francis Rummel, undated, Joseph Francis Rummel Papers, Archives of Archdiocese of New Orleans, hereinafter cited as JFR Papers; New Orleans *Times-Picayune*, May 27, June 15, 24, July 3, 1954.

forces with the agricultural establishment in supporting S.B. 127. Union attorney C. Paul Barker said that the New Orleans Retail Association solicited $100,000 from its members to support S.B. 127. At a legislative committee hearing on the matter, Cane League attorney Paul G. Borron submitted letters from the governors of North Dakota, Virginia, Georgia, South Dakota, and Nebraska, justifying right-to-work laws in their respective states.[13]

Obviously, the Right-to-Work Council's blitzkrieg had swayed legislators in 1954. F. A. Graugnard, Jr., a member of the House Committee on Capital and Labor, opposed the majority of his committee which drafted an unfavorable report on S.B. 127. Cane country legislators, including D. Elmore Becnel (St. John), Bryan Lehmann, Jr. (St. Charles), Richard Guidry and R. J. Soignet (Lafourche), Clarence Savoie (Assumption), Clarence Aycock and E. J. Grizzaffi (St. Mary), Carroll Dupont (Terrebonne), and F. A. Graugnard, Jr. (St. James), voted for the bill. Several other legislators, whose parishes contained both agricultural and industrial interests, voted against final passage of S.B. 127 after attempts to modify the bill failed. State Senator Clyde C. Caillouet, whose district included the important sugar parishes of Lafourche, Terrebonne, and Assumption, voted against S.B. 127 because certain objectionable features of the bill "could be the cause for the complete destruction of the union."[14]

During the 1954 right-to-work struggle, both antiunion Catholic laymen and church leaders assumed positions more extreme than those taken during the 1953 cane-field strike. Church leaders displayed more unanimity in opposing right-to-work than they had ever mustered in support of collective bargaining for unionized cane-field workers. T. M. Barker and F. A. Graugnard, Jr., who had clashed earlier with Archbishop Rummel over agricultural union problems, seemed less awed by episcopal authority and, indeed, eager to use conflicting Catholic opinion to challenge the archbishop's views. Archbishop Rummel's statements on right-to-work represented an economic and political opinion, they argued, not a definitive ruling on dogma and doctrine. As leaders of Catholic Laymen for Right-to-Work, they consulted with clergymen who opposed the archbishop's stand. They ran newspaper ads stating

13 *Lafourche Comet* (Thibodaux), April 29, May 6, 13, 20, 23, June 7, July 4, 1954; New Orleans *Times-Picayune*, May 26, June 3, 14, 1954.

14 *Louisiana House Journal*, 1954, pp. 1967–68; Clyde Caillouet to E. J. Clement, June 11, 1954, in possession of Mr. Clement; *Louisiana Senate Journal*, 1954, pp. 452–59; New Orleans *Times-Picayune*, May 26, June 3, 14, 1954.

that Pope Pius XII opposed labor monopoly, or the union shop. They accused opponents of right-to-work of attempting "to convert a political or economic question into a Religious Dispute." They also implied that spokesmen for the archbishop stressed doctrine "in direct conflict with other learned and holy men of the church." Barker inquired—in a tone suggesting surprise—why the archbishop had sent him material regarding right-to-work. Rummel replied that he had sent material to all Catholics who had signed the right-to-work newspaper ads, as an alternative to making a statement about the ad because "at that time I considered it inopportune to issue any statement of resentment or criticism of what many interpreted as an act of disloyalty."[15]

Father Twomey, who was serving as regent of the law school and directing the Institute of Industrial Relations at Loyola University, represented Archbishop Rummel at legislative hearings in Baton Rouge during the summer of 1954. He called the Catholic Laymen for Right-to-Work "a phony front" bent on giving the church an antilabor appearance. The laymen erred in two important areas, Twomey told members of the Senate Committee on Industrial Relations. First, they said church authorities had incorrectly interpreted papal encyclicals. Then, they suggested that the Catholic church did not really sympathize with problems of workingmen. Archbishop Rummel's telegram to the same committee declared that S.B. 127 "is insincere because, while it pretends to guarantee the right to work, it actually frustrates that right, in effect exposing labor to lose security, a decent standard of living and humane working conditions." Later, Twomey, testifying before the House Capital and Labor Committee, explained a subtle point regarding freedom of thought for Catholics: they could decide things for themselves, "but when serious moral implications" arose, they erred in equating "their own conclusions with those of their recognized spiritual leader."[16]

Right-to-work proponents found few priests who agreed with their stand, but when they did find a convenient Catholic source, they used it for maximum effect. At a legislative hearing Graugnard embarrassed

15 T. M. Barker, interview, May 10, 1972; T. M. Barker to Rummel, December 30, 1954, Rummel to Barker, January 10, 1955, both in unlabeled folder, JFR Papers; New Orleans *Times-Picayune*, June 27, 1954; clippings, Jerome Drolet Scrapbook, lent to the author.

16 Charles Plauché, interview, March 22, 1972; clippings from The *Wage Earner*, [June, 1954], The *Catholic Mind*, September, 1954, pp. 561–76, both in Drolet Scrapbook.

Father Twomey by reading long excerpts from a book by Notre Dame University professor Edward A. Keller, C.S.C., who believed that Pope Pius XII had criticized labor monopoly and, in effect, had endorsed right-to-work. Monsignor George Higgins insisted that Pius XII had referred to Marxist unions in Europe, not to compulsory unionism in America. Monsignor John Ryan had defended the closed shop. Confused by inquiries regarding S.B. 127, the editor of *Catholic Action of the South,* the official journal of the Archdiocese of New Orleans, finally asked Archbishop Rummel to clarify his stand. The Reverend James Stovall, a Methodist minister from Baton Rouge, told a legislative committee that S.B. 127 encouraged "union busting." Monsignor Irving A. DeBlanc, chaplain at Southwestern Louisiana Institute at Lafayette, criticized S.B. 127 with approval of Bishop Jules Jeanmard. The Catholic Committee of the South claimed that S.B. 127 pitted class against class and set the stage for "economic warfare and intense bitterness among ourselves."[17]

Father Twomey, an intense man who threw himself into conflicts with great vigor, learned a great deal from his unsuccessful clash with right-to-work forces during the summer of 1954. He was disappointed and surprised at being labeled prolabor for his activities with the Industrial Relations Department at Loyola. An idealist who once complained in letters to members of his religious order that Jesuit law schools did not produce "socially alert graduates," Twomey thought that defeat by right-to-work proponents had made Archbishop Rummel aware, for the first time, of the strength of the opposition he faced when he spoke out on matters not strictly spiritual. Perhaps, the setbacks in the cane-field strike and in the legislature contributed to the caution Archbishop Rummel exercised later when he denounced segregation openly but moved slowly to effect real change. Twomey, nonetheless, found at least four positive gains from the unsuccessful right-to-work fight: first, the church won support from workingmen; second, church leaders found a forum for discussing social doctrine; third, the struggle helped swing M. F. Everett, editor of *Catholic Action,* into a more aggressive posture; and finally, the struggle brought into the open "compartmen-

17 "Random notes on R.T.W. fight in Louisiana, April–July 1954" folder, Drolet Scrapbook; M. F. Everett to Rummel, April 27, 1954, in unlabeled folder, JFR Papers; John C. Cort, "The Battle Over 'Right-to-Work'," *Commonweal,* April 22, 1955, pp. 75–77; New Orleans *Times-Picayune,* May 29, June 1, 1954.

talized" Catholics who only supported social and economic doctrine as generalities. At times "compartmentalized" Catholics did not even bother with the amenities of religious argument. One, who advocated a hands-off policy, wrote Archbishop Rummel: "I believe that every shoemaker should stick to his own last." Another suggested that the archbishop did not realize the difficulties of dealing with union workers. By getting involved in political controversies, still another hinted, the church invited threats of an overthrow of authority.[18]

Even though Father Drolet did not officially represent the Archdiocese of New Orleans in the legislative struggle, he managed to sling a few barbs at the American Sugar Cane League, provoking intense controversy. "They used our farmers," Drolet wrote, "to put over the RTW bill to break the back of city workers' unions." He charged the Cane League with running a closed shop of its own by deducting dues of 1.5 cents per ton before grinding a farmer's cane. He goaded Malcolm Dougherty by asking if he would encourage a secret election so farmers could vote whether or not they wanted to pay dues to the Sugar Cane League. When Dougherty, the Cane League, and the Right-to-Work Council ignored his requests, Drolet challenged them to name two genuine sugar farmers in Lafourche and Terrebonne parishes who were not members of the Cane League. The League deducted "dues," of $22.50 a year from cane payments to farmers with fifty acres, he charged. In July, T. M. Barker responded in a strongly-worded statement: "There are at least 700 Louisiana sugar cane growers who are not members of this organization, but whose sugar cane is processed into sugar by Louisiana processors. I make this statement to publicly clarify any misunderstanding which may have resulted from false and malicious statements made in the public press by certain irresponsible persons." Drolet also criticized Lafourche Parish legislators Richard Guidry and R. J. Soignet, who had voted for S.B. 127, and Governor Kennon, who had signed it into law, but praised State Senator Clyde Caillouet, who had voted against it. Kennon supporters in the area fired

18 Raymond Witte, interview, February 20, 1974; Louis Twomey to Irvin DeBlanc, July 8, 1954, in "Louisiana Sugar Cane" folder, Louis Twomey Collection, Document Center, Loyola University, New Orleans, Louisiana, hereinafter cited as LTC. W. Leppert to Rummel, May 29, 1954, Edwin Grant to Rummel, May 28, 1954, Lucien S. Miranne to Rummel, June 2, 1954, all in unlabeled folder, JFR Papers.

back "An Open Letter to Father Drolet," insisting that those criticized by Drolet were, in fact, fine men.[19]

Organized labor in Louisiana engineered the repeal of right-to-work in 1956 more easily than many observers had expected. There was no flare-up involving church, union, agricultural establishment, and chamber of commerce because the church did not wage an active campaign and organized labor forced the agricultural establishment into accepting an accommodation. During the 1956 regular session of the Louisiana legislature, which seemed preoccupied with measures to thwart racial integration of the public school system, union leaders, who felt betrayed by events in 1954, moved forward with a carefully orchestrated plan to repeal Act 252 of 1954. The repeal bill, including a provision that would make right-to-work apply to agriculture only, followed a direct legislative route. Clearly, organized labor had decided to concede an agricultural right-to-work provision to farm legislators, who complained of strikes during harvesting season, but the agricultural establishment, again showing a preference for general right-to-work, refused to support repeal of Act 252. Without the full backing of liberals in the Catholic church, H. L. Mitchell, who spoke for agricultural workers in the state, made only feeble complaints—and most of these he directed against industrial union brethren, who, he knew, had sacrificed farm workers for the good of more numerous industrial unions. Besides, the agricultural right-to-work law, the *coup de grace* to an already dying operation, hardly figured in the decline of Mitchell's union.

State Representative Bryan Lehmann, Jr. of St. Charles Parish introduced two measures dealing with right-to-work during the 1956 regular session. House Bill 250 called for repeal of Act 252, the 1954 right-to-work statute; and House Bill 255 provided for an agricultural right-to-work measure. Legislators who had supported an agricultural right-to-work bill in 1954 opposed legislation that would apply to industrial unions as well. These included Lehmann, D. Elmore Becnel, and B. B. Rayburn in the Senate. They hoped to remedy this situation by repealing right-to-work except as it applied to agriculture. But the agricultural establishment favored a broader, more general law. The Cane League would not support an agricultural bill unless it included plant workers processing food, Graugnard, a legislator and the president of the Sugar

19 Unidentified clippings, 1954, Drolet Scrapbook; *Lafourche Comet* (Thibodaux), April 29, May 20, July 8, 1954; Baton Rouge *State Times*, May 11, 1954.

Cane League, said. Lehmann's companion bills went to the House Committee on Labor and Industry; it reported favorably on them and scheduled both for consideration on June 5 by the entire House sitting as a committee of the whole. The House passed H.B. 250 by a vote of 57 to 44 and H.B. 255 by an even more lopsided margin, 67 to 29. Cane country legislators Eugene Gouaux and Francis Dugas of Lafourche voted against both measures. Risley Triche of Assumption voted against repealing right-to-work but in favor of the agricultural right-to-work bill. However, Becnel, Lehmann, and legislators from industrial sections provided the margin of victory. Governor Earl Long, a neutral on the matter, came to hear part of the lengthy floor debate on the measures.[20]

On June 6, Senate leaders received the companion bills from the House and assigned them to the Committee on Industrial Relations, which reported both bills favorably on June 12. Two days later the Senate passed H.B. 250 by a 21-to-18 vote. Two senators, A. O. Rappelet and Alvin Stumpf, representing six big cane country parishes voted for the measure, but Clifton Gaspard, whose district included important cane-growing St. Mary Parish, voted against the bill. Support from industrial areas helped pass the repeal, which Governor Long signed into law on June 21.[21]

The agricultural right-to-work bill (H.B. 255) ran into problems in the Senate when agricultural lobbyists added amendments favoring special interest groups. Representative Fruge of rice-growing southwest Louisiana, won committee approval for an amendment that included "the irrigation, harvesting, drying, and milling of rice and/or harvesting of crops, livestock and other agricultural products and making raw sugar into brown sugar." Sylvan Friedman of Natchez failed to win committee approval for an amendment to include the processing of cottonseed. The Sugar Cane League hoped to include the transportation of sugarcane by the grower from the field to the mill. On June 14 the Senate passed H.B. 255 by a 38 to 1 vote and sent it back to the House with amendments. On July 5, however, the House rejected by a large margin the Senate amendments to H.B. 255 and asked that the Senate set up a conference committee to reconcile House and Senate versions. A six-man conference committee finally agreed on a report. The result,

20 *Louisiana House Journal*, 1956, pp. 706–709; New Orleans *Times Picayune*, June 6, 1956; Baton Rouge *State Times*, May 22, 1956.

21 *Louisiana Senate Journal*, 1956, pp. 401, 615, 751–54; New Orleans *Times-Picayune*, June 22, 1956.

Act 397 of 1956, incorporated amendments added by rice and cotton interests, but excluded the transportation of sugarcane, rice, or cotton by the grower from the field to the mill because the legislators feared incurring the wrath of the powerful teamsters union if they included transportation.[22]

These restrictions to H.B. 255 indicated obvious reasons for continued efforts by the agricultural establishment to retain a general right-to-work law. First, a general law covered many nonfarm jobs specifically excluded from "agriculture" in H.B. 255. By joining industry leaders in opposing repeal of Act 252, farmers gained legislative support from the Chamber of Commerce and other business lobbies. Besides, organized labor had helped to defeat legislators who voted for Act 252 in 1954, and a farm-industry coalition could counter future union threats. Dougherty explained his group's position by saying that an agricultural right-to-work law could not stop strikes at gins, driers, canning factories, milk-cooling plants, and sugar mills. Graugnard of the Cane League agreed: "There would be no point in harvesting sugar cane, if the cane could not be ground, and this could be the case, if cane mill workers were not protected by the right to work act."[23]

In 1956 the agricultural establishment used the tactics that had worked well in 1954. Once again, the Lafourche Parish Farm Bureau held a barbecue and invited legislators. Francis Dugas, Eugene Gouaux, and A. O. Rappelet promised not to vote for repeal of right-to-work. T. M. Barker informed members of the executive committee of the American Sugar Cane League that he would fight attempts to repeal Act 252 through the Free Enterprise Association just as he had done earlier with the Right-to-Work Council and Catholic Laymen for Right-to-Work. Free Enterprise ran large newspaper advertisements, some of which referred to "union overlords." After Senator Rappelet voted for both H.B. 250 and for H.B. 255, a cane country weekly called his action "a double cross vote." Union member George Parr, in a letter to the editor, defended those who had voted against right-to-work. Bryan Lehmann, Jr. told constituents that general contractors, not small farmers, opposed H.B. 255.[24]

22 *Louisiana Acts of the Legislature*, 1956, 776–79; *Louisiana Senate Journal*, 1956, pp. 751–54, 2101–102, 2342–43; *Louisiana Senate Calendar*, 1956, pp. 292–93; New Orleans *Times-Picayune*, July 10, 1956.

23 Marshall, *Labor in the South*, 294; *Lafourche Comet* (Thibodaux), June 14, 1956; New Orleans *Times-Picayune*, May 20, 1956.

24 American Sugar Cane League, Minutes of Executive Committee Meeting,

Undoubtedly, industrial union leaders abandoned agricultural union members in 1956 and supported an agricultural right-to-work law in order to repeal Act 252 of 1954. For some time Mitchell had complained of statements from national and state union leaders suggesting the futility of organizing agricultural workers. George Meany had infuriated Mitchell in 1955 when he told AFL convention delegates that farm workers would not benefit from union membership. E. H. "Lige" Williams likewise incurred Mitchell's wrath by blaming the NAWU for passage of right-to-work in 1954 and for attempting to bypass the NAWU to form an AFL federal labor union for agricultural workers. Worst of all, Mitchell knew that Williams had publicly called him "the prostitute of the labor movement." Williams all but announced his decision to abandon agricultural unions completely after passage of Act 252 in 1954. "We are genuinely sorry for Louisiana's agricultural workers," he said. "We trust they will soon realize the folly of joining causes that can only result in detrimental effects to them."[25] He seemed to be blaming Mitchell's constituents for causing farm groups to combine with industrialists for passage of right-to-work legislation.

After its introduction, Mitchell had asked the secretary-treasurer of the State Federation of Labor how the agricultural right-to-work bill had come to be introduced. His colleague, Galarza, felt certain that Williams had had a hand in introducing H.B. 255. Later, Mitchell sent telegrams to George Meany, Walter Reuther, and Governor Long venting his feelings. "Labor diligently sponsored House Bill 255, applying right-to-work provisions to agricultural workers only," he wrote. He asked Governor Long to sign H.B. 250 but to veto H.B. 255. Galarza, too, repeated details of the double cross of the NAWU at an AFL-CIO meeting in Denver, Colorado. Galarza claimed that Victor Bussie, who replaced "Lige" Williams as president of the state AFL-CIO in 1956, admitted conceding H.B. 255 in order to obtain repeal of Act 252. Mitchell planned to air his gripes about the whole matter at an AFL-CIO executive committee meeting that Bussie also planned to attend.[26]

Nicholls State University Library, Thibodaux, Louisiana, February 29, 1956, p. 5; *Lafourche Comet* (Thibodaux), May 24, June 21, July 19, 1956; New Orleans *Times-Picayune*, May 31, June 3, 5, July 10, 1956; Baton Rouge *State Times*, March 2, 1959.

25 New Orleans *Times-Picayune*, July 3, 1954.

26 H. L. Mitchell to Fay Bennett, April 16, 1956, Mitchell to E. J. Bourg, May 31, 1956, Ernesto Galarza to Mitchell, June 5, July 17, 22, 1956, Minutes of National Executive Board Meeting of the NAWU, June 16, 1956, Mitchell to

Both the National Agricultural Workers Union and the Louisiana Labor Council, AFL-CIO, felt obligated to explain H.B. 255. To document the NAWU version of the double cross Galarza wrote a twenty-one–page pamphlet entitled *Dateline for a Deal*, a calendar of events leading to passage of the agricultural right-to-work law. Galarza called H.B. 255 the only right-to-work law in America sponsored by a state AFL-CIO union. Upset that the state labor organization had not consulted with the NAWU before supporting H.B. 255, Galarza resented the setback to unionized agricultural workers. "For the first time," he wrote, "these workers found the way to stand up and demand that they be treated with respect, and for the first time they learned the lesson on labor's national solidarity."[27] Pressed to explain NAWU charges, the Louisiana Labor Council convened a special executive board meeting in Baton Rouge. The Council defended its decision to forsake its agricultural union brethren, whose 1953 strike, a Council report stated, led to the 1954 right-to-work law. The Council called that strike "a direct challenge to a traditional system in one of Louisiana's oldest and most basic industries. And it was interpreted as a flagrant insult to the men of stature and influence who controlled the system." The report explained that antilabor forces, who had tried for years to pass a right-to-work law, succeeded with backing of the agricultural establishment. Earlier NAWU strikes in rice, strawberries, dairy operations, and shallots had created "a backlog of highly resented NAWU efforts in agricultural regions." This "brought the anti-union pot to the boiling point."

In August, 1956, Mitchell and Galarza appeared before the AFL-CIO Executive Board to charge Victor Bussie and the Louisiana AFL-CIO with helping to pass an agricultural right-to-work law. George Meany appointed Joe Curran of the National Maritime Union and Richard Walsh of the Theatrical Stage Employees Union to study Mitchell's charges. They recommended that the AFL-CIO approve the action of the state AFL-CIO.[28] Clearly, Mitchell's impoverished NAWU, which had relied on charity from the industrial unions for years, was in no position to over-

---

Galarza, July 30, 1956, George Meany to Mitchell, August 6, 1956, all on Roll 39, Southern Tenant Farmers Union Papers, housed in the Southern Collection (and photoduplicated by the Microfilm Corporation of America in 60 rolls) University of North Carolina, Chapel Hill, hereinafter cited as STFU, with box and folder or roll number.

27 [Galarza], *Dateline for a Deal*, August 20, 1956, Roll 39, STFU.

28 Paul Jacobs, "The Labor Movement Cripples a Union," *Reporter*, November 1, 1956, pp. 19–20.

turn action by the entire Louisiana AFL-CIO. Besides, Mitchell's criticism of national union leaders obviously had not been forgotten.

Mitchell realized that airing his complaints against the state AFL-CIO before the recently merged national AFL-CIO virtually ended all hope of his continuing to receive subsidies from wealthy industrial unions. The AFL-CIO never forgave him for what he said and wrote about state and national union officials for their part in the right-to-work settlement. But that hardly mattered now—Mitchell's NAWU had never recovered from the effects of the 1953 cane-field strike, the fines levied against dairy farmer locals, and the Mathews strike in 1954. The right-to-work debacle simply made agricultural union operations more difficult and created a rift between the NAWU and industrial unions in the state. In March, well before the legislative session, Mitchell had explained his economic status to a trusted supporter. "Our financial situation is desperate. Unless there is some help forthcoming in the next two weeks we are going to have to fold the Union and seek some means of earning a living." In July, after learning that plantation workers in Florida had received slight wage increases after the Agriculture Department hearings, he wrote Galarza in Louisiana: "I think that just for the record, you and Frank [Lapeyrolerie] should appear on August 2, so we can take credit for whatever increase is handed out to plantation workers."[29] The NAWU, once a forceful voice in the cane country, could now only go through the motions of representing agricultural workers.

29 Mitchell, interview, April 12, 1971; Mitchell to Bennett, March 13, 1956, Mitchell to Galarza, July 17, 1956, all on Roll 39, STFU.

Epilogue

Change and Continuity in the Cane Country

In the 1970s some aspects of the sugar industry remain as they were in antebellum days, while others have taken on an entirely new dimension. Fewer workers, laboring on larger sugar plantations, use more mechanized equipment than ever before.[1] Since the late 1950s, there has been little interaction among the three protagonists in the cane country —the agricultural establishment, the Catholic church, and the National Agricultural Workers Union. In a sense, each adjusted to religious, economic, political, and social changes as best it could. Mitchell's union did not survive, and the Cane League and the Catholic church moderated their demands and tried to avoid controversies that would alienate the public.

Both union leaders and spokesmen for the cane industry felt that their struggle was also a moral conflict, which, when won, would benefit the general public. Both believed in conspiracy theories about their economic adversaries. Union leaders knew the agricultural establishment would never voluntarily surrender any of its advantages. Agricultural interests disliked making concessions for fear that each year union demands would increase. Growers subscribed to broker politics which most benefited those groups with a strong, unified voice and viewed the matter as an adversary situation. They had the apparatus to protect their interests and used it fully. Workers—protected for a while by a weak union voice and then by no voice at all—had only public opinion, support of some Catholic church leaders, and the meager protection of the

1 U.S. Department of Agriculture, *Agricultural Manufacturing and Income Statistics for the Domestic Sugar Areas, 1968* (Washington, D.C.: Policy and Program Appraisal Division, 1969), Vol. II of 2 vols., in USDA, *Sugar Statistics and Related Data*, 1–8; Charles Roland, *The Improbable Era: The South Since World War II* (Lexington: The University Press of Kentucky, 1975), 23.

Sugar Act to fall back on. In the 1970s, however, neomuckraker journalists succeeded in generating more adverse publicity about the poverty
and the living and working conditions in the sugar industry than H. L.
Mitchell's union or Catholic social action leaders ever did.

Of the three groups involved so intimately in the lives of sugarcane
plantation workers since World War II, the NAWU underwent the most
drastic change. This change came mostly because H. L. Mitchell, the
longtime agricultural labor leader who was nearing retirement age, no
longer felt he could hold together his weakened union after suffering
defeats on a number of fronts.

When Mitchell's union career ended in the mid-1970s, he had spent
forty stormy years working with agricultural laborers. After the NAWU's
decline in the late 1950s, his friend Patrick Gorman had helped find a
spot for him with the Amalgamated Meatcutters and Butcher Workmen
of North America as head of an agricultural division. When the Butchers merged with the United Packinghouse Workers of America in 1968,
Mitchell became director of the Agricultural and Allied Workers Union
Local 300, a semiautonomous, free-wheeling body that organized fishermen, rice mill workers, plantation workers, and several quasi-union
groups in the Gulf South.

Mitchell's career as leader of the Southern Tenant Farmers Union
during the New Deal years gave him a place in history, and in 1958,
when he participated in the Columbia University Oral History project,
he was especially conscious of his historical role. The following year,
when the moribund NAWU celebrated its twenty-fifth anniversary,
Mitchell published a booklet subtitled *The Story of a Union That Refused to Die.* This final utterance was an epitaph to enshrine the idealism of his NAWU.

Because he had feuded with both AFL and CIO leaders, the AFL-CIO
did not choose Mitchell to direct its drive in the 1960s to organize
agricultural workers in California. Instead Cesar Chavez and younger
leaders began the campaigns among Mexican-American laborers in the
fields and vineyards and won enormous publicity. Mitchell believed
that he had been a precursor to Chavez among California agricultural
workers: "Maybe I was kinda like a John the Baptist to Cesar Chavez,
to sum it up." Mitchell felt that one of his most significant contributions had been publicizing the plight of the agricultural workers. He
realized that changes in sugarcane production brought on by increased
mechanization, had created a need for a new kind of organization.

"Somewhere out there, there is a Cesar Chavez in the black belt," he said. "We want to find him."

The NAWU fought many tough battles against the American Sugar Cane League and other lobby groups, but it never recommended terminating the Sugar Act, even after it had come under heavy fire. Galarza, who had made detailed studies of the sugar industry for the NAWU, realized that price fluctuations and high fixed costs posed serious problems for growers. On many plantations, expensive mill and harvesting equipment is used for only nine weeks of the year. Unlike critics who called sugarcane production a subsidized industry that should be allowed to die a natural death, the NAWU urged continuing support for the industry as long as its labor force received adequate compensation and fringe benefits.

Because Mitchell and his colleagues spent so much of their time struggling with NAWU finances, they failed to articulate their goals and long-range objectives. Nor did the NAWU capitalize fully on the vulnerable position of the subsidized sugar industry in its propaganda war with the American Sugar Cane League. Often the union was overwhelmed by the effective publicity from the agricultural establishment. Shrewdly associating its own ends with the general well-being of the cane country, the Cane League succeeded in equating the aims of the NAWU with the greed of outside agitators and Communists. The NAWU's problems were intensified by its inability to get along with other unions in the state or with the AFL-CIO. Undoubtedly, leaders of other unions grew weary of Mitchell's constant pleas for financial aid for his disadvantaged agrarians. By the late 1950s the impoverished and demoralized NAWU could only go through the motions of being a voice for sugar plantation workers.

As if to ensure that unions would not easily rise again to threaten the status quo, Louisiana passed a right-to-work law in 1976, the twentieth state to embrace right-to-work. The legislature, meeting in regular session, passed House Bill 637, which became Act 97, a general right-to-work law, thereby joining twelve other states in legislating an end to the union shop. The others are Alabama, Georgia, Iowa, Nevada, North Carolina, South Carolina, North Dakota, Tennessee, Texas, Utah, Virginia, and Wyoming. Seven states accepted right-to-work by constitutional amendment: Arizona, Arkansas, Florida, Kansas, Mississippi, Nebraska, and South Dakota. In the legislative struggle over H.B. 637 Edward Steimel, president of the Louisiana Association of Business and

Industry, claimed that if Louisiana hoped to attract new industry, it would have to pass right-to-work to prove that organized labor did not dominate the state. Victor Bussie, president of the Louisiana AFL-CIO, argued that the main purpose of the law was to lower wages, not to bring in new industry.[2] Steimel's LABI used sophisticated television advertising in a publicity campaign which associated organized labor with corruption, violence, and autocratic domination of workers, and, despite a determined effort by Bussie to correct this impression, antiunion forces won a surprisingly lopsided victory in the legislature. Louisiana once again had a general right-to-work law.

With a right-to-work law safely on the books and the moribund NAWU out of the picture, sugar producers and processors have relied on their lobby group, the American Sugar Cane League, to help with congressional problems relating to falling sugar prices, cutbacks in domestic production quotas, and minimum wage legislation. The League also provided complex data on which the United States Department of Agriculture based the prices of sugarcane and wage rates for plantation workers. Senator Ellender, whose seniority gave him a strong voice in agricultural matters, probably did more to protect the industry than any other elected official and deserved the plaudit, "first friend of the domestic sugar industry," bestowed on him by industry leaders. He pushed through amendments to the original Sugar Act that extended its life in 1948, 1951, 1956, 1961, 1965, and 1971.

Aside from denying allegations about deplorable conditions for plantation workers, the Cane League, in the absence of any union opposition in recent years, expends most of its energies lobbying. Spokesmen for the League constantly bombard federal agencies with pleas for larger domestic sugar quotas and higher sugar prices. They persistently block attempts by reformers to bring agricultural workers under workmen's compensation and minimum wage provisions, claiming the industry cannot afford higher labor costs. Sugar lobbyists also complain about freight rates and attempt to win reductions from regulatory agencies. When nutrias, the prolific fur-bearing mammals from South America, multiplied rapidly in south Louisiana and caused problems by destroying sugarcane, the lobbyists sought aid from state and federal sources. They

2 See Newton Renfro, New Orleans *Times-Picayune*, March 14, 15, 16, 17, 1976, for an excellent four-part feature summarizing arguments for and against the controversial legislation.

requested federal funds to control the nutria and won approval from
the Louisiana Wildlife and Fisheries Commission to trap and poison
nutrias in their fields. Throughout the entire period they have supported
local and national groups promoting right-to-work legislation.[3]

But the Cane League could not prevent the wave of critical articles
about the sugar industry from appearing. In May, 1972, *Saturday Review* published a scathing feature-length indictment of the Louisiana
sugar industry written by Peter Schuck, a young lawyer associated with
Ralph Nader. According to Schuck, the sugar lobby had, for years,
thwarted attempts by liberals in Congress to provide agricultural workers the benefits of National Labor Relations Board jurisdiction, unemployment compensation, and minimum wage coverage. The sugar
industry hired as lobbyists, Schuck said, retired USDA bureaucrats who
had administered the Sugar Act during their government tenure, and in
1970, American taxpayers spent $400 million to keep the domestic
price of sugar higher than the world market price.[4] Schuck wrote that
the USDA had paid out an additional $93 million in benefit payments
to limit production, and in 1969, South Coast Corporation had received
$297,000, Southdown, $185,000 in benefit payments.[5] Yet, according
to Schuck, the average sugarcane plantation worker with a family of six
received only $2,635 a year, $1,900 less than the poverty level for a
farm family, and $1,000 less than the average income for a farm-
worker family. Housing conditions remained substandard in many cases,
he felt, and welfare officials discriminated against blacks.

In 1973, less than a year after Schuck's devastating attack, Patsy Sims,
a freelance writer, completed "Behind the Cane Curtain," a series of
fifteen muckraking articles published serially by the New Orleans *States-
Item* during March and April. Quoting planters whose ideas seemed to
derive from the world of William Faulkner and Erskine Caldwell more

3 American Sugar Cane League, Minutes of Executive Committee Meetings,
Nicholls State University Library, Thibodaux, Louisiana, *passim.*

4 U.S. Department of Agriculture, *Supplies, Distribution, Quota Operations,
Prices and International Data Through 1968* (Washington, D.C.: Policy and
Program Appraisal Division, 1969), Vol. I of 2 vols., in USDA, *Sugar Statistics
and Related Data,* 146–47, shows that the average domestic price for raw sugar
usually ran 2 or 3 cents higher in the United States than on the world market.
In 1966, 1967, and 1968 the price averaged over 4 cents higher in the United
States. The 11 million tons needed annually in the U.S. would have cost $440
million less at world prices just 2 cents lower than domestic prices.

5 *Congressional Record,* 93rd Cong., 1st Sess., 1973, Vol. 119, Part 11, pp.
E2838–40.

than from the post 1960s civil rights movement, she demonstrated that paternalism still flourished in the cane country. Then, just before the start of the harvest season in 1974, the *Wall Street Journal* published a front-page story by Richard Shaffer describing depressed conditions for cane-field workers, many of whom were black and living below the poverty level. Average income for the 16,000 cane workers in 1973, he pointed out, was $3,420. In describing living conditions, he observed that "deplorable housing still abounds in the state's 17-parish sugar belt."[6]

Because the Cane League influences public opinion in the cane country, to criticize the sugar industry is to provoke the wrath not only of the Cane League and the Farm Bureau but of newspaper editors, businessmen, and political leaders as well. Local governmental officials, enraged by criticism of governmental practices, threatened damage suits against the neomuckrakers of the 1970s. Even minor functionaries not mentioned by name in these critical articles threatened legal action, presumably to vindicate their damaged reputations.

Nonetheless, consumer groups and soft drink and candy manufacturers finally pressured Congress, with the support of a Republican administration, into allowing the Sugar Act to expire in 1974. Critics claimed that for years the Act had rewarded domestic producers at taxpayers' expense and had enriched lobbyists who obtained quotas for nations that exported sugar. For a number of reasons, the sugar industry did not support a bill to reinstate the Sugar Act in 1975. For one thing, industry leaders feared that a new sugar law would place minimum wage restrictions on all phases of operation. Besides, sugar prices in 1975 reached an all-time high of 64.5 cents per pound. (Domestic producers claimed that they needed a price level of between 17 to 20 cents per pound to remain healthy.) Moreover, the League had lost its principal architect of sugar legislation, Senator Ellender, who died in 1972.

When sugar prices fell to 12.35 cents per pound in August, 1976, producers had second thoughts about the need for some type of federal legislation to stabilize sugar prices. Industry spokesmen called for tripling the tariff on sugar or for establishing some kind of price supports, but Agriculture Department officials did not favor abolishing the free market system for sugar, although they acknowledged that prices had fallen dangerously low for growers. The agricultural establishment,

6 Patsy Sims, "Behind the Cane Curtain," New Orleans *States-Item*, March–April, 1973; Richard Shaffer, "Left Behind: For a Plantation Hand, Progress for Blacks Seems Far Removed," *Wall Street Journal*, October 17, 1974.

which was clamoring for programs to avert economic disaster in the cane country, appealed to congressional delegations for assistance. The Carter administration has inherited the usual barrage of propaganda from the sugar lobby bent on obtaining some form of agricultural subsidy for sugarcane.

In any event, Cane League officials, in time, found ways to counter charges by critics. In their angry denials, leaders in the sugar industry concentrated mostly on demonstrating that workers earned more than $2,600 per year and that housing was better than critics suggested. T. M. Barker supplied evidence that field employees of Valentine Sugars earned considerably more than Schuck stated, but admitted that his company probably hired more Acadians and fewer blacks than did most cane plantations. He defended his company's housing policy and suggested that Schuck had displayed anti-Catholic bias in his criticism of Bishop Maurice Schexnayder of Lafayette.

Schuck had, indeed, reserved some of his choicest barbs for the Catholic church, for its negative role in the cane country, despite the fact that it was one of the first groups to have come to the aid of plantation workers. He singled out Bishop Maurice Schexnayder of the Diocese of Lafayette, which has the largest black Catholic population in the United States, for actually undermining efforts by young priests and nuns to assist plantation workers. Schuck charged that Bishop Schexnayder had called in Father Frank Ecimovich, who had been working among canefield laborers, for a meeting with irate sugar growers. Planters told Ecimovich to mind his own business, and they made his stay in the area uncomfortable. After Ecimovich left the diocese, Sister Anne Catherine, a Dominican nun, took over direction of the Southern Mutual Help Association, an organization dedicated to improving the life of poor workers through cooperative educational, welfare, health, and consumer-oriented projects. Veteran labor priest Vincent O'Connell has also worked with the SMHA, which receives funds from the Department of Health, Education, and Welfare and from the National Sharecroppers' Fund.

Since 1954 when Catholic laymen had teamed up with industrialists to pass a right-to-work law in Louisiana, the Catholic church has reduced its overt partisan involvement in controversial social action causes. Once considered the third party in the struggle between agricultural unionists and the agricultural establishment, church leaders in the Archdiocese of New Orleans became more circumspect in their support for controversial social action programs. Several factors accounted for this change. First, the victory by right-to-work supporters in 1954 surprised and disturbed Archbishop Rummel. His spokesman, Father Twomey, thought that for the first time the prelate realized how forcefully Catholics could oppose their spiritual leader in economic and political matters. Failing health also reduced the archbishop's ability to participate in social action. And, finally, the archbishop became preoccupied with the racial integration of the parochial schools in the Archdiocese of New Orleans. He had denounced segregation publicly, but he was wise enough to move very cautiously toward integration.[7] Catholic schools were dependent for survival on governmental aid—aid that could be denied by segregationists who held important positions in the state legislature and on congressional committees. Senator Ellender, for instance, had assisted Catholic clergymen in many ways, but he made clear his opposition to racial integration of schools.

For a while during the 1960s, when the NAWU seemed likely to collapse completely, church leaders considered reorganizing stranded union members into a Catholic union. Most of the orthodox union leaders— and even the atypical H. L. Mitchell—saw the folly of resorting to such a vestige of the past, however. They considered a Catholic union an anachronism not unlike the old Catholic workingmen's associations which were closely tied to immigrant Irish and German workers, and the Catholic union movement never really made much headway. Perhaps the Catholic church has simply fallen back into its more traditional, conservative role of the past. Indeed, one might argue that the entire social action program inspired by Archbishop Rummel represented an idealistic departure from usual church policy. Now, having failed to bring sweeping changes, Catholic leaders have slipped back into more familiar routines.

In 1976 the *Clarion Herald*, newspaper of the Archdiocese of New Orleans, in a three-part feature, showed how Catholic programs designed to help plantation workers had changed.[8] Moderately critical of the sugar industry, author Renée Pitre concentrated on the productive work of the Southern Mutual Help Association. She also outlined significant changes in the sugar industry itself. Sister Anne Catherine and

7 Edward Haas, *DeLesseps S. Morrison and the Image of Reform: New Orleans Politics, 1946–1961* (Baton Rouge: Louisiana State University Press, 1974), 254–55.

8 *Clarion Herald*, January 15, 22, 29, 1976.

B. Bernard Broussard of the SMHA office in Abbeville work with sugar-cane laborers who earn an average of slightly more than $3,000 per year, about $2,000 less than the government standard for farm workers. SMHA leaders blame the poverty on the traditional system of plantation labor, which has survived since the days of slavery, not on sugar planters themselves. The general public, Sister Anne Catherine thinks, helps to perpetuate the ways of the past that keep a worker psychologically dependent on the free house the planter still provides, often with good intentions. Leaders of the SMHA include Father Vincent O'Connell, who knows that attempts to unionize plantation workers have not changed the system nor solved their problems. SMHA leaders do not feel that leaving the plantation is a viable alternative for plantation workers. Instead they develop health, housing, and education programs. Useless and needless poverty, O'Connell feels, is the common enemy.

Recent census figures indicate that Schuck, Shaffer, Sims, and other critics are right about poverty in Louisiana's sugar country, particularly among blacks. However, their implication—that distressed conditions are common only in the cane country and are due primarily to the machinations of the sugar industry—is simplistic and misleading. Two extenuating circumstances mitigate the brunt of their charges. For one thing, poverty levels in other southern states and in sections of Louisiana outside the cane country are as distressing as figures for the sugar bowl. In addition, the importance of plantation labor continues to decline in the cane country where mechanization continues at a rapid rate. Only 17,000 workers (blacks and whites) earned their living on sugar plantations in 1974, whereas census figures for 1970 show that the population of blacks alone was over 100,000 in eleven of the biggest sugar parishes. This pattern repeats itself in other agricultural areas where the relative importance of farm labor as a means of employment has declined in recent years. In 1960, Louisiana farm laborers comprised 3.8 percent of the state's labor force; in 1970 this figure had dropped to 2.4 percent. In contrast to this, a greater percentage of black workers depends on farm labor for employment. Six and one-half percent of the black population of Louisiana (1.08 million—30 percent of Lousiana's total population of 3.64 million in 1970) earns its living performing farm labor as opposed to only 1.2 percent of the white population. However, the paucity of detailed information on labor, tabulated by race, crop, and specific farm occupation, makes generalizing about the cause of economic distress speculative at best.

Most assuredly, the economic distress of blacks in five leading sugarcane parishes far exceeds that of whites. In Assumption Parish 58.7 percent of all black families (803 families) live below the government poverty level, while 30.2 percent of all families (1328 families) in the parish live below the poverty level. In Lafourche figures are comparable: 48.6 percent for black families; 15.4 percent for all families. The pattern repeats itself in other important sugar parishes: St. Charles has 40.2 percent of black families and 16.3 percent of all families below the poverty level. Percentages for St. Mary are 46.3 and 19.0 respectively. Terrebonne has poverty statistics of 45.8 percent for black families and 15.3 for all families. If one extrapolates farm census figures and calculates for white families only, the discrepancy between white and black families is even greater. For instance, in St. Mary about 11.0 percent of the white population falls below the poverty level compared to 46.3 for black families.

Other census information for 1970 sheds light on the subject but does not give an adequate tabulation by race among cane-field laborers. Total farm laborers listed by parishes show 589 in St. Mary, 512 in Assumption, 454 in Lafourche, 328 in St. James, and 284 in Terrebonne. Median annual income of farm workers in these important sugar parishes ranged from a high of $2,826 in Lafourche, down to a low of $1,872 in Terrebonne, but the economic woes of blacks in Louisiana cannot be blamed on the sugarcane industry alone. St. Mary Parish census figures list a total of only 589 farm laborers, yet 2,662 families, nearly half of St. Mary's 17,000 blacks, live below the poverty level. Clearly, other economic activities must also share part of the blame. Even if many of these oppressed blacks are vestiges of yesteryear's plantation labor system, the sugar industry cannot bear sole responsibility for their plight nor be expected single-handedly to devise ways for them to adjust to other types of productive work.[9]

Some aspects of the sugar industry have changed dramatically since the 1950s. The number of workers hired during peak harvest season, for instance, declined from 34,000 in 1951 to half that number in 1973. These plantation workers, whose racial and financial backgrounds are difficult to profile, earned an average of 45 cents per hour in 1951, 62 cents in 1956, $1.12 in 1963, $1.53 in 1969, and $2.05 in 1973.

9 U.S. Department of Commerce, Bureau of the Census, *1970 Census of Population: General Social and Economic Characteristics—Louisiana* (Washington, D.C.: U.S. Government Printing Office, 1972), 155, 331–36, 347, 349–54, 367–72.

Because many of them work only during the nine- or ten-week grinding season, determining their average annual salary is difficult. Census figures seem to indicate that fewer workers, using more sophisticated equipment on larger farms, have produced efficiently in recent years, despite complaints from cane growers about rising labor costs. For instance, the number of man-hours of work required to harvest one acre of sugarcane declined from 101 in 1953, to 80 man-hours in 1963, to only 42 man-hours in 1973. Likewise, the number of man-hours needed to produce a ton of sugarcane declined for the same periods from 4.9 to 2.8 to 2.0. Meanwhile, sugarcane production trends in Louisiana over the past two decades indicate stability: 5.7 million tons in 1953, 8.5 million in 1963, and 6.5 million in 1973. Growers have also increased their average yield per acre from 20 tons in 1953 to 28.9 in 1963 to 20.6 tons in 1973. A decline in the number of sugarcane farms in the last twenty years indicates that farms are increasing in size, probably because of greater use of machinery and high fixed costs. Over 4,000 sugar farms produced cane in 1953; 2,308 operated in 1963; and by 1973 there were only 1,290 cane farms in the state.[10]

The controversy lingers as some conditions change and others remain untouched by time. A wall of ignorance, poverty, discrimination, and defeatism, some observers feel, still surrounds the cane country today, but luckily it is not reinforced by the common use of tyranny, intimidation, fear, or strongarm tactics. Unfortunately, though, its shadow stretches far past the tall sugarcane to other sections of the South. Sugar planters, like members of the agricultural establishment in other sections of the country, are only partly to blame for it. Today the idealistic effort of the Southern Mutual Help Association to improve conditions is a modern alternative to union tactics of the past. The SMHA carries on with benefit of clergy—at least some of the clergy—who have aspirations of one day tearing apart the cane curtain that still encircles the sugarcane country of Louisiana.

10 *Sugar Statistics*, 1975, II, 1–8, 83.

Only the principal materials consulted for this study are included in this essay. Footnotes provide exact citations.

Manuscripts and State Documents

The confidential role of each of the three main groups emphasized in this study—the Catholic Church, the agricultural establishment, and the National Agricultural Workers Union—is documented in at least one significant collection of manuscripts and papers. The Southern Tenant Farmers Union papers, housed in the Southern Collection at the University of North Carolina, and photoduplicated in 60 reels by the Microfilm Corporation of America, is a voluminous collection that covers H. L. Mitchell's forty-year union career from 1933 to 1973. Although the STFU papers cover many subjects, the collection is especially useful in dealing with the inner workings of the agricultural union leadership. The papers of Archbishop Joseph Francis Rummel, which the author was privileged to use in 1972, are not yet open to researchers. The archbishop's letters to and from sugar planters, businessmen, politicians, and laymen indicate his extensive efforts to implement idealistic Catholic social doctrine. The Allen J. Ellender papers housed in the Archives of Nicholls State University in Thibodaux, Louisiana, form a massive collection covering the senator's career from 1937 until his death July 27, 1972. Although it is accessible to researchers only on a limited basis, the collection is a major source of information about agriculture, education, labor, race relations, and politics. The senator, who served on the Agriculture Committee throughout his Senate career, was an important part of the argricultural establishment. His papers prove how effective he and his colleagues could be in shielding their pet farm projects from critics. The minutes of the executive committee meetings of the American Sugar Cane League, microfilmed on reel 11 of the Sugar Archives, also at Nicholls State University, give an inside view of Cane League officials' reactions to challenges from the NAWU and from social action priests.

A number of smaller collections also provide useful information. Several folders of the Catholic Committee of the South papers housed in the Amistad Research Center at Dillard University in New Orleans document Archbishop

Rummel's concern that the CCS had become bureaucratic. Father Jerome Dro-let's personal scrapbooks, which were lent to me, contain letters and vital bits of information to illuminate several problem areas. I also used the papers of the late Reverend Louis Twomey, S.J., housed in the Document Center at Loyola University.

Official proceedings of the Louisiana legislature cover the right-to-work struggles in 1946, 1954, 1956, and 1976 fully. Most useful are the *House Journal*, the *Senate Journal*, and the House and Senate calendars for various sessions.

Interviews

Many clergymen, labor leaders, spokesmen for the sugarcane industry, public officials, and citizens of the cane country agreed to discuss (most of them on tape) the subject matter of this study. Their partisan comments contributed valuable information on church-labor political and economic developments in mid–twentieth century Louisiana's cane country. NAWU president H. L. Mitchell, who participated in the Columbia University Oral History project in the late 1950s, graciously gave many hours of his time to discuss his union's efforts in Louisiana. NAWU organizers, Frank Lapeyrolerie and Henry Pelet, talked to me about their day-to-day personal contact as it concerned plantation workers. E. J. Bourg of the State Federation of Labor talked about statewide labor problems.

T. M. Barker described the sugar economy, labor activities, and Catholic social doctrine, as well, and Florence LeCompte, Senator Ellender's personal secretary in Washington for many years, patiently answered many questions about the senator's personal lifestyle and habits. Charles Logan, former regional director of the National Labor Relations Board in the New Orleans area and occasional advisor to Archbishop Rummel, provided his candid opinions of a number of people involved in labor disputes. Frank Wurzlow, Jr., an Ellender aide in Washington for many years, discussed sugar legislation.

Others with knowledge of the sugar industry who helped by describing specific incidents include Warren Harang, E. J. Clement, Charles Breaux, Guy Thibodaux, Edmond Becnel, Jr., Etienne LeBeouf, Abdon Portier, Auguste Landry, Emile Bourgeois, Nelson Melancon, Pete Ledet, Dan Mack, and Ernest Gaudet.

Father Vincent O'Connell, S.M., never tired of talking about social action struggles, past and present. He enjoyed the confidence of labor leaders but never convinced conservative sugar growers that he was not a left-winger. Msgr. Charles Plauché of New Orleans, who served as chancellor of the Archdiocese of New Orleans under Archbishop Rummel, shared his firsthand knowledge of the controversial men and matters with which the archbishop dealt. Bishop Joseph Vath of Birmingham, Rummel's personal secretary and vice-chancellor, likewise remembered the toughness of the archbishop in deal-ing with influential Catholics. The Jesuits, Charles O'Neill and Thomas Payne of Loyola University, shared information and ideas with me, especially regard-ing the role of their deceased former colleague, Louis Twomey. Raymond Witte noted the racial implications (and humor too) of the archdiocesan su-gar program, and Father Jerome Drolet talked briefly about his career. A number of parish priests—including Will Todd, Joseph Chotin, Roland Boud-reaux, and Monsignor Daniel Becnel—discussed the intricacies of parish ad-ministration.

Francis Dugas and Marc Picciola provided the legislative point of view by talking about their careers in the Louisiana legislature during the time of right-to-work controversies. My colleague, Paul Leslie, has shared his knowl-edge of Earl Long and Louisiana politics with me over the past several years.

Newspapers

Big-city dailies in Louisiana usually provided extensive coverage of dramatic labor-management clashes and political campaigns. In New Orleans the *Times-Picayune*, the *States*, and the *Item* (now the *States-Item*), and in Baton Rouge the *Morning Advocate* and the *State Times* provided full details about most events. *Catholic Action of the South*, the official publication of the Archdiocese of New Orleans, printed surprisingly little controversial material. Its conservative editor apparently hoped to avoid confrontation with Catholics by keeping social action matters out of print. Small-town weeklies in the cane country usually picked up items covered by larger papers for their news col-umns and added their own touch. Among those consulted were the *Lafourche Comet* (Thibodaux), the *Assumption Pioneer* (Napoleonville), the Donald-sonville *Chief*, the Lafayette *Daily Advertiser*, the *St. Charles Herald* (Hahn-ville), and the Houma *Courier*. From time to time the New York *Times* re-ported Louisiana subjects.

Secondary Materials

The list that follows contains only those materials on labor, agriculture, and Catholic social doctrine that contributed most directly to my work.

C. Vann Woodward's *Origins of the New South, 1877–1913* (Baton Rouge, 1951) and George Tindall's *Emergence of the New South, 1913–1945* (Baton Rouge, 1967) are basic for any study dealing with the twentieth-century South. Charles Roland's *The Improbable Era: the South Since World War II* (Lex-ington, 1975) interprets life since the war in broad generalizations. In *Farmer Movements in the South, 1865–1933* (Berkeley, 1960) Theodore Saloutos touches briefly on a vast range of protest activity. Murray Benedict's *Farm Policies of the United States, 1790–1950* (New York, 1966) is a useful general work. Stuart Jamieson, *Labor Unionism in American Agriculture* (Washington, 1945) discusses many largely unsuccessful attempts to organize agricultural workers. F. Ray Marshall, *Labor in the South,* (Cambridge, 1967) surveys a great deal of union activity, mostly since the 1930s. F. Ray Marshall and Lamar B. Jones, "Agricultural Unions in Louisiana," *Labor History,* III (Fall, 1962), briefly reviews many isolated union clashes. Marion P. Tullier's "The Development of State 'Right-to-Work' Legislation," (M.A. Thesis, Louisiana State University, 1959), is an excellent study of the legal ramifications of right-to-work laws, which does not, however, explore fully the economic, political, and religious motives in the Louisiana legislative disputes.

Several important works deal with the early career of H. L. Mitchell and the STFU. David Conrad's *The Forgotten Farmers: The Story of Sharecroppers in the New Deal* (Urbana, 1965) and Donald Grubbs' *The Cry From Cotton: The Southern Tenant Farmers Union and the New Deal* (Chapel Hill, 1971) are thorough studies that incorporate the essence of a number of articles dealing with specific aspects of Mitchell's career. Two fine studies deal with the sugar industry: Alfred S. Eichner's *The Emergence of Oligopoly: Sugar Refining as a Case Study* (Baltimore, 1969), which explains the influence of the Havemeyer sugar trust on raw sugar producers; and the standard work on the sugarcane industry of the South, J. Carlyle Sitterson's *Sugar Country: The Cane Sugar Industry of the South* (Lexington, 1953), an economic history written from the perspective of industry leaders grappling with the sugar trust, foreign competition, natural disasters, and wildly fluctuating sugar prices. Sitterson, however, viewed labor conflicts in terms of production costs, not as social problems. Donald Holley's "Old and New Worlds in the New Deal Resettlement Program: Two Louisiana Projects," *Louisiana History* (Spring, 1970) looks into the Farm Security Administration experimental sugarcane farm in the late 1930s near Schriever in Terrebonne Parish, which Senator Ellender supported.

On race relations in Louisiana as slavery ended Joe Gray Taylor's *Louisiana Reconstructed, 1863–1877* (Baton Rouge, 1974) is a basic work. Also useful are C. Peter Ripley, "The Black Family in Transition: Louisiana, 1860–1865," *The Journal of Southern History* (August, 1975) and William F. Messner, "Black Violence and White Response: Louisiana, 1862," *Journal of Southern History* (February, 1975). William I. Hair, *Bourbonism and Agrarian Protest: Louisiana Politics, 1877–1900* (Baton Rouge, 1969) views agricultural labor problems of the Bourbon Era in Louisiana and traces attempts by the Knights of Labor to establish a foothold in the cane fields of Louisiana.

Several works help explain the economic-political-racial structure of Louisiana at mid–twentieth century. Wilbur Cash, *The Mind of the South* (New York, 1941), and Roger Shugg, *Origins of the Class Struggle in Louisiana* (Baton Rouge, 1939) are the most notable of the older works. V. O. Key, Jr., *Southern Politics in State and Nation* (New York, 1949), a valuable evaluation of political developments in each of the southern states, has been updated by William Havard (ed.), *The Changing Politics of the South* (Baton Rouge, 1972). T. Harry Williams, *Huey Long: A Biography* (New York, 1969) views the former governor and senator as an enlightened mass leader, while Allan Sindler, *Huey Long's Louisiana: State Politics, 1920–1952* (Baltimore, 1956) and Perry Howard, *Political Tendencies in Louisiana, 1812–1952* (Baton Rouge, 1971) are less impressed with the Kingfish. Both discuss bifactionalism that split the Democratic party into Long and anti-Long factions. A. J. Liebling, *The Earl of Louisiana* (New York, 1961) is a good popular study of Earl Long. Edward Haas, *DeLesseps S. Morrison and the Image of Reform: New Orleans Politics, 1946–1961* (Baton Rouge: 1974) sees the New Orleans mayor's reforms as more theatrical than real.

On modern agricultural and labor policies a number of works proved useful. Grant McConnell, *The Decline of Agrarian Democracy* (Berkeley, 1959) explains the growth of the agricultural establishment in twentieth century America. Richard Kirkendall, *Social Scientists and Farm Politics in the Age of Roosevelt* (Columbia, 1966) and Theodore Saloutos, "New Deal Agricultural Policy: An Evaluation," *Journal of American History* (September, 1974) are both helpful in evaluating the overall impact of the New Deal on agriculture. Rudolph C. Hammack, "The New Deal and Louisiana Agriculture," (Ph.D. dissertation, Tulane University, 1973) is an exhaustive study of how the agricultural establishment in Louisiana reacted to New Deal farm policies. Michèle B. Francois, "Federal Regulations, Processing Costs and Scale of Plant in the Louisiana Sugar Cane Industry," (Ph.D. dissertation, Tulane University, 1971) blamed governmental policies for hindering development of larger, more efficient sugar plants, but did not assess effects of the Sugar Act on consumers and farm laborers. Irving Bernstein's *The Lean Years: A History of the American Worker, 1920–1933* (Boston, 1960) and *The Turbulent Years: A History of the American Worker*, 1933–1941 (Boston, 1970) are excellent for discussion of labor trends before World War II. Thomas Krueger, "American Labor Historiography, Old and New: A Review Essay," *Journal of Social History* (Spring, 1971) is a concise review of recent trends in labor history.

George G. Lewis and John Mewha, *History of Prisoner of War Utilization by the United States Army, 1776–1945* (Washington, 1955) and Joseph Butler, "Prisoner of War Labor in the Sugar Cane Fields of Lafourche Parish, Louisiana: 1943–1944," *Louisiana History* (Summer, 1973) describe POW camps in the cane country, but do not question the racial or economic implications of Cane League recommendations.

Studies of national church leaders helped to put the role of social activists in Louisiana into perspective. John T. Ellis, *The Life of James Cardinal Gibbons* (Milwaukee, 1963), Francis L. Broderick, *Right Reverend New Dealer: John A. Ryan* (New York, 1963), and George Flynn, *American Catholics and the Roosevelt Presidency, 1932–1936* (Lexington, 1968) all elaborate on the part different leaders played in shaping social thought through the 1930s. Wilfrid Sheed, "America's Catholics," *New York Review of Books* (March

7, 1974) and Robert Cross, *The Emergence of Liberal Catholicism in America* (Cambridge, 1958) discuss liberal trends in twentieth-century Catholicism. David J. O'Brien, "American Catholic Historiography: A Post-Conciliar Evaluation," *Church History* (1968) reviews the merits of various works on American Catholicism. J. B. Gremillion, *The Journal of a Southern Pastor* (Chicago, 1957), Jean Eyraud and Donald Millet (comps. and eds.), *A History of St. John the Baptist Parish With Biographical Sketches* (Marrero, Louisiana, 1939), and Roger Baudier, *The Catholic Church in Louisiana* (New Orleans, 1972) all touch on Catholic social action in Louisiana. John Payne's dissertation: "A Jesuit Search for Social Justice: The Public Career of Louis J. Twomey, S.J., 1947–1969" (University of Texas, 1976), traces the career of an idealist social leader. Michael Harrington, "Catholics in the Labor Movement: A Case History," *Labor History*, I (Fall, 1960), looks into the Association of Catholic Trade Unionists (ACTU) movement.

Index

crat charges, 134; and Ste. Marie, 154, 168–70; and Mathews strike, 168–71; and Msgr. Perino, 170; mentioned, 105, 127, 135, 136
Ducos, Frank, 148
Dugas, Felix, 147, 150, 153, 155, 177
Dugas, Francis, 191, 192
Duhe, J. P., 137
Durbin, Gilbert: and 1953 strike, 143, 150; and evictions, 145; mentioned, 39, 137, 146, 185

Ecimovich, Frank, 203
Edwards, Lewis, 110, 165
Efferson, J. N., 88, 109, 123–24
Elizabeth strike, 183
Ellender, Allen: labor policy of, 23–27, 38, 42; as agrarian politican, 24, 27, 28, 41, 43, 70, 72–81, 89, 130, 200; criticism of, 65–66, 149; legislative techniques of, 78; as segregationist, 80–81, 204; and displaced persons, 95–96; and 1953 strike, 142, 144; on right-to-work, 181; death of, 202; mentioned, 20, 21, 29, 39–40, 48, 100, 113, 128, 156
Evictions, 38–40, 143–46
Eyraud, Jean, 62–63, 136, 144

Fair Labor Standards Act, 14
Farm Bureau: and sugar wage hearings, 46; and right-to-work, 183 185, 192; mentioned, 16, 69, 77, 98, 100, 104, 107, 180
Farmers' Union, 69
Farm Security Administration, 23
Farwell, Charles, 79, 84,88, 132, 152
Federal Bureau of Investigation, 100, 134
Federal Mediation and Conciliation Service, 141

Ferris, Josiah, 113
Fleming, Raymond, 38
Forstall, George, 100–101
Fournet, John, 163
Freedmen's Bureau, 3
Free Enterprise Association, 192

Galarza, Ernesto: early life of, 44; in 1953 strike, 140, 149; in Mathews strike, 165, 166, 168–71; critical of the CIO, 170–71; pessimism of, 178; on right-to-work, 194; mentioned, 33, 111, 115, 120, 135, 158, 162, 199
Gibbons, James, 51–52
Godchaux Sugars, Inc.: in 1953 strike, 139, 156; mentioned 34, 76, 121, 125, 126, 135, 145, 161
Godchaux Sugars, Inc. v. Paul Chaisson, 163–64
Goldberg, Arthur, 164
Gooseberry, Richard, 6–7
Gorman, Patrick, 44, 175–76, 198
Gouaux, Eugene, 191, 192
Graham, Frank, 113, 151–52
Graugnard, F. A., 58
Graugnard, F. A., Jr., 185, 186, 190–91, 192
Green, William, 26, 46, 115, 116
Grevemberg, Francis, 152
Guerre, L. F., 84
Guidry, Joe: Acadian organizer, 105–106, 121; called strike meeting, 129; feuded with E. H. Williams, 172; mentioned, 105, 127, 131, 155, 162, 166, 175, 177–78
Guidry, Richard, 185, 186, 189
Guste, Robert, 155

Haas, Francis, 64
Hasiwar, Henry: early career of, 44–45; and strawberry farmers, 98, 163, 165, health of, 110–11, 115;

119, 144
Our Lady of Prompt Succor Church,
104–105
Overton, John, 26, 27, 73, 84

Papal infallibility, 49
Parker, I. Lee, 46, 106–107
Parr, George, 168–71, 175, 176–77,
192
Patterson, Roy: criticism of,
109–110; removal of, 136
Patton, James G., 46
Pelet, Henry, 115, 116, 127,
168–71, 176–77
Peltier, Harvey, 39, 175
Perez, Leander, 19, 28
Perino, Dominic, 63, 136
Picciola, Marc J., 182
Pieper, Fred, 60, 63
Pitre, Renée, 204–205
Plauché, Charles, 62, 108, 126, 136,
170, 173
Poindexter, J. E., 153
Pollitt, Daniel, 101–102, 164
Polmer, Mervin, 40
Ponder, A. L., 164
Populism, 8–9, 13
Poverty, 205–207
Prejean, A. P., 145, 153
Prisoners of war, 63, 81–86, 89
Producers' and Manufacturers' Pro-
tective Association, 72
Production and Marketing Adminis-
tration, 114, 115
Propaganda, 102–104, 139, 146–59
passim
Prostitution, 134. See also Jeanette's

Quota on imported sugar, 73–76

Rainach, W. M., 183
Rappelet, A. O., 191, 192
Rayburn, B. B., 183–84, 190

Realty Operators. See Southdown
Reintjes, William H., 61
Rerum Novarum, 51–53, 60, 66,
179
Reuther, Victor, 168, 171, 172
Reuther, Walter, 28, 111, 172–73,
178, 193
Richard, Fernand, 145, 151
Right-to-work, 21, 22, 166, 170,
173, 174, 179–95, 199–200
Right-to-Work Council, 184, 185
Robinson, Joseph, 72–73
Roosevelt, Eleanor, 32
Roosevelt, Franklin, 54, 55, 74–76
Rummel, Joseph Francis: early career
of, 57–61; and social action,
60–61, 66–67, 204; and strawberry disputes, 98–99; resisted
pressure from cane growers, 114,
143–44; growers refused to meet
with, 124, 126, 132–33; aided
striking workers, 144; and right-
to-work, 182, 183–90; mentioned,
37, 93, 104, 108, 138, 154–55,
165, 170, 177
Ryan, John A., 53–55, 60, 188

St. Benedict the Moor Church, 114
Ste. Marie, Eddie J., 154, 168–69
Savoie, Clarence, 75, 76, 113–14,
125, 135, 150, 152–53, 182,
186
Schachter, Leon, 43, 44
Schexnayder, Maurice, 203
Schuck, Peter, 201, 205
Selective Service Act, 23
Senior, Clarence, 32–33
Shaffer, Richard, 202, 205
Shrimpers: unions of, 18–19;
strikes of, 19
Sigur, Alexander, 105, 120, 136,
185
Simpson, John A., 69, 99

Sims, Patsy, 201–202, 205
Sinagra, Charles, 99
Sitterson, J. Carlyle, 5
Smith-Connally Act, 25
Smith, Margaret, 39, 142, 149
Sockrider, Guy W., Jr., 183–84
Soignet, R. J., 185, 186, 189
Songy, Antoine, 167
South Coast Corporation, 40–41,
76, 139, 142, 201
Southdown, 39–40, 76, 87, 127,
131, 139
Southern Mutual Help Association,
203–205, 207
Southern States Industrial Council,
180
Southern Tenant Farmers Union,
31, 32–33, 43, 51, 198
Steimel, Edward, 199–200
Stephens, Tony, 176
Sterling Sugars, 76
Stith, George, 116, 139, 177
Sugar Act: provisions of, 35–36, 42,
74–78; benefit payments of, 42,
75–76; violations of, 42, 122;
criticism of, 198, 199, 201–203;
expiration of, 73, 202; mentioned
35–36, 39, 46, 72, 107, 112,
113
Sugar Cane Workers Organizing
Committee, 114, 119
Sugar Division, 35, 40, 41, 79
Sugar growers, 122, 124–26, 127,
131–33, 137, 141
Sutton, Eddie, 161

Taft-Hartley Act, 14, 26, 28, 106,
142, 162, 180, 183
Talmadge, Eugene, 15
Talmadge, Herman, 15
Tariff, 72
Teamsters. *See* International
Brotherhood of Teamsters

Thibodaux Massacre, 7–8
Thomas, Norman, 32, 33, 113, 148,
153, 157, 165
Toups, Roland, 156, 170
Treadaway, Angelina, 19
Triche, Risley, 191
Truman, Harry S., 28, 86, 87
Turner, Joseph G., 116, 119, 136
Twomey, Louis: early career of,
112; head of Institute of Indus-
trial Relations, 112, 162; and
Time interview, 146–47; and
right-to-work, 183–90; and the
agricultural establishment, 204;
mentioned, 119–20, 136, 139,
145, 175, 176

Union strength in the South, 15
United Cannery, Agricultural, Pack-
ing and Allied Workers of
America, 31–32
United Packinghouse Workers of
America, 161, 175–78
United States Department of Labor,
130
United States Employment Service,
23, 55, 141, 142
Upton, Irving, 127

Valentine Sugars: union of, 110;
mentioned 63, 76, 169
Vath, Joseph, 136
Violet Seafood Workers' Association,
19

Wagner Act, 17, 18, 180, 181
Wallace, George, 182
Wallace, Henry A., 72, 75–76, 78,
79
War Food Administration, 23, 76,
87
War Manpower Commission, 23, 83
Watkins, J. Louis, 155–56, 163–64